BLOOMSBURY
LONDON · NEW DELHI · NEW YORK · SYDNEY

# River Cottage

# FRUIT

## every day!

## Hugh Fearnley-Whittingstall

**Photography by Simon Wheeler**

**Beautiful, bountiful and bouncy,** fruit is a truly fantastic food. It's so delicious and so very, very good for us – and yet it remains ridiculously under-explored in our kitchens. We are, frankly, a nation that still thinks it's a bit racy to slice a banana on to our breakfast cereal. I want to change that. I think it's time to revolutionise the way we eat fruit. A 'piece of fruit' in a lunchbox or at the end of a meal is all very well – but there is so much more we could be doing with fruit, and I'm impatient to get that ball rolling for you.

In part this will mean taking a leaf (or a fruit) from foreign food cultures, for whom including fruits in cooking is often second nature, in savoury recipes as well as sweet: think of the tagines of North Africa where dates, apricots and preserved lemons mingle with tender spiced meats; think of the tart, aromatic flesh of mangoes, papayas and pomegranates in Far Eastern salads and salsas; and we shouldn't overlook sour cherries and tart berries in the soups and stews of Scandinavia and Eastern Europe either. Why should we let these culinary competitors steal a march on us? Do we really think roast pork with apple sauce, fine as it is, is a strong enough entry in the international fruit-in-a-savoury-recipe cookery Olympiad? What about our pears, plums, berries and currants? Don't they deserve a look-in too?

Before we get stuck into the recipes, though, let's remind ourselves why fruits are *so* special. They are the only foods that 'want' to be eaten. To fulfil their evolutionary mission in a competitive world (it's a fruit jungle out there) they have fashioned themselves into pretty much the perfect foodstuff – visually irresistible, cleverly packaged, nutritious and, most importantly, *delicious*. Their consumption is an integral part of their life cycle. We eat a piece of fruit, we spread the seed, the seed grows, the plant fruits. Along with many of our fellow mammals, birds too of course, and other species, fruits have systematically seduced us.

Down the centuries, fruits have had us working on their behalf, nurturing and cultivating them to make them even plumper, juicier and sweeter. Most varieties can now be eaten as soon as they're picked, plucked or cut – raspberries off the cane, cherries off the tree, currants off the bush. And even if you don't grow any yourself, fruit is always accessible: in greengrocers and supermarkets of course, but also on the street. Fruit has beguiled us so much, and we are so proud of our success in growing it, that we can't resist piling it into vast colourful displays of conspicuous delight. Now, in major cities all over the world, fruit stalls come out to greet us on the pavements, to dazzle us with sheer temptation.

And yet I reckon that many of us could do with a fruit boost. I think we know in our hearts that unless we are eating fruit every day, we're probably not eating enough. So why is it that, for so many of us, fruit isn't quite happening? One reason is that we don't always fully understand fruit – when it's in season, how to buy it at its best, what to do with it. Or we take it for granted. The fruit bowl becomes a decorative item, and a symbol of good intentions. If we don't want to munch that apple right now, we'll leave it till tomorrow. Tomorrow comes and, surprise, surprise it isn't looking any more tempting…

I intend to address any such lingering fruit apathy head on, with advice on sourcing, storing, ripening, cooking and eating this amazing resource. You'll find recipes for almost all the seasonal fruit that grows in this country, from the first forced pink rhubarb of January, through juicy early summer berries and high summer plums and gages, to the bounty of our autumn apple and pear harvest – and by no means neglecting the blackberries, damsons, hips and haws that are the season's rich hedgerow pickings. But I don't stop there. I'm all for enjoying fruits from other parts of the world, especially when our own are out of season. Imported fruits are mainly shipped, not flown, so the environmental burden is not so great as with many veg. They are also the agricultural staples of communities that rely on our support. Fairtrade and organic labels flag up the most responsible and sustainable options. So oranges, lemons, limes and clementines, Mediterranean figs, grapes and melons, as well as tropical favourites like bananas, pineapples and mangoes, are all included in my fruit extravaganza.

I hope to refresh your view of all these fruits, and more, and help you put them slap-bang at the centre of your everyday eating, where they belong. So as well as offering my personal versions of fruity classics that we already know and love – the pies, crumbles and cobblers, the ice creams and sorbets, the simple combinations of fruit with cream, custard or meringue – I'll encourage you to start cooking with fruit in some new ways. I want you to put all kinds of raw fruit in your savoury salads, and some savoury things, herbs for example, in your sweet fruit salads. I want to persuade you to put fruit on a pizza (not ham and pineapple, I promise) and into your daily bread. I want you to introduce it to your rich and meaty stews and pies. I want to show you how surprisingly well fruit goes with fish, both hot and cold.

And so… drum roll… I bring you strawberry panzanella; kiwi and apple with tarragon; rocket, pear and raspberry pizza; broad beans, blueberries and bacon; slow-roast lamb shoulder with spiced apricot sauce; chicken, leek and plum pie; banana kedgeree; rhubarb fish parcels with soy and ginger; oysters with apple and shallot vinegar… Well over half my recipes are savoury dishes that I'm sure you won't have tasted before, the rest are sweet treats and puds selected for their sheer fruity intensity. I'm convinced you'll find these recipes inspiring, intriguing and refreshing. They might just change the way you cook – forever!

Punching juicily above their diminutive weight, berries and currants are luscious, generous fruits, rich in vitamins and antioxidants. They are perhaps the most instant fix of summer to be found in a food – that's real sunshine stored in their ripe, sweet juices! Wonderful as they are to cook with, they're best of all neat – or nearly neat. A bowlful of Scottish raspberries, or homegrown alpine strawberries, with nothing more than a shake of sugar and a slosh of cream, is hard to beat. So much so, that we very rarely try…

But that's certainly not the only way to celebrate our best summer soft fruits. They are far more versatile than you may ever have given them credit for. Savoury outings open up a whole new summer vista: strawberry panzanella (page 19) is a cheeky take on the popular classic Italian bread and tomato salad – and I promise you won't mistake it for a pudding. Broad beans, blueberries and bacon (page 20) sounds bonkers I know. But it doesn't just alliterate, it sets your tastebuds alight. And if I say to you 'roast pork with gooseberries and black pudding' (on page 32), I think you might be converted before I even get to the end of the sentence.

Bursting as they are with new possibilities, we have to face a hard fact about berries and currants: shop-bought specimens are often awfully disappointing. Why is it so easy to find insipid strawberries and blueberries, and too-tart raspberries? And why is it so hard to find redcurrants and gooseberries at all? The answer is that the modern marketplace has turned some of these fruits – particularly strawberries and blueberries – from seasonal treats into year-round staples, with under-ripe and underwhelming imported fruit standing in for the real homegrown deal for eight or nine months of the year.

Meanwhile other classics, such as gooseberries, redcurrants and blackcurrants, are almost entirely neglected – when we could be feasting on them from July to September. Did you know that over 95 per cent of all the blackcurrants grown in the UK are used to make a certain well-known blackcurrant drink? I've nothing against this cordial – in fact I think it's great that this household brand continues to use British fruit – but surely we could stake a claim on some of this luscious fruit for our own kitchen forays (if only to make a very grown-up version of that cordial – see page 62 for my delicious homemade cassis).

In short, we view the berry family in a lopsided way – all or nothing – instead of appreciating it for what it is, a collection of highly seasonal fruits that flourish between June and September. We should plunder this glorious summer treasure while the sun shines and pass by the so-so standbys that are pushed at us out of season. So if you're eating raspberries in January, they should be in your homemade jam. And if you're eating strawberries on Christmas Eve, I hope they're in a luscious ice cream or sorbet. (The strawberry yoghurt semifreddo on page 48 is a delicious doddle…)

The supermarket, I'd say, is about the worst place to buy berries and currants. The range is poor, and the quality often poorer. These soft fruits are fragile, so to survive distribution and retain any kind of shelf-life, they are often picked under-ripe. That's the real crime here – these fruits just don't deliver on that sunshine promise unless they have been allowed to bask in those rays.

Go instead to a farm shop selling locally grown fruit, or order berries and currants from the best box scheme that delivers in your area. Best of all, take the family to a pick-your-own farm. These places should be recognised as pillars of our food culture, as important as traditional orchards or regional farmers' markets. Here you can pick punnet upon punnet of super-fresh, properly ripe fruit, choosing exactly what you fancy, and even tasting one or two along the way. You'll be told what's ripest and best on the day. And where else, apart from your own garden, can children see so clearly how food gets from plot to plate? We must cherish these places – as the brutal saying goes, 'use them or lose them'; see the Directory (pages 402–3).

Growing your own is, of course, an even more satisfying way to fill your berry boots. You'll need a bit of space, of course, but maybe not as much as you might think. None of these fruits are difficult to raise and many – currant bushes and blueberries in particular – do well in large pots or containers. City gardens often have the suntraps that will bring out the best in them. Berries are gluttish and you'll get nothing one week and bucket loads the next. A plethora of recipes has been developed over the centuries to cope with this fruity overload: preserves, cordials and liqueurs, summer puddings, ice creams and sorbets. My favourites are here.

And I would always rather freeze ripe berries and currants than buy under-ripe, imported ones out of season. Spread them out on a tray so they freeze without sticking together, then transfer to a plastic tub and return to the freezer. Throwing a handful of frozen blueberries into a winter smoothie, or whipping up an autumnal apple and gooseberry crumble, are ways in which you can enjoy these beautiful berries at their best. Out of season, strictly speaking, yes; but not out of order.

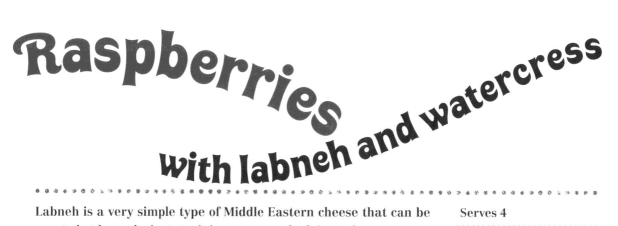

# Raspberries with labneh and watercress

Labneh is a very simple type of Middle Eastern cheese that can be created at home by just straining some good, plain yoghurt. You can also buy labneh in some delis. Its creamy-but-tangy flavour is a lovely foil to peppery watercress and sweet-sharp raspberries. This salad is delicious as a starter, but also works well as part of a spread of mezze-style dishes.

Start by making the labneh, which you need to do several hours in advance, or ideally a day or two before. Put the yoghurt in a bowl, add the ½ teaspoon salt and mix thoroughly. Line a sieve with a square of clean muslin or a clean, thin cotton cloth. Spoon the salted yoghurt into the centre of the cloth, then flip the sides of the cloth over the yoghurt to cover it and place the sieve over a bowl.

Leave in a cool place (the fridge, if you can fit it in) to drain for at least 2 hours (or up to 4 hours), until a significant amount of liquid has drained into the bowl and the yoghurt has the texture of thick crème fraîche or clotted cream. Transfer the labneh to a bowl and refrigerate until needed. You'll probably find that the labneh continues to release liquid – just pour it off before serving.

When you're ready to serve, take a large serving platter and spread the labneh cheese over it in a thick, swirly layer. Tear the watercress over – it should be scattered on like a herb, rather than layered thickly – then add the raspberries. Trickle over plenty of extra virgin olive oil and a healthy squeeze of orange or lemon juice. Season with salt and pepper and serve, with warm flatbreads or pitta breads.

**Serves 4**

500ml plain wholemilk yoghurt

½ teaspoon fine sea salt

2–3 handfuls of watercress

200g raspberries

Extra virgin olive oil, to trickle

A good squeeze of orange or lemon juice

Sea salt and freshly ground black pepper

# Strawberry
## panzanella

Serves 6

300g slightly stale sourdough, ciabatta or other coarse-textured bread

500g strawberries, hulled

4 tablespoons extra virgin olive oil

1 tablespoon balsamic vinegar

½ medium cucumber, chopped

1 small red onion, very finely sliced

1 small fennel bulb, trimmed and finely sliced

1 tablespoon baby capers, rinsed

A few basil leaves, shredded or torn

Sea salt and freshly ground black pepper

**This colourful salad shows how fruit can be used in an unexpected savoury context to create a delightful and original dish. A traditional Italian panzanella majors on tomatoes. Strawberries offer a similar, delicious balance of acidity and sweetness, but have a wonderful fragrance all their own.**

Preheat the oven to 200°C/Gas 6. Tear the bread into bite-sized chunks, scatter on a baking tray and put into the oven for just 5–10 minutes, until lightly toasted. Leave to cool.

Crush half the strawberries with your hands. Put them into a sieve over a large bowl and work them through with the back of a wooden spoon to give a thin strawberry purée. Whisk in the extra virgin olive oil, balsamic vinegar and some salt and pepper.

Quarter the remaining strawberries, or cut them into smaller pieces if they are really big. Put them into a large bowl with the cucumber, onion, fennel, toasted bread, capers and about half the basil. Spoon over the strawberry dressing, toss lightly and leave the salad to stand for 10–15 minutes before serving.

Taste and adjust the seasoning with salt and pepper as needed. Toss the salad gently one more time, scatter over the remaining basil leaves and serve.

# Broad beans, blueberries and bacon

This works amazingly well – the sweet-tart of the berries matching up to the slight bitterness of the beans and the saltiness of the bacon. The shapes of the berries and beans are good together too – pleasing in the mouth. And I always love recipes that alliterate.

Pod the broad beans. Bring a pan of water to the boil, drop the beans in and cook for 3–4 minutes, then drain. Try a couple of the beans. If the skins seem rather bitter, you can skin them. But with small, fresh beans, this shouldn't be necessary. Set the beans aside.

Heat the olive oil in a frying pan and fry the lardons until crisp. Throw in the broad beans and cook for 1 minute more, tossing them with the bacon. Turn off the heat, add the squeeze of lemon juice, some salt and pepper and the blueberries. Toss together well. Leave in the pan so the blueberries warm through – even cook ever so slightly – while you sort out the toast.

Toast the bread and rub lightly with the halved garlic clove. Trickle over some extra virgin oil and pile the broad bean and blueberry mixture on top. Scatter, if you like, with a few thyme leaves. Give it another trickle of olive oil, add a grinding of pepper and serve.

**Variation** The beans and blues combination also works well with goat's cheese. Cook the beans as above, drain and leave to cool, then toss with the blueberries, a little olive oil and some salt and pepper. Serve this with goat's cheese crumbled on top, or dish it up alongside grilled goat's cheese on toast.

## Serves 2

About 750g young broad beans in the pod (200g podded weight)

1 tablespoon olive oil

175g bacon or pancetta lardons (either dice or strips)

A squeeze of lemon juice

75g blueberries

2 slices of sourdough, or other good robust bread

1 garlic clove, halved

Extra virgin olive or rapeseed oil, to trickle

A few thyme leaves (optional)

Sea salt and freshly ground black pepper

# Cucumber and gooseberry soup

Gooseberries give a subtle edge to this refreshing soup. It's great hot but even better, I think, chilled. Either way, a little smoked fish really finishes it off beautifully (see the variation below).

Melt the butter in a large saucepan over a medium heat. Add the onion, cover and let it sweat, stirring occasionally, for 10–15 minutes until softened and translucent.

Meanwhile, peel the cucumbers, halve them lengthways and scoop out their seeds with a teaspoon, then cut the flesh into 2cm slices.

Add the cucumber slices to the onion in the pan, along with the diced potato and gooseberries. Stir over the heat for a minute, then add the stock and some salt and pepper and bring to a simmer. Reduce the heat to low, cover and cook for about 20 minutes until the potato, cucumbers and gooseberries are tender, stirring occasionally.

Transfer the soup to a blender and whiz until smooth (in batches if necessary). Return the soup to the pan and whisk in the crème fraîche. Taste and add more salt and pepper as needed.

If serving hot, ladle the soup into warm bowls, dollop more crème fraîche on top and finish with a trickle of extra virgin olive oil and a grinding of pepper. Alternatively, let the soup cool and refrigerate it for a few hours before serving in chilled bowls, finished in the same way.

## Variations

Flake about 75g smoked trout over the hot or chilled soup to serve.

*Chilled cherry soup* This looks great and is very refreshing. Make the soup as above, omitting the gooseberries, then chill it. Stone and halve or quarter 250g sweet cherries and place in a saucepan with the juice of ½ lemon. Cook gently to a chunky compote, about 10 minutes. Leave to cool, then chill. Serve the soup in chilled bowls, with the cherry compote spooned over the top (it will partially sink and then marble the soup with lovely pink streaks). Finish with soured cream, a trickle of extra virgin oil and a grinding of black pepper.

### Serves 6

A knob of butter

1 small-medium onion, chopped

1kg cucumbers (about 3 large ones)

200g potato, peeled and cut into 1cm dice

100g gooseberries, topped and tailed

800ml chicken or vegetable stock

4 tablespoons crème fraîche or soured cream, plus extra to serve

Sea salt and freshly ground black pepper

Extra virgin olive or rapeseed oil, to finish

# Sausage sandwich with gooseberry ketchup

Traditionally paired with oily fish, tart gooseberries also complement rich meats. Here, I've cooked them into a tangy sweet-sour ketchup to go with sausages in a sandwich. Or you could serve the bangers with soft polenta or creamy mash and the ketchup.

For the ketchup, sterilise a couple of sealable 250ml bottles or jars by washing them thoroughly in hot soapy water, rinsing well then putting on a tray in a low oven (at 120°C/Gas ½) to dry out and warm up.

Put the gooseberries in a pan with 2 tablespoons water and cook over a low heat until they begin to release their juice, then simmer very gently for a few minutes until soft and pulpy. Tip into a sieve over a bowl and rub through with a wooden spoon. You should have about 750ml purée.

Tip the purée into a saucepan and add the sugar, vinegar, mustard, spices and salt. Bring slowly to the boil, stirring to dissolve the sugar, then let it simmer until reduced and thickened to the consistency of a good-quality tomato ketchup, stirring often to stop it sticking and burning on the base of the pan. This will take about 30 minutes; it will thicken a little more as it cools. Pour the ketchup into the prepared bottles or jars, seal and leave to cool completely. This makes around 500ml, so you'll have plenty for other uses (see below). Store in a cool, dark cupboard for up to 4 months and refrigerate once opened.

To cook the sausages, heat the oil in a frying pan over a medium heat, add the sausages and cook reasonably gently, turning them often, until golden brown all over and cooked through. This will take at least 20 minutes. (Or cook them in the oven or under the grill if you prefer.)

Butter the bread, add the hot sausages (sliced in half lengthways if they're thick) and a generous splurge of gooseberry ketchup, and serve.

*Other ways to use your gooseberry ketchup* Serve it dolloped on the side with grilled or barbecued oily fish, such as sardines or mackerel, or herrings fried in oatmeal, or in a smoked mackerel sandwich. It's also very good instead of pickle in a Cheddar sandwich.

**Per person**

A trickle of olive or rapeseed oil

4 chipolatas or 2 fat butcher's sausages

2 slices of good white bread

Butter, for spreading

*For the ketchup*

1kg gooseberries

125g light soft brown sugar

75ml cider vinegar

2 teaspoons mustard powder

1 teaspoon ground ginger

½ teaspoon freshly ground black pepper

½ teaspoon ground cloves

½ teaspoon salt

# Rabbit rillettes with
# gooseberry relish

Serves 8

**For the rillettes**

500g rindless, fatty
outdoor-reared pork
belly, cut into 2–3cm
cubes

1 wild rabbit, skinned
and jointed

1 large sprig of thyme

3 bay leaves

1 garlic bulb, halved
crossways

A good pinch of ground
mixed spice

A good pinch of ground
mace

Sea salt and freshly
ground black pepper

**For the relish**

300g gooseberries,
topped and tailed

1 small or ½ medium
onion, finely sliced,
root to tip

30g caster sugar

2 tablespoons cider
vinegar

**To serve**

Freshly toasted slices
of sourdough or other
good robust bread

**Rillettes is a kind of coarse pâté – a lovely, rich, aromatic meaty mishmash that just begs for something a little sharp and tangy on the side. This super-easy gooseberry relish fits the bill.**

For the rillettes, preheat the oven to 220°C/Gas 7. Put the pork and rabbit pieces in a casserole dish or roasting tin in which they fit quite snugly in a single layer. Add the herbs and garlic and pour over 250ml water. Cover with a lid or foil and cook in the oven for 30 minutes, then lower the oven setting to 140°C/Gas 1 and cook for a further 2½ hours, or until the rabbit is completely tender and can easily be pulled into shreds with a fork. Set aside until cool enough to handle.

Now comes the hands-on bit. Pull all the rabbit meat off the bones, discarding the bones, then shred the meat with a pair of forks, or just with your hands. Put it into a large bowl. Shred the pork in whichever way you find easiest too, making sure you include all the fat. Add to the rabbit and work the two meats together, crushing the fat from the pork belly thoroughly into the mix so it is evenly spread.

Now add the spices and plenty of salt and pepper – you'll probably need ½ teaspoon salt – and some of the flavoursome liquid from the casserole or roasting tin. Stir together, adding more liquid as necessary, until you have a coarse, fairly loose pâté texture. You may not need all the liquid. Taste and add more salt, pepper or spices as needed.

Transfer the mixture to a bowl or jar, cover and refrigerate for at least a day or two, which improves the flavour, and sets the rillettes firm.

To make the relish, put the gooseberries in a pan with the onion, sugar and cider vinegar. Cook over a low heat until the sugar has dissolved and the gooseberries begin to release their juice, then simmer gently for a few minutes until the gooseberries are soft and pulpy. Remove from the heat and leave to cool completely. Taste and add salt, pepper and more sugar or vinegar if you like, keeping it quite tart.

Serve the rillettes with warm toast and the gooseberry relish.

# Mackerel with gooseberry and mint salsa

This lovely, fresh-tasting salsa is best made with tart, firm, early-season gooseberries – the kind you're likely to find in June – rather than the sweeter, softer fruit of late July. As well as mackerel, the salsa is great with other robust or oily fish, such as bream, sardines and trout – particularly when the fish has been cooked on a barbecue.

To make the salsa, slice the gooseberries thickly and put them into a bowl. Add the cider vinegar, sugar and some salt and pepper, mix well, then cover and leave to macerate for at least an hour. Stir in the mint, taste and add a little more salt, pepper or sugar if you like, then it's ready to serve.

If you're barbecuing the fish, first make sure that your barbecue is good and hot, and that the flames have died down to leave glowing coals covered in a layer of white ash. Brush or rub the mackerel with a little oil, then season them inside and out with salt and pepper. Stuff the herbs, if you're using them, inside the fish.

Lay the mackerel on the hot barbecue and cook, without moving, for 2–3 minutes. Turn the fish over and barbecue for another 2–3 minutes or until the flesh is cooked through. Alternatively, you can cook the mackerel under a hot grill. Serve straight away, with the gooseberry and mint salsa.

Serves 3–4

3–4 medium line-caught mackerel, descaled and gutted

A little olive, rapeseed or sunflower oil

A few bay leaves and/or sprigs of thyme (optional)

Sea salt and freshly ground black pepper

### For the salsa

150g tart gooseberries, topped and tailed

1 tablespoon cider vinegar

1 tablespoon caster sugar

About 1 tablespoon finely shredded mint

# Mackerel with redcurrant sauce

**Serves 2**

1 tablespoon olive oil

2 medium line-caught mackerel, filleted

150g redcurrants

A knob of butter

A large sprig of thyme, leaves only

A pinch of sugar

Sea salt and freshly ground black pepper

We all know how well a squeeze of lemon juice works as a seasoning for seafood, so it's no surprise that other tart fruits can be delicious with fish. Both rhubarb and gooseberry are time-honoured partners to mackerel and I'm currently (excuse the pun) very fond of this match, the sharpness of the redcurrants mitigated by a little butter, a pinch of sugar and some earthy thyme.

Heat the olive oil in a large non-stick frying pan over a medium heat. Season the mackerel fillets all over and add to the pan, skin side down. Fry for 2–3 minutes, until the skin is golden, then turn them and fry for a minute or so on the other side until just cooked through. Remove the mackerel fillets to warm serving plates.

Turn down the heat under the frying pan, add the redcurrants and crush them with a spatula to release their juices. Use these juices to deglaze the pan, scraping the bottom with a wooden spatula to release any nice crusty bits created by frying the fish. Add the butter, thyme leaves, sugar and some salt and pepper and let the mixture bubble for a few minutes, stirring regularly, until soft, rich and pulpy.

Now quickly tip the contents of the pan into a sieve set over a warm bowl, pressing with a spoon to extract all the juice. Immediately spoon the sauce alongside the mackerel on the plates. Alternatively, you can sieve the sauce directly on to the plates, which is quicker, if a little less elegant. Either way, serve without delay.

I like a green salad alongside – perhaps based on some lovely soft roundhead lettuce leaves. White beans or Puy lentils in addition would make a slightly more substantial plate of food – a proper main course, rather than a light lunch or hearty starter.

# Roast **pork** with gooseberries and black pudding

Apples are traditionally paired with pork, but gooseberries – which share some of the floral acidity of apples – work equally well. Leave the pork joint uncovered, skin side up, in the fridge overnight, if possible. This helps to dry the skin, which makes for better crackling.

Preheat the oven to 220°C/Gas 7. If it hasn't already been done, score the skin of the pork, using a very sharp blade, such as a Stanley knife, to make long cuts about 2cm apart all over the skin, going through the skin and about 3mm into the fat, but not through to the meat.

Unroll the pork and lay skin side down on a board. Slice into the 'eye' of the meat to create a pocket for stuffing. Open up the meat, season with salt and pepper and crumble over the black pudding. Scatter over 100g of the gooseberries (thickly slicing any large ones first), press down and sprinkle with the sugar. Roll up the joint, enclosing the stuffing, and tie with string. Turn the joint skin side up, wipe the skin dry and place in a roasting tin. Season the skin well with salt and a little pepper.

Roast for 20 minutes, then lower the setting to 170°C/Gas 3 and pour a glass of water into the tin (not over the meat). Roast for a further 1¼ hours – 1 hour 40 minutes until a meat thermometer inserted into the centre of the meat registers 70°C and the juices run clear. Transfer the joint to a warm plate to rest for 20–30 minutes. If the crackling isn't crisp enough, you can slice it off the meat and put it under a hot grill until crackled and blistered, keeping an eye on it as it can quickly burn. Meanwhile, put the remaining gooseberries into the roasting tin with the pork juices and cook in the oven for about 10 minutes until soft.

Serve the pork in thick slices, with spoonfuls of the tart gooseberry compote/gravy from the tin. Serve with roast or mashed potatoes and some leafy greens, such as kale or purple sprouting broccoli.

**Variations** In place of the gooseberries, you could add a good, tart eating apple, peeled and cut into chunky dice, to the stuffing and some wedges of apple to the roasting juices for the final half hour. Or try chunks of rhubarb for a different but equally delicious fruity tartness.

Serves 6–8

1.5–2kg piece of boned and rolled loin of outdoor-reared pork

100g black pudding, skinned

350g gooseberries, topped and tailed

20g soft brown sugar

Sea salt and freshly ground black pepper

# Seared short-cured sirloin with strawberries

**Serves 2 as a main course, 4 as a starter**

2 thick-cut, well-aged sirloin steaks, about 200g each

A little sunflower oil or beef dripping, for frying

*For the short dry cure*

50g fine sea salt

10g caster sugar

10g freshly coarse-ground black pepper

*For the strawberries and dressing*

200g strawberries, hulled

15g caster sugar

Finely grated zest and juice of 1 lemon

50ml rosé wine

2 teaspoons rosewater, or orange flower water (optional)

3–4 lemon verbena leaves, bruised (optional)

*To serve*

A couple of handfuls of small sorrel leaves, or delicate salad leaves

**This recipe was improvised at the Mad Food Festival in Copenhagen by my River Cottage colleagues Gill Meller and Steve Lamb. They were cooking for the whole kitchen team of Noma, recently voted best restaurant in the world. So no pressure then… It went down an absolute storm, and I was hugely proud of them. It may sound a bit outré, but it's actually very simple – a delicious, if unexpected, amalgamation of meaty, fruity and fragrant flavours.**

Combine the ingredients for the dry cure. Scatter half the cure evenly over a plate, lay the steaks on top, then cover them evenly with the remaining cure, rubbing it in lightly with your fingertips. Leave to stand for about half an hour (45 minutes max).

Meanwhile, to make the dressing, put half the strawberries in a bowl with the sugar, lemon zest and juice, wine, rosewater and lemon verbena, if using. Use your hands to crush the fruit together with the flavourings. Set aside to macerate while the steak is curing.

After the allotted time, carefully wash the cure from the steaks under a cold running tap. Pat the steaks thoroughly dry with kitchen paper.

Strain the macerated strawberry mixture through a sieve into a clean bowl. Slice the remaining strawberries thickly into this dressing.

Heat a frying pan over a high heat, then add a dash of oil or dripping. When it is almost smoking hot, add the steaks to the pan. Cook for 2 minutes on each side for rare, 3 minutes each side for medium-rare, or a little longer if you prefer them medium – but they really should be pink in the middle. Remove the steaks from the pan and allow them to rest for a good 5 minutes.

To serve, slice the steaks thickly and arrange over two or four plates, then spoon over the strawberries and their aromatic dressing. Leave for just a minute for the dressing to mingle with the steak juices. Season with a few twists of black pepper and sprinkle with a handful of small sorrel or salad leaves.

# Gooseberry
## and sage focaccia

**Makes 1 large loaf**

500g strong white
bread flour

1 teaspoon easy-blend
yeast

10g fine sea salt

3 tablespoons extra
virgin olive oil, plus
extra to trickle

Cornmeal or polenta,
to dust (optional)

150g gooseberries,
topped and tailed

About 20 sage leaves

Coarse sea salt,
to sprinkle

**This fruity bread is perfect to serve at the table before the rest of dinner arrives. It's also lovely for supper with some salty cheese, ham, or leftover pork or chicken and a few salad leaves alongside.**

Put the flour, yeast and fine salt in a bowl and mix well. Pour in 350ml warm water and the 3 tablespoons olive oil and mix to a very soft, wet elastic dough. If you have a mixer with a dough hook, it will make short work of the kneading. Otherwise, turn the dough out on to a lightly floured surface and knead it by hand for about 10 minutes until smooth and silky. Add more flour if you need to, but keep it minimal.

Put the dough into a lightly oiled large bowl, cover with a clean tea towel and leave to rise in a warm place until doubled in size. This will take at least an hour, probably closer to two.

Preheat the oven to 220°C/Gas 7. Oil a fairly shallow baking tin, about 22 x 30cm, and scatter it with cornmeal or polenta if you have some (to give the focaccia a nice crisp base).

Tip the dough from the bowl straight into the oiled baking tin, without kneading out the air, and press it lightly with your fingertips to roughly fill the tin. Cover again and leave for at least another 30 minutes – up to an hour – until it has risen further and is light and puffy.

Pair each sage leaf with a gooseberry and arrange all over the surface of the focaccia, pressing them into the dough. Trickle generously with more olive oil and scatter with coarse sea salt. Bake in the oven for 10 minutes, then lower the oven setting to 190°C/Gas 5 and bake for a further 15 minutes or so until golden.

Remove the focaccia from the tin and place on a wire rack. Allow to cool a little, then eat while still warm.

**Variations** In place of the gooseberries and sage, try studding your focaccia with redcurrants, seasoned with lots of black pepper as well as the salt. Another delicious idea is to press pieces of peeled pear and chunks of blue cheese into the dough before it goes into the oven.

# Strawberry
## and peanut butter sandwich

This fresh version of the peanut butter and jelly (jam) sandwich so revered over the Pond is, I would propose, an even more delightful combination: nutty, fruity, sweet and just a little bit greedy... a comfort snack of the highest order.

Thickly slice the strawberries. Spread both slices of bread generously with butter, if you like. Spread one slice (or both) thickly with peanut butter and add a good layer of strawberries. Scatter with a little caster sugar (or, if you prefer a more savoury version, a few twists of black pepper) and top with the second slice of bread.

Pressing lightly on the bread to hold everything together, slice in two with a very sharp knife, and serve.

**Variations** This is particularly good if you make your own nut butter, which is surprisingly easy. Almond butter is my favourite, though this works well with peanuts, cashews and hazelnuts too. Just put 200g very lightly toasted blanched almonds in a food processor with a good pinch of salt and whiz until finely chopped. Add 1–2 tablespoons rapeseed, sunflower or coconut oil and process to a creamy paste. You can sweeten it, if you like, with honey or sugar, though I prefer it unsweetened.

There's great mileage in the berry sandwich idea. One of my favourite greedy treats is a strawberry and clotted cream version, made as above but with indulgent thick West Country clotted cream in place of the peanut butter. Or pile lightly crushed raspberries on to the buttered bread and sprinkle generously with sugar before applying the top slice. Arguably slightly more virtuous is a blueberry and honey sandwich or, for a breakfast treat, try blueberry and lemon curd (see page 353).

**Per person**

About 50g strawberries, hulled

2 slices of fresh crusty white bread

Unsalted butter, at room temperature, for spreading (optional)

Crunchy, no-added-sugar peanut butter, to taste

Caster sugar (or freshly ground black pepper), to sprinkle

# Strawberries and blueberries in raspberry sauce

**Serves 4**

200g raspberries

1–2 tablespoons icing sugar

250g strawberries, hulled

250g blueberries

This is a gorgeous fruit salad in its own right, but it can also be served alongside ice cream or pannacotta, or folded lightly through a mixture of crushed meringue and lightly whipped cream to create a sumptuous version of Eton Mess.

Purée the raspberries in a blender or with a handheld stick blender, then push through a sieve into a bowl with a wooden spoon to remove all the pips. Add enough icing sugar to the purée to make it taste pleasantly sweet-but-tart.

Thickly slice the strawberries. Toss them into the raspberry sauce, along with the blueberries and leave for an hour or so in a cool place (not the fridge) to macerate before serving.

**Variations** This simple fruit salad is delicious if you add a little shredded fresh basil or mint along with the raspberry sauce.

# Blackcurrant
## and orange salad
## with mint sugar

This fruit salad is simple to make but packs a serious punch. Sweet orange pieces and sharp little blackcurrants come together in a surprisingly explosive way, with the minty sugar adding a scented, crystally crunch. It's a lovely way to end a summer meal.

Start by making the mint sugar. Either put the sugar and mint into a food processor and blitz them together or, alternatively, finely chop the mint leaves then pound them together with the sugar using a pestle and mortar. Either way, you should end up with a crystalline green, grainy mixture with a texture a little like damp green sand. Set aside. (You may not need all of it for this recipe; see below for other uses.)

Slice all the peel and pith away from the oranges: to do this, cut a slice off the base and stand the orange on a board. Then use a sharp knife to cut down through the peel and pith, slicing it away completely, in sections, so you have a whole orange with no white pith left at all. Now, working over a bowl, slice out the orange segments, letting them drop into the bowl. (Any juice can be strained off and drunk.)

Arrange the orange segments over individual plates. Scatter over the blackcurrants, finish with a generous sprinkling of the minty green sugar and serve.

*Other ways to use your mint sugar* Sprinkle it over strawberries, redcurrants or raspberries, or other soft fruits.

**Variation** For a strikingly different, savoury version of this zesty dish, omit the mint sugar and instead make a dressing with 2 tablespoons extra virgin olive oil, 1 teaspoon cider vinegar, a squeeze of the orange juice, a good pinch of sugar and some salt and pepper. Thinly slice 2–3 tender inner stems of celery or 1 trimmed fennel bulb, scatter these over the orange segments and blackcurrants and trickle with half the dressing. Now flake some smoked trout, mackerel or cooked kipper over the top and finish with the remaining dressing, a few mint leaves or fennel fronds and an extra scattering of black pepper.

### Serves 4

4 medium oranges

100g blackcurrants

### For the mint sugar

75g caster sugar

About 20 mint leaves

# Raspberry sorbet with lavender

Raspberries can be pricey in the shops but this is a great way to use a homegrown glut. Or, if your local pick-your-own farm sells cheap, slightly over-ripe, squishy berries for jam-making, they'll be perfect too. The best lavender to use is tender young leaves and/or the flowerbuds, before they are fully open, in June and early July when the plant is at its sweetest and most fragrant.

Put the sugar in a saucepan with 200ml water. Heat gently, stirring often, until the sugar has dissolved, then increase the heat and bring to a simmer. Allow to simmer for 5 minutes, then take off the heat and stir in the lavender. Set aside to infuse and cool completely.

Whiz the raspberries in a blender to a purée, then pass through a sieve into a bowl to remove all the pips. Strain the cooled, lavender-infused syrup through a sieve on to the raspberry purée, pressing the lavender with a wooden spoon to extract every last drop of flavour. Cover and chill in the fridge.

Churn the chilled mixture in an ice-cream maker until just set, then transfer to the freezer to set solid. (Alternatively, freeze in a plastic container for about an hour until it is starting to solidify around the sides. Mash the frozen sorbet into the liquid centre with a fork, and then return to the freezer. Repeat at hourly intervals until soft-set, then let it freeze solid.)

Transfer the sorbet to the fridge about 20 minutes before serving, to soften a little. Scoop into glasses or on to plates and scatter over a handful of raspberries, if you like. Lavender and lemon shortbread biscuits are the perfect complement.

**Variation** You can also make this sorbet with a mixture of raspberries and strawberries.

**Serves 4**

125g caster sugar

1 tablespoon roughly chopped lavender leaves and/or flowerbuds

500g raspberries

*To serve (optional)*

About 125g raspberries

Lavender and lemon shortbread biscuits (see page 357)

# Strawberry yoghurt semifreddo

A semifreddo (literally 'half-frozen') is a very simple Italian iced pud, usually made with egg yolks and sugar whipped into a sort of mousse. This means it doesn't require churning in the way that an ice cream does. There's also yoghurt in the mix here, which gives the finished dish a lovely light tang.

Line a 1kg loaf tin, about 22 x 11cm, with cling film (if you make the loaf tin slightly wet first, it helps the cling film to cling).

Whiz the strawberries in a blender to a purée, then pass through a sieve into a bowl to remove all the pips.

Put the egg yolks and sugar in a large bowl over a saucepan of just-simmering water and whisk for 5–10 minutes with an electric whisk, until thick, pale and creamy; don't let the bowl get too hot or the eggs may start to scramble. The mixture should 'hold a trail' when you lift the beaters (i.e. a ribbon of the mixture should clearly be seen to sit on the surface before sinking back in).

Carefully fold the strawberry purée into the moussey egg mixture using a large metal spoon or spatula, then cover and chill in the fridge.

Put the cream and yoghurt into a bowl. Slit open the vanilla pod, scrape out the seeds with the tip of a small, sharp knife and add them to the bowl. Whisk together until the mixture just holds very soft peaks.

Gently fold this creamy mixture into the chilled strawberry mix with a large metal spoon, trying to keep in as much air as possible. Then pour into the prepared tin and freeze until solid.

Transfer the semifreddo to the fridge 30 minutes before serving to soften. Cut into thick slices and serve with extra strawberries.

Serves 8

300g strawberries, hulled, plus extra to serve

6 large free-range egg yolks

175g caster sugar

100ml double cream

150ml plain wholemilk yoghurt

1 vanilla pod

# Thyme-scented raspberries with yoghurt and crumble

**Serves 4**

350g raspberries

2 tablespoons caster sugar

1 teaspoon chopped thyme

About 125ml thick, plain wholemilk yoghurt

'Independent crumble' (see page 84)

This simple dish follows one of my favourite pudding formulas, combining something sharp and fruity (raspberries), with something creamy (yoghurt) and something crunchy and crisp (the crumble). It's incredibly easy and it looks as good as it tastes.

Crush about a quarter of the raspberries in your hands to get the juices flowing, then put them into a bowl with the uncrushed berries, sugar and chopped thyme. Mix gently, cover and leave to macerate for an hour or so.

To serve, divide the raspberry compote between serving bowls. Spoon the yoghurt over the fruit and scatter the crumble generously on top.

**Variation** Try adding a few blueberries to the raspberries. You could also substitute the raspberry-dressed strawberry and blueberry salad on page 43 for the raspberry compote.

# Gooseberry,
## elderflower and almond
# cobbler

It's not essential to use fresh elderflowers here but if you can get hold of a few creamy heads (usually from late May to the end of June) they will lend a lovely, subtle floral flavour to this pud. The best elderflower heads are those where only some of the flowers are fully open, and some still just tight white buds.

Tie up the elderflower heads, if using, in a piece of muslin. Put the gooseberries, 100g sugar and the lemon zest in a pan. If you are using fresh elderflowers, add 3 tablespoons water. If you're using the cordial, add it with just 1 tablespoon water. Stir over a low heat until the fruit starts to release its juices. Add the bundle of elderflower, if using, bring to a gentle simmer and cook for about 5 minutes until the fruit is soft but not too mushy. Press the elderflower bundle down into the fruit to encourage the flower heads to release their fragrance. Set aside to infuse while you make the topping.

Preheat the oven to 190°C/Gas 5. Sift the flour, baking powder and salt into a bowl. Add the butter and rub it in with your fingertips until the mixture resembles coarse breadcrumbs. Stir in the ground almonds and sugar. Beat the egg together with the milk and stir lightly into the flour mix, bringing it together into a soft, sticky dough (much looser than a conventional scone dough); try to avoid overworking the dough.

Remove the elderflower heads from the gooseberry compote. Taste it and add more sugar if necessary. Different gooseberries vary in their sweetness and personal taste is a factor. I like the gooseberry compote to be pleasantly sweet, but with the tartness of the gooseberries still right up there.

Transfer the gooseberry compote to a wide, shallow oven dish, about 1.5 litre capacity. Spoon the scone dough on top in 6–8 large dollops) and scatter the flaked almonds on top of the dough. Bake for about 30 minutes, until the scone topping is well risen and golden. Poke a toothpick or skewer into one of the 'cobbles' to check that it is cooked right through. Serve hot or warm, with double cream or custard.

Serves 6–8

10 freshly picked heads of elderflower, or 2 tablespoons elderflower cordial

750g gooseberries, topped and tailed

100–125g caster sugar

2 strips of lemon zest

### For the cobbler topping

100g plain flour

1½ teaspoons baking powder

A pinch of salt

35g cold butter, diced

75g ground almonds

35g caster sugar

1 large free-range egg

75ml milk

A handful of flaked almonds

# Raspberry ripple chocolate ice cream

**Makes about 600ml**

**For the raspberry purée**

300g raspberries

50g caster sugar

**For the ice cream**

200ml whole milk

300ml double cream

200g dark chocolate (about 70% cocoa solids), quite finely chopped

4 large free-range egg yolks

100g caster sugar

Plain shortbread biscuits (see page 357), to serve (optional)

Chocolate and raspberries are such a winning combination, and this is a very neat way of serving them together: gorgeous, ridiculously chocolatey, and a little bit unexpected.

To make the raspberry purée, put the berries, 2 tablespoons water and the sugar in a pan and bring to the boil. Simmer for a few minutes until the fruit has collapsed, then press through a sieve and return to the pan. Boil for 6–7 minutes to reduce and thicken the purée, stirring often so it doesn't stick and burn. Leave to cool, then chill thoroughly.

For the ice cream, put the milk and cream in a saucepan and heat to just below boiling. Take off the heat, add the chopped chocolate and leave for a few minutes to melt, stirring from time to time. It's unlikely to all melt completely smoothly at this point, but don't worry.

Whisk the egg yolks and sugar together thoroughly in a bowl, then pour on a little of the hot chocolate cream and whisk together. Return this to the pan with the rest of the chocolate cream. Put back over a medium heat and cook gently, stirring all the time, until the custard thickens and the chocolate is completely melted and amalgamated. Don't let it boil or it will 'split'. Pass through a fine sieve into a clean jug, leave to cool completely, then chill in the fridge.

Once cold, spoon the thick chocolate custard into an ice-cream maker and churn until soft-set. (Alternatively, freeze in a plastic container for about an hour until solidifying around the sides. Mash the frozen sides into the liquid centre with a fork, and return to the freezer for another hour. Repeat this at hourly intervals until soft-set.)

Transfer the soft-set ice cream to a shallow freezer container. Add the raspberry purée in spoonfuls and ripple it through, leaving some nice thick streaks of raspberry. Put into the freezer to freeze solid.

Transfer the ice cream to the fridge about 30 minutes before serving to soften slightly. This is fabulous served with plain shortbread biscuits.

# Strawberry
## and red wine granita

I've always loved a granita, the simplest of all frozen desserts. In this one, the combination of strawberries and fruity red wine makes for a richly flavoured and rather grown-up iced pud.

Halve the strawberries and put them into a saucepan with the sugar and wine. Leave to stand for half an hour.

Bring the strawberry mix to a simmer, stirring to dissolve the sugar, then cook gently for 10 minutes – at never more than a subtle simmer. Purée the mixture in a blender, then pass through a sieve into a bowl to remove the pips and leave to cool.

Stir the lemon juice into the cooled liquid and taste. You can add more sugar at this point if you like – the easiest thing is to whisk in some icing sugar – but don't make it too sweet or you'll mask the other flavours. Pour the liquid into a shallow freezer container and freeze until solid – give it at least 12 hours.

Take the granita out of the freezer about 20 minutes before serving and test the consistency. You'll probably find that it's soft enough to scratch with a fork straight away – the alcohol and the sugar stop it from freezing absolutely solid. In this case, put it back in the freezer until you're ready to serve. If, however, it does seem very hard, leave it out of the freezer.

Use a fork to scratch the frozen purée into crystals – the finished granita should have a texture rather like a coarse sorbet, or fruity snow. Pile the crystals into serving glasses or bowls. Serve immediately, as it is, or topped with a generous, snowy cap of cream if you prefer.

**Variation:** *Rhubarb and Champagne granita* Simply replace the strawberries with rhubarb and use Champagne or good sparkling wine instead of the red wine. You can add the finely grated zest and juice of an orange to the rhubarb and wine before you cook it, but it's not vital. You can also replace 25g of the sugar with 1 tablespoon honey. There's no need to sieve the purée if it's well blended.

**Serves 6–8**

500g strawberries, hulled

100g caster sugar

400ml light, fruity red wine such as Beaujolais, Tarrango or any Gamay

Juice of ½ lemon

A little icing sugar (optional)

# Blackcurrant curd

This variation on the classic lemon curd is tart, sweet, rich and completely delicious. The curd doesn't keep for very long once opened, so it makes sense to preserve it in small jars.

Sterilise 5 small (250–300ml) jars by washing them thoroughly in hot soapy water, rinsing well then putting them upside down on a tray in a low oven (at 120°C/Gas ½) to dry out and warm up.

Put the blackcurrants in a saucepan with the lemon juice. Bring slowly to a simmer, stirring often until the fruit starts to release its juice, then simmer gently for 5–10 minutes until the blackcurrants have collapsed. Rub this mixture through a fine sieve into a heatproof bowl to obtain a smooth purée.

Add the butter and sugar to the blackcurrant purée and set the bowl over a pan of simmering water. Stir until the butter has melted and the mixture is smooth. Take off the heat and let it cool for a minute – you don't want it to be too hot when you pour the eggs in, or they will scramble. It should be cool enough that you can comfortably put your finger into it. Pour in the strained beaten egg, whisking all the while.

Return the pan to the heat and stir the mixture over the simmering water until it is thick and creamy. This will take at least 10 minutes. It should register 82–84°C on a sugar thermometer. If the mixture does get too hot and start to scramble, take it off the heat and whisk vigorously until smooth. As soon as it has thickened, pour the curd into the warm jars and seal. Leave to cool completely.

Store the blackcurrant curd in the fridge and use within 4 weeks. Once opened, it should be used within a week.

*Eating your curd* Spread it on scones, dollop on eggy bread or rice pudding, or try it rippled into a muffin mix before baking. It's also exquisite in the middle of a sponge cake. Or, with a blob of yoghurt and a few fresh berries, it makes a great, quick pud.

**Makes 5 small jars**

500g blackcurrants

100ml lemon juice

125g unsalted butter

450g granulated sugar

200ml strained beaten egg (4–5 large free-range eggs)

# Strawberry and elderflower cocktail

**Serves 4**

250g strawberries, hulled, plus a few extra to serve

150ml elderflower cordial

About 30 ice cubes

About 200ml good vodka

**I have to warn you: this drink is dangerous. Fragrant, fruity and delectably thirst-quenching, it slips down very easily.**

Roughly chop the strawberries, put into a blender with the elderflower cordial and pulse to a thin purée (or blitz together in a jug, using a handheld stick blender). You can make the purée smooth or, as I prefer, leave it a little coarse with small nuggets of strawberry.

Crush the ice. If you have a very robust blender, it may be up to this job. Alternatively, put the ice cubes in a tough plastic bag or wrap in a robust tea towel, and bash them with a rolling pin. Divide the crushed ice between four glasses (ideally chilled).

Pour 30–50ml vodka over the ice in each glass and top up with the strawberry and elderflower purée. Give each glass a good stir and top with a few slices of strawberry (or even a sprig of elderflower if you have any). Drink straight away, with a straw, if you prefer.

Variations
You can make a milder drink by topping up with a little soda water or sparkling water, or replacing the alcohol altogether with sparkling water or apple juice. (The same applies to the following cocktail.)

*Raspberry and mint cocktail* In a blender, purée 400g raspberries with 100g caster sugar and the roughly torn leaves from a large bunch of mint (around 50g). Leave for an hour or two for the flavours to mingle and develop, then pass the purée through a sieve to remove the raspberry pips. Pour this purée over vodka and ice, as above.

# Blackcurrant liqueur

This homemade version of crème de cassis is essentially the late, great Jane Grigson's recipe, from *her* Fruit Book. It has a deliciously rounded, smooth flavour that's perfect in a kir or kir royal (combined with white wine, or sparkling wine, respectively). You can also use it in puddings such as the sorbet on page 237. Or simply trickle it over vanilla ice cream, or apple pie, or both!

Combine the blackcurrants and wine in a glass or ceramic bowl and leave to macerate for at least 24 hours (and up to 48).

Purée the blackcurrants and wine in a food processor, then tip into a sieve lined with muslin or a clean cloth. Leave to drip for several hours, then squeeze out the last of the juice by twisting the edges of the cloth together with your hands. Measure the juice into a large saucepan. For every 100ml juice, add 60g sugar. Heat gently, stirring frequently, until the sugar dissolves.

You now need to cook the syrup at the lowest possible temperature – to quote Jane Grigson, 'regulate the heat so that the liquid keeps above blood heat but well below simmering and boiling points'. This helps to ensure that the pectin in the fruit isn't released, which would cause the liquid to set into a gel once cooled. You might find it helpful to use a heat-diffusing plate on the hob, and even to turn the heat off every now and again for a minute or two, to keep the liquid below simmering. Cook it like this for about 2 hours, skimming off any scum that forms. It will reduce slightly and become a little more syrupy, though it can be hard to detect this while it's still hot. Leave it to cool completely.

Meanwhile, sterilise your bottles, and their lids or caps, by washing in very hot, soapy water (use a bottle brush), rinsing well and then putting them on a tray in a low oven (at 120°C/Gas ½) for 20 minutes to dry out. Leave to cool.

Measure the cooled syrup, then stir in one part vodka to three parts syrup. Decant into the cold, sterilised bottles. Store for at least 2 weeks before drinking.

**Makes about 1 litre**

500g blackcurrants

500ml fruity red wine, such as Beaujolais or Tarrango

About 500g granulated sugar

About 300ml vodka

Strictly speaking, rhubarb shouldn't be in this book. As the stem of a leafy plant, it can't even *begin* to claim it's a fruit. It's really rather odd to think of it as one – yet, lover of rhubarb that I am, I wouldn't have it any other way. And since I am no taxonomic disciplinarian, I welcome it on to these pages with open arms.

Of course, how this interloper has inveigled its way into the fruit-pudding pantheon is not really a mystery. Down the ages, cooks have recognised its almost berryish tartness and its obliging tendency to collapse into a juicy compote when gently heated. Rhubarb has become such a hero of hot crumbles and cold fools that, for many households, these are pretty much the only ways it is prepared. That's no great surprise. These two puds can be so very good that to visit each of them a few times a year keeps most rhubarb fans quite content.

But surely we shouldn't settle for mere contentment. How about excitement? We should also address the bewildering fact that many people remain underwhelmed by rhubarb. If you are not as enamoured of the blushing stems as I am, I wonder whether that's because you've only experienced lacklustre versions of that crumble (perhaps the topping was too stodgy to live up to its name) and that fool (maybe over-stewed, stringy rhubarb mixed with over-whipped, lumpy cream)? And even if you *love* rhubarb, I bet there are all kinds of ways to enjoy it that you haven't yet explored. Either way, I intend to launch a whole new raft of recipes into your rhubarb repertoire.

So whilst the simplest of compotes, served with cream and a good biscuit, will always have a place in my heart, I've allowed my rhubarb thinking to stray *way* outside the old-school box. My default rhubarb cooking vessel has changed from saucepan to roasting tin: I find that oven-baking, rather than poaching, lets the rhubarb keep its shape and colour and thereby more of its texture and charm. I've used this technique in a number of recipes, including the rhubarb and strawberry compote on page 88, where the chunky pieces of rhubarb jumble with thickly sliced raw strawberries, and the rhubarb and ginger cheesecake on page 92, where they are arranged pertly over the top.

On the savoury side, rhubarb's sharpness makes it a shoo-in with rich meats and oily fish – not a new idea, but an under-explored one. Roast goose with rhubarb stuffing (page 74) and rhubarb fish parcels with soy and ginger (page 72) not only take advantage of its fat-cutting edge, but show that it sometimes makes sense to deploy rhubarb like the vegetable we've forgotten it is. (Though please *don't* extend this notion to cooking with the leaves – they are poisonous!)

I would also press you to try it raw, or almost raw, from time to time. Provided it's young and tender (i.e. forced, or of the early spring outdoor crop), then thinly sliced or finely chopped, it's a revelation. The rhubarb and orange salad on page 82 uses just the heat of a syrup to slightly tenderise otherwise raw rhubarb, while the rhubarb and carrot salad on page 68 uses the crunch of raw stems as though they were a tart kind of celery. These may be fairly unusual approaches, but they are in no way outlandish – try them and you'll see they make perfect sense.

Besides choosing the right partners for rhubarb, the knack with these recipes is in controlled texture and accurate sweetening. But there are other ways of countering rhubarb's astringency, besides the simple addition of sugar or honey. Orange zest, vanilla, rosewater, ginger – even herbs such as thyme or rosemary – can all be used to enhance and aromatise rhubarb. When it's tweaked in this agreeable way, I tend to find it needs less sweetening. (In my recipes I err on the side of under- rather than over-sweetening rhubarb, so by all means taste and add more sugar if you find it too tart.)

Rhubarb comes in two distinct seasonal incarnations. The early crop, from late December to April, is 'forced' in dark sheds and turns out slender, tender and an outrageous Barbie pink. This coquettish stem is replaced in late spring by its big brother, outdoor-grown rhubarb, whose strong, broad shaft has a much darker crimson hue. These siblings may look different, but they work similarly in recipes. Forced rhubarb is a tad more delicate and effervescent, the outdoor crop more fibrous and sour, so it may require a little more sugar. But either type can be used in any of my recipes.

Although the plant is native to Siberia, I think of rhubarb as one of ours. The best of the early crop indisputably comes from Yorkshire, from the area known as the 'rhubarb triangle', where the climate and soil suit the plant perfectly. Yorkshire rhubarb now has PDO (Protected Designation of Origin) status, and deservedly so. Supermarkets will often stock cheaper continental imports, but it's really worth seeking out the homegrown stuff.

Rhubarb is also the gardener's favourite, a stalwart of the veg patch and allotment. I often see ready-to-plant rhubarb crowns on sale for pence at farmers' markets and outside garden gates. Anyone who can offer it well-manured soil and a bit of space will be rewarded with a ready crop through spring and summer. There could be no better way to give this honorary, and honourable, fruit the full kitchen run-around than with fine, crimson-flushed stems you've raised yourself.

*Rhubarb*

# Raw rhubarb and carrot salad

Colourful, crunchy and packed with bright, sharp flavours, this is a winning salad for the winter months when forced pink rhubarb is in season, though you can also make it later in the year with maincrop outdoor rhubarb and little summer carrots.

For the dressing, whisk the ingredients together thoroughly in a bowl, or shake in a screw-topped jar to emulsify.

Peel the carrots and cut into julienne strips (or grate them coarsely if you prefer). If using baby summer carrots, just cut them lengthways into quarters, or eighths. Put them in a bowl.

If you're using maincrop, outdoor-grown rhubarb, use a vegetable peeler to remove the outer skin, which can be overly fibrous. If you have very tender, forced pink rhubarb, this won't be necessary, and it's nice to keep that lovely pink colour. Either way, slice the rhubarb very thinly, across the stems and on a slight diagonal.

Add the rhubarb to the carrot, pour over the dressing and mix well. Leave to stand for 10 minutes or so, then spread the mixture on a plate (or two plates).

Tear or crumble the cheese over the top, then scatter over the walnuts. Add a grinding of pepper and serve straight away.

**Variations** Raw celeriac or beetroot, cut into julienne, can stand in very nicely for the carrot. Or use two, or all three, of these roots.

Serves 2

About 125g carrots
(2 medium, 1 very
large, or a handful
of baby carrots)

About 125g rhubarb
(a couple of good
stems), trimmed

75g soft or crumbly
goat's cheese or other
crumbly, salty white
cheese, such as
Caerphilly

25g walnut halves
(or broken bits)

### For the dressing

3 tablespoons extra
virgin olive oil

1 teaspoon cider
vinegar

1 teaspoon Dijon
mustard

1 teaspoon honey

Sea salt and freshly
ground black pepper

# Sausages and scrambled eggs with rhubarb

**Serves 2**

1 tablespoon sunflower oil

2 butcher's sausages or 4 chipolatas

100g rhubarb, trimmed

2 knobs of butter

1 teaspoon soft brown sugar (or caster sugar)

A few thyme leaves

4 free-range eggs, lightly beaten

Sea salt and freshly ground black pepper

**Rhubarb and custard? Not quite. Granted, there is a hint of that divine partnership in this intriguing dish but the sausages anchor it firmly in the savoury camp.**

Put a non-stick frying pan over a medium heat and add the oil. Add the sausages and cook them, relatively gently, turning often, until nicely browned and caramelised on the outside and cooked right through to the middle. This will take a good 20 minutes. Transfer to a warm dish and keep warm. (Alternatively, you could cook the bangers in the oven or under the grill if you prefer.)

In the meantime, cut the rhubarb into 5–6cm lengths.

Pour off any excess fat from the frying pan and add a knob of butter. When foaming, add the rhubarb, sugar, thyme leaves and some salt and pepper. Fry the rhubarb very gently for 5–6 minutes, turning a few times, until just tender but still holding its shape. Transfer the rhubarb to a warm dish, draining off the excess liquid – save a little if you fancy spooning it over the rhubarb to serve; keep warm.

Wipe out the frying pan with a wad of kitchen paper. Add another knob of butter to the pan and turn the heat down as low as possible. Add the beaten eggs and some salt and pepper and cook gently, stirring, until the eggs are lightly scrambled but still nice and loose.

Serve the scrambled eggs straight away, with the sausages, rhubarb and a little of their juice if you like. Grind over a little salt and some pepper and serve with hot buttered toast on the side.

**Variations** This quirky scrambled egg and rhubarb combination also works with other rich, salty, meaty breakfasty items, such as bacon and black pudding.

# Rhubarb
## fish parcels with soy and ginger

Cooking fish 'en papillote' like this is such a neat and efficient way of combining it with lots of lovely, aromatic flavours. Rhubarb, with its sour notes, is not unlike lemon in the way it seasons fish, and it works deliciously with ginger, leeks and salty soy. You can use any firm fish fillets here, from chunky white fish – like pollack and coley – to more robust fish, such as black bream and grey mullet.

Preheat the oven to 190°C/Gas 5.

Put the leek, rhubarb and ginger into a large bowl. Add the soy sauce, chilli, some black pepper and a pinch of salt and mix well. Add the fish fillets to the bowl and turn them in the mixture, rubbing the seasonings into the flesh.

Take four sheets of baking parchment, each about 45 x 35cm. With the shorter edge towards you, fold each in half to give you doubled sheets, about 22.5 x 35cm. Now fold 2cm over, twice, on each of the shorter sides, to seal them. Scatter a little of the rhubarb mixture inside each 'bag'. Place a fish fillet on top, skin side down, then add the remaining rhubarb mixture and all its liquid. Fold over the open edge of the parcel to seal it.

(Alternatively use foil. Lightly oil 4 thick foil squares, about 30cm, add the rhubarb mixture and fish, as above, and scrunch the foil up around the fish. Crimp the edges together well, but leave some air inside, so each piece of fish is sealed in a baggy foil parcel.)

Transfer the parcels to a large baking tray – or, even better, two trays. You want space between them so the hot air can circulate. Bake for about 15 minutes, or a little longer if your fish fillets are very thick.

Carefully open one parcel and check that the flesh is opaque all the way through and flakes easily off the skin. When the fish is cooked, transfer the parcels directly to warm plates. Serve with plain rice and steamed or stir-fried garlicky greens. Eat everything in the parcel, trickling any juices over the rice.

**Serves 4**

1 large leek, trimmed, washed and thinly sliced

150g rhubarb, trimmed and thinly sliced

A fat, thumb-sized piece of ginger, peeled and thinly sliced

3 tablespoons soy sauce

½–1 red chilli (not too fiery), deseeded and finely sliced (or a good pinch of dried chilli flakes)

4 chunky fish fillets, about 150–175g each

Sunflower oil, for oiling (if using foil)

Sea salt and freshly ground black pepper

# Roast goose with rhubarb stuffing

The festive availability of plump, free-range goose usually coincides with the start of the forced rhubarb season – in December. It's a match made in heaven, as the sharp, acidic rhubarb cuts the richness of the meat perfectly. Here rhubarb cooks with a few aromatics inside the goose to a tasty compote. Ideally, leave the goose uncovered overnight in the fridge, so the skin is nice and dry.

Preheat the oven to 220°C/Gas 7. To make the rhubarb stuffing, heat the oil in a frying pan, add the onion and fry gently for 10–15 minutes, until soft and golden. Tip into a bowl and mix with the rest of the ingredients, plus a good pinch of salt and a few twists of pepper.

Pull out any obvious lumps of fat from the goose cavity. If necessary, blot the skin dry with kitchen paper, then prick it all over with a fork and season generously with salt and pepper. Put the stuffing into the cavity; there will still be room for hot air to circulate inside as the bird roasts. Put the goose on a rack in a large roasting tray.

Roast the goose for 30 minutes, then lower the oven setting to 160°C/Gas 3 and cook for another 1½–2½ hours, depending on the size and meatiness of the bird; start checking after 2 hours total time by piercing the body at the point where the leg joins the breast – the juices should run clear. (A meat thermometer pushed into this joint should register 75°C.) After about 1½ hours, carefully pour off (and save) the fat that has collected in the tin, retaining the darker juices beneath. When cooked, leave the bird to rest in a warm place for 20–30 minutes.

To make the gravy, pour off most of the remaining fat from the roasting tin, leaving the dark juices behind. Place over a low heat. If you like a thickened gravy, mix in a little flour. Pour in the wine, scraping up the sediment to deglaze the pan. Strain the liquor into a clean saucepan, add the stock and boil hard until reduced to a rich syrupy gravy. Add a touch of redcurrant or crab apple jelly and adjust the seasoning.

Carve the goose and serve with the rhubarb stuffing, gravy, potatoes (roasted in goose fat) and seasonal veg.

## Serves 6

1 goose, 4.5–5kg, with neck and giblets

Sea salt and freshly ground black pepper

### For the rhubarb stuffing

1 tablespoon rapeseed, sunflower or olive oil

1 onion, finely chopped

400g rhubarb, trimmed and cut into 2–3cm lengths

2 small or 1 large apple (cookers or eaters), peeled, cored and chopped

4–6 bay leaves, torn

2 teaspoons chopped rosemary

Finely grated zest of 1 small lemon

A pinch of sugar

### For the gravy

2–4 teaspoons plain flour (optional)

½ glass of white wine

500ml goose stock, made from the giblets and neck, or chicken stock

1 teaspoon redcurrant or crab apple jelly

# Quick **rhubarb** pickle

**Serves 4–6**

150g early-season forced rhubarb, trimmed

1 medium carrot, peeled

½ small onion, finely chopped

3 tablespoons cider vinegar

1–2 tablespoons caster sugar

½ teaspoon crushed coriander seeds (or a couple of pinches of ground coriander)

2 bay leaves, torn

Sea salt and freshly ground black pepper

**This bright, light pickle is a great way to use raw rhubarb, making the most of its delectable crunch and vibrant acidity. It's particularly good with rich terrines, cold pork or chicken, and good Cheddar.**

Using a very sharp knife, cut the rhubarb into 2–3mm dice. Dice the carrot into similar-sized pieces. Combine the rhubarb, carrot and onion in a bowl.

Add the cider vinegar, 1 tablespoon sugar, the coriander, bay leaves and some salt and pepper. Mix thoroughly to dissolve the sugar, then leave to stand for 10–15 minutes.

Taste the pickle and adjust the seasonings and sweetness as you like. It's now ready to serve.

If you want to keep the pickle (for up to 24 hours), drain off the excess vinegar so it doesn't get over-pickled and store in a sealed plastic container in the fridge.

**Variation: *Rhubarb and wasabi pickle*** This is a lovely fresh and fiery take on the pickled rhubarb idea. Prepare the vegetables as above. To make the dressing, put 2 tablespoons cider vinegar, 2 tablespoons sugar and ¼ teaspoon wasabi paste in a small bowl. Add some salt and pepper and whisk to amalgamate. Taste and add a little more wasabi if you like. Pour this over the prepared veg and proceed as above.

# Two-course lamb and rhubarb pasty

This crisp-crusted pasty gives you both main course and pud in one, an echo of the traditional Cornish pasties eaten by tin-miners that had meat at one end and jam or fruit at the other. Lamb and rhubarb is just one version; other meaty, fruity options are explored below.

To make the pastry, put the flour and salt in a food processor and blitz briefly (or sift into a bowl). Add the butter and blitz (or rub in with your fingertips) until the mix resembles breadcrumbs. Mix in the milk, little by little, until the pastry just comes together. Turn on to a lightly floured surface, knead briefly into a ball, then wrap and chill for 30 minutes.

Preheat the oven to 180°C/Gas 4. Line a large baking sheet with baking parchment. Combine the lamb, potato, onion, Worcestershire sauce and melted butter in a bowl. Season well with salt and pepper and stir well.

Cut the rhubarb into 2–3cm pieces and combine with the sugar. Make sure the rhubarb is dry – excess water may make the pastry soggy.

Roll out the pastry on a lightly floured surface to a 4–5mm thickness and, using a plate as a template, cut four 20cm circles. Place a quarter of the lamb filling on one pastry circle, positioning it so it roughly fills a quarter of the pastry, leaving a 2cm margin at the edge. Put a quarter of the rhubarb beside it. Brush the margin with eggwash and fold the pastry over to encase the filling. Crimp the edges with your fingers to seal. Repeat this process for the remaining 3 pastry rounds.

Brush the tops of the pasties with eggwash. Covering the rhubarb side with greaseproof paper, sprinkle the rosemary and flaky salt over the lamb half. Move the paper to the other side and dust the rhubarb half with the sugar. Transfer to the lined baking sheet and bake for 35–40 minutes until golden. Let cool slightly – or completely – before eating.

**Variations** The two-course pasty is ripe for customisation. Try pork and a tart Bramley apple compote, beef with blackberries and diced pear, or chicken with quartered, sugared plums or gages. And by all means experiment with cherries, blueberries and blackcurrants as well.

## Makes 4

### For the pastry

400g plain flour

A pinch of salt

200g cold unsalted butter, cut into cubes

About 75ml cold milk

### For the fillings

250g lean lamb (leg or chump), cut into 3cm chunks

100g peeled potato, cut into 3–4mm pieces

1 small-medium onion, finely chopped

2–3 shakes of Worcestershire sauce

25g butter, melted

250g rhubarb, trimmed

50g caster sugar

Sea salt and freshly ground black pepper

### To finish

Eggwash (1 egg beaten with 1 tablespoon milk)

1 tablespoon chopped rosemary

Flaky sea salt

2 tablespoons caster sugar

# Rhubarb and orange salad

This fresh, fragrant salad from River Cottage head chef Gill Meller hangs on a lovely balance of acidity and sweetness. The rhubarb is lightly poached by the hot syrup, resulting in a distinctive, not-quite-crunchy texture that contrasts with the juicy orange segments. Made with forced pink rhubarb in winter, it's wonderfully fresh-looking, but it's equally delicious in spring and summer with outdoor rhubarb.

Cut the rhubarb stems on a slight angle into thin slices, just 2–3mm thick. Put the rhubarb slices into a heatproof bowl.

Carefully pare the zest from half of 1 orange, using a vegetable peeler or zester, taking care to avoid taking any bitter white pith. Set aside.

Slice all the peel and pith away from the oranges: to do this, cut a slice off the base and stand the orange on a board. Then use a sharp knife to cut down through the peel and pith, slicing it away completely, in sections, so you have a whole orange with no white pith left at all. Now, working over a bowl, slice out the orange segments, letting them drop into the bowl. Squeeze any juice out of the remaining orange membranes into the bowl too.

Strain off the juice from the bowl of orange segments into a measuring jug. Make up the quantity to 100ml with water if needed. Tip this liquid into a small pan and add the sugar, star anise, saffron, honey and pared orange zest. Bring this mixture to a simmer, stirring to dissolve the sugar and honey, then immediately pour over the sliced rhubarb in the bowl. Stir well and then leave to cool completely.

Once cooled, add the orange segments to the rhubarb and syrup. Toss gently, then leave to stand until you're ready to serve. (Or refrigerate if making in advance, taking it out of the fridge an hour before serving.)

Serve the salad in dishes or on plates, with the syrup spooned over. On its own it's lovely and fresh-tasting, but it can be served with thick yoghurt, and a tuile or shortbread biscuit (see page 357), if you want to make a greedy pud of it.

## Serves 4

200g rhubarb, trimmed

2 oranges

100g caster sugar

2–3 star anise

A good pinch of saffron strands

2 tablespoons honey

# Rhubarb fumble

I do like a fumble. It's nothing more than a fruit fool topped with a separately made crumble – an idea I came up with a few years back, which I'm pleased to see is catching on! In this case, the fool part is rhubarb mingled lightly with a sweet vanilla-laced custard. The crunchy, nubbly topping finishes it off perfectly. The beauty of this approach is that you can serve all the elements hot, all cold, or at room temperature (which is my preference), or a bit of both.

To make the 'independent crumble', preheat the oven to 180°C/Gas 4. Put all the ingredients into a large bowl. Rub together with your fingertips until you have a crumbly dough, then squeeze in your hands to form clumps. Crumble these on to a large, lipped baking tray and spread out evenly. Bake for about 25 minutes until golden brown and crisp, giving the whole thing a good stir halfway through. You can let the crumble cool for just 10 minutes or so and use it still warm, or leave it to cool completely. You'll have more than you need for this recipe, but it stores well in an airtight container for a couple of weeks and can be used to top all sorts of fruity and/or creamy puds.

Cut the rhubarb into 4–5cm lengths and put into a large saucepan with the sugar and orange juice. Heat gently until the juices start to run, then give it a stir. Cover and cook gently, moving the pieces around carefully once or twice to ensure even cooking, for 10–15 minutes, until tender to the point of a knife. Ideally, you want most of the pieces to hold their shape. Either keep warm, or allow to cool, then chill.

To make the custard, put the cream, milk and vanilla pod in a saucepan and bring to just below the boil, then set aside to infuse for 10 minutes. Beat the egg yolks, sugar and cornflour together in a bowl until smooth then slowly pour on the hot cream, whisking all the time. Pour back into the pan and heat gently, stirring with a wooden spoon, until the mixture is thick enough to coat the back of the spoon; don't let it boil. Strain and either leave it to cool or serve it straight away.

Serve the rhubarb with the custard and a liberal scattering of crumble.

Serves 4

**For the 'independent crumble'**

225g plain flour

A pinch of fine sea salt

200g cold unsalted butter, cut into cubes

150g granulated or demerara sugar

100g medium oatmeal, ground almonds or porridge oats

**For the rhubarb**

400g rhubarb, trimmed

40g caster sugar

2 tablespoons freshly squeezed orange juice (or water)

**For the custard**

125ml double cream

125ml whole milk

½ vanilla pod, slit open lengthways

2 large free-range egg yolks

40g caster sugar

1 teaspoon cornflour

# Rhubarb mousse

## Serves 4

500g rhubarb, trimmed

125g caster sugar

50ml freshly squeezed orange juice (or water)

Enough sheets of leaf gelatine to set 500ml liquid

1 large free-range egg white

150ml double cream

### To finish (optional)

50g rhubarb, cut into 2–3mm thick slices

1 tablespoon caster sugar

### To serve (optional)

St Clements shortbread biscuits (see page 357) or brandy snaps (see page 182)

**This creamy, fruity mousse is a delightful, silky way to enjoy the tart flavour of rhubarb. For a textural contrast, I like to serve it topped with sugared slices of raw rhubarb and a shortbread biscuit or brandy snap, but it's also lovely just as it is.**

Cut the rhubarb stems into 3–4cm pieces and put into a saucepan with the sugar and orange juice. Bring to a simmer and cook gently, stirring frequently, for about 15 minutes until the rhubarb is completely soft and broken down.

Meanwhile, calculate how much gelatine you'll need to set 500ml liquid; different brands vary but the pack should tell you how much each leaf sets. (Your mixture will be more than this volume, but you want a fairly soft-set mousse.) Place the required gelatine leaves in a bowl of cold water for about 10 minutes to soften.

Use a handheld stick blender to purée the cooked rhubarb until smooth (or blitz it in a blender and then return to the pan).

While the rhubarb purée is still hot, drain the soaked gelatine leaves and squeeze to remove excess water, then stir into the purée. You want it to dissolve completely into the rhubarb, so stir well for a good minute. (If your rhubarb has cooled down, heat it again gently before adding the gelatine, but don't let it boil or it will be too hot.) Leave the rhubarb mixture to cool to room temperature.

In a clean bowl, whisk the egg white until it holds firm peaks, then fold it carefully into the cooled rhubarb purée, using a large metal spoon.

In another bowl, whip the cream until it just holds soft peaks – if too stiff it will be difficult to fold in smoothly. Fold it very gently into the rhubarb mixture, keeping in as much air as possible. Spoon the mousse into 4 glasses and refrigerate for at least 6 hours to set before serving.

If you want a contrasting crunchy finish, toss the sliced raw rhubarb and sugar together, then arrange on top of the mousses. Serve straight away, with shortbread biscuits or brandy snaps if you like.

# Roast rhubarb with raw strawberries

These two fruits make marvellous bedfellows; they are very good in a pie or crumble together, but this colourful compote/salad is a wonderfully fresh way to enjoy them.

Preheat the oven to 150°C/Gas 2.

Cut the rhubarb into 5cm pieces and put into a wide oven dish, ideally in one layer. Sprinkle with the sugar and orange juice. Cover with foil and bake for 25–45 minutes until tender and juicy, stirring carefully to turn the pieces over after the first 10 minutes. Check the rhubarb after 25 minutes – and regularly thereafter – poking it gently with the tip of a small knife: you want to catch it just at the point when it's perfectly tender but still holding its shape.

Carefully transfer the rhubarb to a bowl with all the juice or syrup from the dish and leave to cool completely.

Thickly slice the strawberries, then gently stir into the cooled rhubarb. Taste and add a little more sugar if you think it's needed.

Either serve the compote straight away, or leave it for a few hours in a cool place, stirring very gently once or twice, to allow the strawberries to macerate and release some of their juices. (The compote can be kept in the fridge for a day, but after that the strawberries will become a bit soggy.)

Serve in glasses or bowls – either straight up, or with cream, crème fraîche or plain yoghurt. And if you want to make a treaty pud of it, serve with a tuile or two or a shortbread biscuit (see page 357).

**Variations** To make a straight rhubarb compote, with the fruit holding its shape, simply omit the strawberries. To ring the changes, you can add a little orange zest to the rhubarb before baking, or replace the sugar with honey. For a delightful perfumed version of the dish, stir in a few drops of rosewater or orange flower water just before serving.

## Serves 4

6 stems of rhubarb (about 500g), trimmed

50g caster sugar

Juice of 1 orange

250g strawberries, hulled

# Ricotta beignets with rhubarb purée

I often like my rhubarb cooked fairly carefully so it retains its shape (see the compote on page 88), but there are other times when I want it collapsed into a purée – it's particularly comforting to eat and ridiculously easy to cook. The beignets it's served with here (that's just a posh word for fritters) are delectable, and a very good recipe to have up your sleeve.

For the rhubarb purée, cut the rhubarb into 5cm lengths and put into a pan with the sugar and the orange zest and juice. Bring to a simmer and cook gently for about 15 minutes, stirring regularly and fairly briskly to help the rhubarb to break down into tender strands. Set aside to cool. You can either serve it at room temperature, or chill it.

Shortly before serving, make the beignets. Beat the ricotta and sugar together in a bowl, then add the eggs and vanilla and beat until smooth. Add the flour and salt and beat into the wet ingredients to make a smooth, thick batter.

Heat a 3–4cm depth of oil in a deep, heavy-based pan to about 160°C; if you drop a tiny bit of the batter into the oil, it should fizz gently and turn light golden in about a minute. You don't want the oil any hotter or the beignets will over-colour on the outside before they are cooked in the middle.

Drop heaped teaspoonfuls of the batter into the hot oil, about 4 or 5 at a time, depending on the size of your pan. Cook for about 5 minutes, turning the beignets regularly in the oil, until they are puffed up and a rich, golden brown all over. Transfer to a plate lined with kitchen paper to drain while you cook the remaining batter. Dredge the hot beignets with icing or caster sugar and serve with the rhubarb purée.

**Variations**  These little doughnuts are gorgeous with many other fruits: try them with an apple compote (such as the one on page 177), spiced up with cinnamon and cloves, for instance. If you're feeling really indulgent, they also go well with ice creams, such as the banana one on page 306, and my strawberry yoghurt semifreddo (see page 48).

## Serves 6

### For the rhubarb purée

500g rhubarb, trimmed

150g caster sugar

Finely grated zest and juice of 1 small orange

### For the beignets

175g ricotta

50g caster sugar

2 large free-range eggs

1 teaspoon vanilla extract

100g self-raising flour

A pinch of salt

Sunflower or vegetable oil, for frying

Icing sugar or extra caster sugar, to finish

# Rhubarb and ginger cheesecake

This is a recipe you can come back to throughout the year, using different fruits in season (see the variations below). I like it made with cream cheese for that authentic cheesecake tang, but you can use mascarpone for a slightly milder flavour if you prefer.

Lightly butter a 20–23cm springform cake tin, line the base with baking parchment and lightly butter the paper.

To make the base, blitz the biscuits in a food processor (or bash in a bag with a rolling pin) until fairly fine. Pour the melted butter through the feed tube, pulsing as you go, until the mix looks like wet sand. (Or mix the butter with the bashed crumbs in a mixing bowl.) Tip into the prepared tin and press in firmly with the bottom of a glass or ramekin so you get an even layer. Chill the base while you make the filling.

For the filling, beat the cheese, ginger, ginger syrup, sugar, orange zest and juice together until well blended. Add the cream and beat until the mixture thickens enough to hold its shape. Spoon on to the biscuit base and spread into an even layer. Chill for 4 hours or overnight, until firm.

For the rhubarb, preheat the oven to 150°C/Gas 2. Cut the rhubarb into 4cm lengths and place in a wide oven dish, ideally in one layer. Sprinkle with the sugar, orange zest and juice. Cover the dish with foil and bake as for roast rhubarb (see page 88) for 25–45 minutes, until tender and juicy. Leave to cool completely, then drain off the juice (it's delicious, so save to pour over ice cream or use in a drink or smoothie).

Run a thin knife around the edge of the cheesecake and release the side of the tin. Serve with the cold baked rhubarb on top or on the side.

**Variations** For the topping, instead of rhubarb, use fresh raspberries or macerated strawberries (or the combo on page 43), or a lightly cooked blackcurrant purée, flavouring the filling with seeds from a vanilla pod rather than ginger, and using plain digestives for the biscuit base if you prefer. Or, in winter, try diced mango with passion fruit pulp, using lime zest and juice in place of the orange in the filling.

Serves 8

*For the biscuit base*

85g butter, melted, plus extra for greasing

200g ginger biscuits

*For the filling*

400g cream cheese (or use mascarpone, if you prefer)

3 balls of preserved stem ginger, finely chopped, plus 3 tablespoons syrup from the jar

25g caster sugar

Finely grated zest and juice of ½ orange

200ml double cream

*For the rhubarb*

400g rhubarb, trimmed

75g caster sugar

Finely grated zest and juice of ½ orange

When perfectly ripe, the stone fruits – defined by the single seed-nut encased inside their flesh – are among the hardest to get into your kitchen or even home from the shops. If you want to avoid peach juice on the steering wheel then it's probably safest to put the fruit in the boot, not on the passenger seat. Such restraint allows a more unbridled passion to unfurl later, in the privacy of your own home. (My wife likes to eat apricots in the bath.)

While stone fruits can and will be eaten hand to mouth, sometimes in near frenzy, their ripe, succulent flesh happily submits to all kinds of hedonistic sweet scenarios. Classics like peaches and cream with meringue (page 137) will always please the crowd. But there are darker, racier treats to be had too, like my cherry, honey and chocolate dippers (page 141), cherry chocolate tart (page 134) and peaches with red wine and black pepper (page 124).

More surprising is the way the raw fruits can bring a balance of sweetness and tartness to savoury salads and salsas. They will kick off vegetables (raw and cooked), leaves and herbs, nuts, seeds and cheeses. Try fresh apricots with celery, pecans and crumbly cheese on page 100, or the peach, watercress and redcurrant salad on page 98, or a plum, mint and red onion salsa on page 121.

When cooked, possibilities both sweet and savoury abound, as the juices start to flow and mingle with contiguous ingredients. There are crumbles, of course, but with a difference – how about plum crumble with honey and rosemary (page 127)? And I'll encourage you to push the boundaries of meat-plus-fruit, too, with slow-roast lamb shoulder with spiced apricot sauce (page 112), duck and plum salad (page 104) and venison stew with damsons (page 116).

Recipes that use raw stone fruits generally demand ripe specimens in near perfect nick. The cooked repertoire, however, is more forgiving. Just as well, since it isn't always possible to source these fruits as ripe as you might like. Cherries, apricots and peaches are notable culprits. They can grow well in the British Isles, and I urge anyone with a sunny sheltered corner in their garden to have a go. But they do like sunshine, and it's no surprise that continental crops have all but ousted the homegrown harvest. The wavering exception is cherries – a few English cherry orchards, and even a couple of Scottish ones, are, through careful choice of varieties and clever marketing, enjoying something of a revival. These cherries deserve our support, see the Directory (pages 402–3).

But if you want to eat peaches, apricots and cherries at all often (and why wouldn't you?) you'll inevitably be buying mostly fruit imported from Southern Europe and beyond. Unfortunately this is no guarantee of quality or ripeness. The prevalent supermarket practice of offering a higher-priced premium product labelled as 'ripe and ready to eat' only serves to emphasise that much of their fruit is picked and stored fatally unripe and may *never* be ready to eat.

The answer is to shop around, taste samples when you can (not easy in a supermarket, though you might get away with filching a cherry without troubling the store detective) and, when you hit the ripeness jackpot, fill your boots. Grocers and those big fruit stalls that set up on city pavements in the summer months will often invite you to taste – a slice of peach, or a cherry – to pull you in. Take full advantage.

Plums and their siblings – gages and damsons – are a different story. They adore our climate, and we excel at growing them. They are among my favourite fruits to cook, their flavour intensifying and becoming more complex as they bubble away and the tannins in the skin infiltrate the flesh and juice. This transformation to a more complex, layered flavour is why plums make such fabulous jams (page 144), crumbles (page 127) and ice creams (page 138). The Victoria, our most popular variety, is a case in point. Straight from the tree it's a bit tart and bittersweet. But those drawbacks become qualities as you simmer them into a compote or bake them in a pie with a bit of added sugar to offset the acid edge. If you want to eat Victoria plums raw, let them ripen in a warm room for a day or so and they will mellow. Large and jolly, Marjorie's Seedlings also sweeten up nicely in a sunny summer.

But if it's raw plum flesh that you hanker after, you can't beat a gage – green, golden or occasionally flushed with red. Smaller, sweeter and rounder than other plums, you rarely see greengages in the shops so there's a particularly strong case for growing your own.

Damsons are often seen as a hedgerow fruit, though these are generally garden escapees. You'll find them in wild places but also urban sites, including allotments and waste ground. It is possible to enjoy damsons straight off the tree, but only if you've found the right variety growing in a sunny spot and they're burstingly ripe. Generally, I cook and sweeten them to reveal their superb, complex winey flavours.

All these stone fruits can be grown domestically, and garden centres and nurseries will happily advise you on your choice. Dwarf varieties take up next to no space and can be grown in large pots or containers. Peaches, apricots and cherries in particular crave sun and shelter, which means they'll fare better in a small urban garden than a windswept rural expanse. City dwellers take note… you can trump the country bumpkins with your homegrown peaches.

# Peach, watercress and redcurrant salad

This is a stunningly colourful salad with a host of peppery, sweet, sour and nutty flavours. Serve it as a starter – or add some bread and a hunk of crumbly white cheese, such as Lancashire, and it becomes a lovely light meal in its own right.

Put the almonds in a dry frying pan over a medium heat and toast them lightly, tossing them often to prevent burning, until patched with golden brown. Tip on to a plate to cool.

If your peaches are spot-on ripe, just halve, stone and cut each half into 5 or 6 slices. If, however, they are not perfectly ripe, it's a good idea to cook them gently first. Heat a trickle of sunflower oil and a little nut of butter in a frying pan over a low to medium heat. Add the peach wedges and cook lightly (gently bubbling in the butter, but barely sizzling) for just a minute or two on each side until tender. Remove from the pan and leave to cool until warm or at room temperature.

For the dressing, put the ingredients into a small jar with some salt and pepper, put the lid on and shake to combine, or whisk together in a jug to emulsify.

Spread the watercress out on a large serving platter. Arrange the peach slices, cooked or raw, on the leaves. Scatter over the toasted almonds and then the redcurrants.

If you've fried the peaches, pour a little of the dressing into the pan to deglaze it, using a spatula to scrape up any little bits of caramelised peach from the bottom, then trickle over the salad.

Trickle the dressing over the salad, stopping when you feel it has enough (you might not need all of it). Give the salad an extra grinding of pepper and serve.

**Serves 4**

75g blanched almonds

2 ripe peaches or nectarines

A trickle of sunflower oil and a nut of butter (if cooking the peaches)

4 good handfuls of watercress

50g redcurrants (or blueberries)

Sea salt and freshly ground black pepper

*For the dressing*

3 tablespoons extra virgin olive oil

1 tablespoon lemon juice

A scrap of honey (about ¼ teaspoon)

# Apricots with celery, pecans and crumbly cheese

Fresh apricots have the most beautiful colour – that tawny yet bright yellow-orange – and a glorious sweet-tart aromatic flavour to match. In this simple salad, a take on the classic Waldorf I suppose, they are a vivid and exciting element in an otherwise tried-and-trusted formula: tart fruit, salty cheese, crunchy nuts and something green.

Halve the apricots and remove the stones, then cut them into slim wedges. Divide between individual plates or bowls.

Thinly slice the celery, on the bias, and distribute the celery slices over the apricots. Scatter over the pecans and crumble over the cheese. Trickle with a little extra virgin olive oil, sprinkle with salt and pepper, then serve.

**Variations** If you can't get hold of apricots, slices of crisp apple or ripe pear, or sweet, tart greengages or plums, will be delicious. You can also vary the cheese – try a soft fresh goat's cheese or ricotta.

Serves 4

8 large or 12 small ripe apricots (about 250g)

4 tender inner stems of celery

100g pecan nuts (or walnuts)

125g Lancashire, Cheshire, mild Cheddar or other crumbly white cheese

Extra virgin olive oil, to trickle

Sea salt and freshly ground black pepper

# Sardines and plums with soy and chilli

**Serves 4**

500g plums or greengages

4 tablespoons soy sauce

4 garlic cloves, thickly sliced

1 large medium-hot red chilli, deseeded and sliced

A thumb-sized piece of ginger, peeled and thinly sliced or cut into julienne

8 large fresh sardines or 4 medium line-caught mackerel, gutted but left whole

Sea salt and freshly ground black pepper

For this flavourful dish, you need ripe fruit that will soften and eventually collapse on cooking. Victorias, Marjorie's Seedlings and greengages are all ideal and they coincide nicely with the finest, plump Cornish sardines available in late summer/autumn. The recipe works well with mackerel too. If you're not getting a nice, juicy result before the fish goes in, feel free to add a little more soy and an extra splash of water to the roasting tray.

Preheat the oven to 190°C/Gas 5.

Halve the plums, remove the stones and place cut side up in a roasting tray. Sprinkle with the soy sauce, 4 tablespoons water, the garlic, chilli and ginger. Roast in the oven for 10–15 minutes, or until the plums are soft and have released lots of juice.

Slash the sides of the sardines a few times with a sharp knife so the flavourings can penetrate. Place the fish on the tray and turn them over so both sides are well coated with the fruit juices and flavourings. Season the fish with salt and pepper and return the tray to the oven for about 15 minutes or until the fish are cooked through.

Transfer the fish to warm plates and spoon the collapsed plums or greengages with all their juices and flavourings over and around them. Serve with plain rice and a green vegetable such as pak choi.

# Duck and plum salad

Crispy roast duck with a spicy plum sauce is a time-tested classic. This gorgeous warm salad is a particularly lovely and effortless way to enjoy the combination, using whole fresh fruit.

Preheat the oven to 170°C/Gas 3.

Heat a trickle of oil in a large frying pan over a fairly high heat. Season the duck legs with salt and pepper, add them to the pan and brown them well all over, then transfer to a roasting dish.

Roast the duck legs in the oven for 1 hour, then turn the oven setting up to 190°C/Gas 5, add the whole plums to the dish and return to the oven for 30 minutes. Transfer the duck and plums to a warm plate and set aside to rest while you make the dressing.

Whisk the dressing ingredients together thoroughly in a bowl. Pour off the duck fat from the roasting dish into a bowl (save it for roasting potatoes), leaving behind the sticky flavourful meaty residues. Pour the dressing into the hot roasting dish and combine it with the meat residues, scraping them up from the base of the pan with a spatula.

Divide the salad leaves between serving plates. Tear the warm duck meat and crisp skin off the legs in rough pieces and add to the plates, along with the soft plums. Trickle the dressing from the roasting dish over the salad and finish with a scattering of sesame seeds. Serve straight away.

## Serves 2

A trickle of sunflower oil (or a little duck or goose fat)

2 free-range duck legs

2 large or 4 small plums or greengages

2 handfuls of salad leaves, such as rocket or baby spinach, or a mix

1 teaspoon sesame seeds

Sea salt and freshly ground black pepper

### For the dressing

1 teaspoon soy sauce

1 teaspoon honey

A small scrap of garlic, grated or mashed

2 teaspoons rice vinegar or white wine vinegar

2 tablespoons sunflower oil

# Pigeon breasts with morello cherry sauce

**Serves 4**

8 pigeon breasts, skinned

1 tablespoon olive oil

A sprig of thyme, leaves only

2 tablespoons white wine

Sea salt and freshly ground black pepper

### For the cherry sauce

350g morello cherries, stoned

1–2 bay leaves

A sprig of thyme

1–2 tablespoons sugar

Morellos are sour cherries, a bit too tart to eat raw but excellent in cooked dishes. Their July season is short and they're not easy to buy, so grab them if you get the chance. Your best bet may be to finagle some from a friend's garden (the morellos I use are all homegrown). You can also buy them frozen – these will work well in this recipe, but they release a lot of juice so you may not want to dish it all up.

To make the sauce, put the cherries in a pan with the bay, thyme and sugar and add 1 tablespoon water (but not if using frozen cherries). Bring to a simmer and cook very gently for a few minutes until the fruit is soft but not collapsed. Taste and add a little more sugar if needed, but keep it quite tart. Set aside.

Toss the pigeon breasts with the olive oil, thyme leaves and some salt and pepper. Heat a frying pan over a medium-high heat and add the pigeon breasts. Cook for 1 minute, turn the breasts over and cook for another minute, then turn again. Toss them in the pan for a couple more minutes. Slice one pigeon breast in half. If it is nicely pink in the middle, remove all the breasts from the pan and set aside to rest on a warm plate. If it still looks very raw, cook for another minute or two.

Pour the wine into the hot pan to deglaze it, letting it bubble briefly while you scrape up any caramelised bits with a spatula. Add the cherry sauce and stir briefly to combine with the pan juices, then taste and add more salt and pepper as needed.

Cut each pigeon breast on the diagonal into 4 or 5 slices. Arrange on warm plates. Add the warm cherry sauce and it's ready to serve. Plain boiled potatoes and beetroot make this a lovely salt-of-the-earth dish. Or serve with wilted, buttered spinach or greens and buttery crushed new potatoes if you fancy something a tad more sophisticated.

**Variations** As you might imagine, this tart morello sauce also works well with duck – try replacing the bay and thyme with a star anise and a stick of cinnamon. It's also good with fish – I like it with hot-smoked trout or mackerel, or oily fish such as sardines and sprats.

# chicken, leek and plum pie

A chicken pie is a wonderful thing: all savoury, succulent comfort. I've never been a fan of gloopy, flour-thickened pie fillings. This one is light and juicy – the thin juice deliciously flavoured by the fruity sharpness of the plums and the savoury edge of the leeks.

Preheat the oven to 190°C/Gas 5.

Melt the butter with a trickle of olive oil in a large frying pan over a medium heat and add the leeks and garlic. As soon as they are sizzling, reduce the heat, cover and let the veg sweat for about 10 minutes, stirring occasionally, until tender. Transfer to a 1.5 litre pie dish.

Increase the heat under the pan to high and add a little more oil. Add half the chicken, season with salt and pepper and brown all over, then remove with a slotted spoon and set aside on a plate. Repeat with the remaining chicken, then return the first lot of chicken to the pan.

Reduce the heat under the pan and pour in the wine. Bubble briefly, scraping up any nice caramelised bits from the bottom of the pan. Add the bay leaf, lemon zest and stock and simmer for about 10 minutes.

Meanwhile, halve the plums and remove the stones, then cut each half into 3 or 4 slices, depending on size. Tip the contents of the pan into the pie dish, add the plums and mix well with the leeks. Taste and add more seasoning if necessary.

Roll out the pastry on a lightly floured surface until large enough to cover the pie generously. Brush the rim of the pie dish with a little beaten egg, then lay the pastry lid over the filling and press the edges down firmly on to the rim of the dish to seal. Trim off the excess pastry.

Brush the pastry lid with more egg, and cut a few long slits so that steam can escape. Bake for about 30 minutes, until puffed up and golden brown. Serve with mash and steamed greens or broccoli.

**Variation** Replace the plums with 150g stoned prunes.

## Serves 4

25g butter

A little olive oil

2 large leeks, trimmed, washed and cut into 1cm thick slices

1 garlic clove, chopped

About 500g boned, skinless, free-range chicken thighs, cut into large chunks

100ml white wine

1 bay leaf

A couple of strips of lemon zest

150ml chicken stock

About 250g plums or greengages

About 200g puff or rough puff pastry (ready-made all-butter puff is fine)

A little beaten egg

Sea salt and freshly ground black pepper

# Pork chops
## with peaches and sage

The delicate balance of acidity and perfumed sweetness that you find in peaches is a great partner to a nicely browned pork chop. This is a lovely, original dish for a summer barbecue, but you can also pan-fry your pork chops and bake your peach parcels – in a preheated oven at 180°C/Gas 4 for about 20 minutes.

Halve the peaches and remove the stones. Take a sheet of foil, lay a quarter of the sage in the middle and place two peach halves, cut side up, on top. Put a nut of butter in each peach cavity and season with salt and pepper. Bring up the foil around the fruit and crimp the edges together to seal and create a parcel. Repeat with the remaining sage and peaches.

If you're barbecuing, first make sure that your barbecue is medium-hot (not *too* fierce) and that the flames have died down to leave glowing coals covered in a layer of white ash.

Put the foil parcels on the barbecue rack and let them cook for 25–30 minutes. Meanwhile, brush the pork chops with a little oil and season them well with salt and pepper. Put them on the barbecue to cook next to the peaches, giving them around 10 minutes each side, or until nicely coloured and cooked through with all their juices running clear.

To serve, put the chops on warm plates with the foil parcels beside them so everyone can open their own parcel and release the fragrant, fruity aromas from inside. This is very good with a potato salad, creamy mash or rice.

### Serves 4

4 ripe peaches or nectarines

A large bunch of sage (75–100g)

50g butter, in pieces

4 outdoor-reared pork chops

A little sunflower or olive oil, for brushing

Sea salt and freshly ground black pepper

# Slow-roast lamb shoulder with spiced apricot sauce

Lamb and apricots is a stunning combination, the tangy sharpness of the fruit being the perfect foil to the meat's fatty richness. This dish works best with mature lamb that has a reasonable covering of fat – or hogget or mutton if you can get it.

Preheat the oven to 220°C/Gas 7. Put the lamb into a large roasting tin, season it well with salt and pepper and trickle over a little olive oil. Roast for 30–40 minutes until starting to colour. Take out of the oven.

Pour a glass of water into the tin (not over the meat), cover with foil and return to the oven. Lower the setting to 120°C/Gas ½ and cook for a further 6 hours, or until the meat is very tender and falling off the bone, adding another glass of water halfway through if the tin is dry.

Meanwhile toast the fennel and coriander seeds, cinnamon, cardamom, peppercorns and star anise in a dry frying pan over a medium heat for a few minutes until fragrant. Allow to cool, then crush together as best you can using a pestle and mortar (they won't be eaten so needn't be fine). Combine the crushed spices with the chilli flakes and paprika.

After the 6 hours, spoon off the excess fat from the lamb roasting tin, leaving the dark juices. Arrange the apricot halves around the lamb and scatter the spices and garlic over them (not over the meat). Return the tin to the oven for 25–30 minutes, or until the apricots are tender and breaking down. Remove the lamb to a warm plate or board to rest.

Use a spatula to scrape all the fruit, spice and sticky lamb juices from the tin into a sieve – you can use a splash of hot water to help loosen the very last of the goodness in the tin. Then rub through the sieve into a bowl to create a rich, spiced apricot sauce. Taste it and add more salt and pepper if required. If it's very thick, loosen with a little more water.

Thickly slice the lamb, or shred it with two forks if you prefer. Serve with the warm, spicy apricot sauce poured over and scattered with a few torn mint leaves if you have any. A green salad and a big bowl of fluffy couscous go very well alongside.

### Serves 6–8

1 shoulder of mature lamb, or mutton or hogget, on the bone

A little olive oil, to trickle

2 teaspoons fennel seeds

3 teaspoons coriander seeds

1 cinnamon stick, broken in half

10 cardamom pods

1 teaspoon black peppercorns

2 star anise

2 teaspoons dried chilli flakes

2 teaspoons sweet smoked paprika

10–12 apricots, halved and stoned

4 garlic cloves, finely sliced

Sea salt and freshly ground black pepper

Mint leaves, to finish (optional)

# Spicy lamb burgers with greengages

**Serves 4**

*For the burgers*

500g minced lamb

1 medium onion, finely diced

2 garlic cloves, crushed or finely grated

½ medium-hot red chilli, deseeded and finely chopped

1 teaspoon ground coriander

½ teaspoon fine sea salt

1 teaspoon freshly ground black pepper

A little olive oil for cooking

*For the roast fruit*

4 large greengages (or plums)

25g soft butter

2 teaspoons caster sugar

Freshly ground black pepper

*To serve*

4 baps or slices of sourdough bread

A handful of coriander leaves (optional)

**The natural sweet-sour quality of greengages – and plums – makes them sure-fire winners with well-flavoured meats, especially if they have been roasted with a little butter, sugar and black pepper to coax all that luscious flavour out of them.**

In a bowl, thoroughly mix the lamb with the onion, garlic, chilli, ground coriander, salt and pepper, with your hands. Cover and refrigerate for at least a few hours, preferably overnight, to let the flavours mingle.

To check the seasoning, break off a small nugget of the mixture and fry it until cooked, then taste. Add more pepper or salt to the remaining meat mixture, if you think it is needed, then divide into 4 equal portions and shape into burger patties.

Preheat the oven to 190°C/Gas 5. Halve and stone the greengages and put them, cut side up, in a small oven dish. Smear a little of the butter over each one, sprinkle with the sugar and give them a light grinding of pepper. Roast for 10–20 minutes or until juicy and tender. Different varieties of fruit will cook differently in the oven – some may collapse quite quickly and others will hold their shape even after 30 minutes. As long as they are tender and juicy, it doesn't matter – and if they collapse into a jammy mess, they will still be very good spooned on to the burgers. Leave in their dish to cool a little.

Brush the burgers lightly with a little olive oil, then fry or grill them on both sides until well coloured and cooked through. The time taken will depend on the thickness of the burgers, but well-done burgers will probably take 4–5 minutes each side.

Serve the hot burgers in baps or on sourdough bread, or just on their own, each with a pair of juicy, fragrant greengage halves on top, as well as some of the tangy fruit juices and pulp and, if you have them, a few coriander leaves.

**Variation** If you can get hold of some flavourful fresh apricots, they make a stunning alternative to the greengages in this dish.

# Venison stew with damsons

The rich, tannic flavour of unsweetened damsons is a fantastic counterpoint to venison in this luscious, dark hearty stew. You can use beef instead of venison if you prefer – a good stewing cut such as shin will work, though it may take longer to cook to tenderness.

Heat 2 tablespoons olive oil in a large flameproof casserole, add the onions and sweat gently for 10 minutes or so, stirring once or twice.

Meanwhile, heat 1 tablespoon olive oil in a large frying pan. Add the pancetta and fry until it has released some fat and taken on some colour. Transfer it to the casserole, leaving most of the fat behind in the frying pan. Add the garlic, thyme and bay leaves to the casserole too.

Now brown the venison in the pancetta fat in the frying pan over a medium-high heat, in 3 or 4 batches, making sure you don't crowd the pan. Don't season it at this stage as the pancetta is quite salty. Transfer each batch to the casserole with the pancetta and onions once it is browned and add a little more oil to the frying pan if you need to.

When all the meat is browned, pour the wine into the frying pan over a moderate heat to deglaze it, scraping up any caramelised bits from the bottom. Tip this over the meat in the casserole. Add the honey and enough stock to barely cover the meat (add a little water if you don't have enough stock). Bring up to a simmer.

Cover and cook on the hob at a very gentle, low simmer (or in the oven at 120°C/Gas ½) for 2–2½ hours or until the venison is tender. Take the stew off the heat, immediately add the damson halves, re-cover and leave for 20–30 minutes to allow the damsons to soften in the residual heat. Taste the stew and add more salt and pepper if needed, then serve, with buttery mashed potatoes and lightly cooked greens.

**Variation** You can also make this with frozen damsons. Allow them to defrost, by which time they will be soft, then simply squeeze the stones out of them. Add the damson flesh and juice to the stew once it has finished cooking and leave for 20–30 minutes.

## Serves 6

3–4 tablespoons olive oil

2 onions, sliced

250g pancetta, cut into chunky cubes

2 garlic cloves, chopped

A couple of large sprigs of thyme

3–4 bay leaves

1.5kg venison shoulder and neck, or haunch, cut into large chunks

150ml red wine

1 tablespoon honey

About 500ml chicken, beef, venison or game stock

500g damsons, halved and stoned

Sea salt and freshly ground black pepper

# Parsnips with plum sauce

**Serves 4–6 as a snack or side dish**

1kg smallish parsnips

2–3 tablespoons rapeseed or olive oil

Sea salt and freshly ground black pepper

*For the plum sauce*

500g plums

4 garlic cloves (unpeeled), bashed

2 star anise

1 cinnamon stick

1 tablespoon olive oil

25g soft brown sugar

1 tablespoon honey

2 tablespoons cider vinegar

1 teaspoon English mustard

A good pinch of cayenne pepper

Sea salt and freshly ground black pepper

This sweet-sour, sticky plum sauce from Nikki Duffy is an ideal way to use the last fat plums of summer. It pairs brilliantly with new season parsnips to make a lovely, unusual accompaniment to roast chicken or pork. It's also fun to serve these crispy roast parsnip chips – with the sauce for dipping into – as a canapé or party nibble.

Preheat the oven to 190°C/Gas 5. For the plum sauce, halve the plums (don't bother to take out the stones) and put them in a roasting dish, cut side up. Add the garlic, star anise and cinnamon and trickle over the olive oil. Roast for 20–30 minutes until soft, bubbling and juicy. Leave to cool a little, then remove the whole spices and garlic.

Rub the roasted plums through a sieve into a saucepan and add the sugar, honey, cider vinegar, mustard and cayenne. Bring to a simmer and simmer for 10–15 minutes, until the sauce is thickened, stirring often to prevent it burning on the bottom of the pan. Take it off the heat, taste and add salt and pepper, as well as more sugar or vinegar to get the sweet/sour balance that you like. Leave to cool.

Heat the oven to 190°C/Gas 5 again, if necessary. Peel the parsnips and trim their tops and tails. Now slice them lengthways into quarters, to create long, tapering 'chips'. These need to be quite slender so, if your parsnips are on the fat side, cut the quarters in half again.

Put the parsnip chips in a roasting tray. Trickle over the oil, give them a good shake of salt and pepper, then toss thoroughly. Roast for 40–50 minutes until the parsnips are tender all the way through and starting to crisp and caramelise at the thin tips, giving them a good stir halfway through. Serve at once, with the plum sauce on the side, for dipping.

**Variation** Take the parsnips out of the oven when they're a couple of minutes off being done to crispy perfection. Spoon about half the plum sauce over the parsnips in their dish, and turn the parsnips a bit, to partly coat them. Return to the oven for 10 minutes, or until sticky and fragrant. This is a great version to accompany roast poultry, game or pork. Serve the rest of the plum sauce on the side.

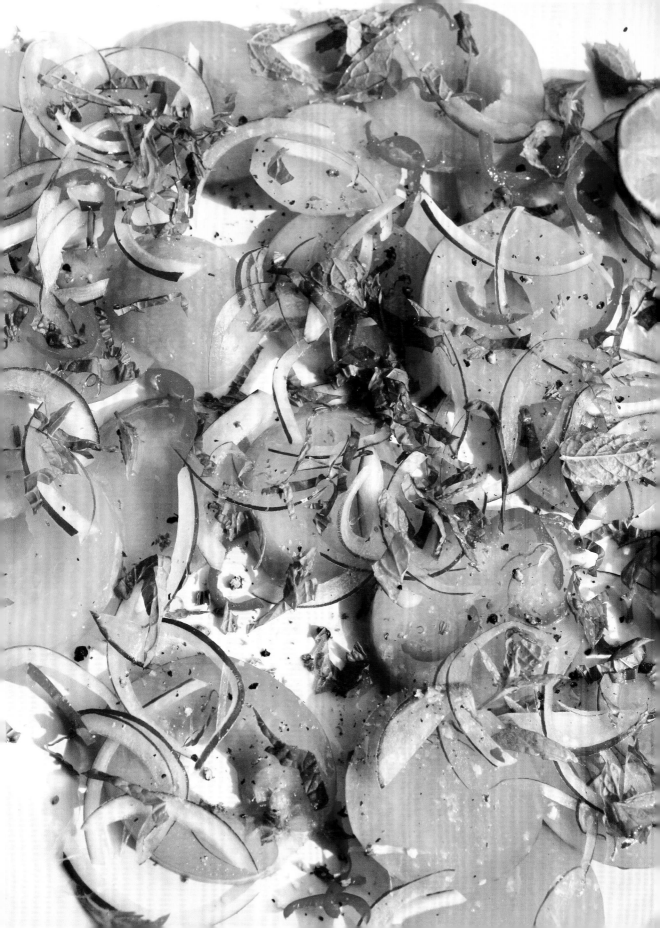

# Plum salad with onion, chilli, lime and mint

**Serves 4–6**

3–4 just-ripe or slightly under-ripe plums or greengages

½ small red onion (or 1 large shallot)

1 small, medium-hot red chilli

1 lime

A trickle of extra virgin olive oil

A handful of mint leaves, roughly shredded

Sea salt and freshly ground black pepper

This fabulously zingy savoury plum salad tastes as great as it looks. Try it alongside simply grilled or barbecued poultry or fish.

Halve the plums and remove the stones, then slice each half into 2–3mm thick rounds. Lay the plum slices over a large serving platter.

Finely slice the onion, from root to tip, and scatter over the plums. Halve and deseed the chilli, then finely slice and distribute over the salad. Grate over the zest of the lime, then squeeze on the juice of about half of it.

Give the salad a trickle of extra virgin olive oil and season with salt and pepper, then finish it off with a scattering of shredded mint and it's ready to serve.

### Variations

This is also delicious with nectarines or peaches in place of the plums.

*Plum, mint and red onion salsa* You can use the same ingredients to make a delicious salsa to serve with burgers or fish. Simply dice rather than slice the plums, onion and chilli, then mix together with the rest of the ingredients, seasoning with salt and pepper to taste.

# Peaches
## with red wine and black pepper

Peaches are one of several fruits – strawberries are another – that get a surprisingly pleasing lift from a judicious seasoning of freshly ground black pepper. This lovely, light summer dessert is incredibly easy, yet sophisticated. You can peel the peaches first if you prefer (see below) but it's not essential.

Quarter the peaches and remove the stones, then slice the fruit thinly and place in a bowl or plastic container. Stir the sugar and pepper into the wine, then pour over the peaches. Cover and leave in the fridge for 24 hours, giving the peaches a gentle stir about halfway through.

Serve chilled in wine glasses, so you can knock back the remaining liquor once the peaches have been eaten.

**Variations** You can also make this dish with ripe or *almost* ripe plums or gages, or apricots, while sliced strawberries make a lovely addition to the peach version.

*Peeling peaches* If you want to peel your peaches, first fill a large bowl with just-boiled water, and another with very cold water. Cut a cross in the base of each peach then immerse them in the hot water. Leave for about 20 seconds, then transfer them to the cold water for a few seconds. Start peeling off the skins. If the skins aren't coming away easily, return the peaches to the hot water for few seconds then repeat. It is much easier to peel peaches if they are ripe. If yours are under-ripe, you may have to pare off the skin (with as little flesh as possible), using a small, sharp knife.

**Serves 4**

3 large, ripe peaches or nectarines

50g caster sugar

¼ teaspoon freshly ground black pepper

½ bottle of light, fruity red wine – a Gamay such as Beaujolais, or Tarrango

# Plum crumble
## with honey and rosemary

**Serves 6**

**For the fruit**

35g butter

1kg plums or greengages, halved and stoned

2 tablespoons runny honey

1 teaspoon finely chopped rosemary, or thyme, or young lavender leaves (optional)

75g soft brown sugar

**For the crumble topping**

150g plain flour

A pinch of salt

125g cold butter, diced

75g light brown or caster sugar

75g ground almonds

**This is a really juicy crumble with that gorgeous 'bubble-through' effect as the hot plum juices erupt through the crisp, golden topping. A little aromatic rosemary – or thyme or lavender – enhances the plums, but the crumble is still very good without the herb.**

Preheat the oven to 190°C/Gas 5.

Start with the crumble topping. Sift the flour and salt into a large bowl, then add the butter and lightly rub into the flour with your fingertips, until the mixture resembles coarse breadcrumbs (or do this in a food processor). Stir in the sugar and ground almonds. Set aside.

For the fruit, melt the butter in a large frying pan over a fairly high heat, add the plums, honey, rosemary and sugar and toss in the sizzling butter. Cook for a few minutes, keeping the heat fairly high, until the plums are reasonably soft but not collapsing and the juices are starting to caramelise. Transfer to an oven dish, about 22cm in diameter.

Squish the crumble mix into lumps with your hands, then crumble it over the surface of the fruit so you get a nice, uneven, nubbly texture. Bake for 25–30 minutes, until the crumble topping is golden brown and the plums are bubbling away underneath. Serve with cold cream.

### Variations

This lovely crumble topping works on top of other fruits, of course. Try it over the gooseberry and elderflower mix on page 52, or the Bramley apple compote on page 177. I also love the following:

*Rhubarb and strawberry crumble* Cut 300g rhubarb into 5mm–1cm slices. Toss in a pie dish with 300g halved strawberries, 100g caster sugar and the finely grated zest of 1 lemon. Let stand for 30 minutes, stir once more, then top with the crumble mix and bake as above.

*Pear and blackberry crumble* Peel, core and roughly chop 4 or 5 just-ripe medium pears (a good 500g prepared weight). Toss in a pie dish with 200g blackberries, 50g caster sugar, the finely grated zest of 1 lemon and half its juice. Top with the crumble mix and bake as above.

# Damson and walnut praline sundae

You might think there's quite a lot of sugary sweetness in this recipe but there is also the divine, rich tartness of the damsons and the delicate bitterness of the walnuts in the praline. It all balances out beautifully. Making your own praline is pretty simple but you can use a bought praline or nut brittle if you like.

To make the compote, put the damsons in a saucepan with 100g sugar and 2 tablespoons water. Bring to a simmer and cook gently, stirring regularly, for 5–10 minutes until the fruit has broken down and the stones are coming free. Pick out all the stones, then taste the compote. Sweeten it further if you like but keep it quite tart to balance the other sweet ingredients in the sundae. Leave to cool, then chill.

If you are making your own praline, lightly oil a baking sheet (or line it with baking parchment or a non-stick silicone mat). Put the sugar in a heavy-based saucepan (ideally stainless steel rather than black-based, so you can see the colour of the caramel). Place over a medium heat and move the sugar around a little with a spatula from time to time until melted. Continue to cook for a minute or two until the liquid sugar has turned to a golden caramel, watching it closely all the time. As soon as it has reached a deep golden brown, remove from the heat and stir in the nuts. Immediately pour on to the prepared baking sheet and leave to set.

When set hard, break the praline into small pieces with a blunt object such as a rolling pin. Store in an airtight container until needed.

When ready to serve, put a generous spoonful of damson compote in each of four sundae dishes. Add a sprinkling of praline, then another spoonful of compote and some more praline. Top with a generous scoop of vanilla ice cream.

**Variation** You can make an equally delicious version of this sundae using plums rather than damsons. You'll need less sugar, though, to keep that lovely fruity acidity, so cook the plums with just 25g sugar and add more only if you need to.

Serves 4

*For the praline*

A little sunflower oil, for oiling

100g caster sugar

50g walnuts, roughly broken up, or whole hazelnuts

*For the damson compote*

500g damsons

100–125g caster sugar

*To serve*

4 scoops of vanilla ice cream (homemade or the best you can find)

# Roasted peach melba

**Serves 4**

2 large or 4 medium peaches or nectarines

2 tablespoons caster sugar

A large knob of butter

1 vanilla pod

*For the raspberry sauce*

350g raspberries

About 2 tablespoons icing sugar

About 1 tablespoon orange juice, and/or a good squeeze of lemon juice

*To serve*

4 scoops of vanilla ice cream (homemade or the best you can find)

**This is my take on the classic dish created by Escoffier in 1893 in honour of Dame Nellie Melba. Roasting the peaches with the sugar, butter and vanilla makes them extra rich and toffeeish, but if you can find some beautifully ripe specimens oozing with sweet juices (not easy in the UK), you can forgo the roasting and use them raw.**

Preheat the oven to 190°C/Gas 5.

Halve the peaches and remove the stones, then place the fruit cut side up in an ovenproof dish. Sprinkle over the sugar and put a scrap of butter in each peach cavity. Slit the vanilla pod open, scrape out the seeds with the tip of a small, sharp knife and distribute over the peaches. Snip the vanilla pod into 8 pieces and put one or two in each peach cavity. Roast the peaches for about 20 minutes, maybe a little longer, until tender and slightly caramelised.

While the peaches are cooking, make the sauce. Put half the raspberries in a blender with 2 tablespoons icing sugar and the citrus juice and whiz briefly to a purée. (Or simply crush them with your hands and whisk in the sugar.) Press the purée through a sieve into a bowl to remove the seeds. Taste and add more sifted icing sugar if you like, but keep it pleasantly tart. Add the remaining raspberries and turn to coat in the sauce.

When you are ready to eat, place the hot peach halves in individual dishes. Spoon the raspberries and their sauce alongside and add a scoop of vanilla ice cream to serve.

**Variations** The hot/cold of the roasted peach and the ice cream is a key factor in this gorgeous pud, but it works well with chilled crème fraîche, or whipped cream sharpened with a little natural yoghurt, in place of the ice cream.

# Apricot fool

Fools are among the simplest of puddings and they really show off the wonderful flavours of fresh fruit. You can use all sorts of puréed cooked fruit to make a fool or 'fumble' (see the variations below).

Set aside 4 apricots. Halve and stone the rest of the fruit and place, cut side down, in a steaming basket or a large sieve over a pan of boiling water. Cover and steam for about 5 minutes until the fruit is soft.

Tip the apricots into a sieve over a bowl and rub through. While the purée is still hot, add 35g of the sugar and stir until dissolved. Leave to cool completely, then refrigerate. Taste the chilled purée: it should be pleasantly tart; add a little more sugar if you think it needs it.

Shortly before serving, put the cream, yoghurt and remaining 40g sugar in a large bowl. Slit the half vanilla pod open and scrape out the seeds with the tip of a small, sharp knife into the bowl. Beat until the mixture holds soft peaks.

Slice or chop the 4 reserved apricots, discarding their stones. Divide half the cream mixture between six glasses or sundae dishes. Spoon half the apricot purée on top. Scatter over the pieces of apricot, then add another layer of cream and another of apricot purée. Use a fork or spoon to roughly marble the cream and fruit together. Scatter toasted flaked almonds on top of each fool and serve straight away.

## Variations

In place of apricots, you could use plums, rhubarb, blackcurrants or gooseberries, adjusting the sweetness of the cooked purée accordingly. And you can turn any of these fools into 'fumbles' by topping with my 'independent crumble' (see page 84) instead of toasted almonds.

*Dried apricot fool* Put 250g unsulphured dried apricots in a pan with 350ml orange juice (from 4–5 large oranges, or use freshly squeezed juice from a bottle or carton) and simmer gently for 10 minutes. Leave to cool completely, then purée – or simply break up the fruit with a fork. Marble this purée into the cream and yoghurt mixture as above.

---

**Serves 6**

500g apricots

About 75g caster sugar

200ml double cream

200ml plain wholemilk yoghurt

½ vanilla pod

A good handful of flaked almonds, lightly toasted

# cherry chocolate tart

Deliciously rich and dark but not too sweet, this is a properly luxurious pudding – ideal for a special occasion. If you back yourself in the pastry stakes, do make the chocolate pastry; alternatively, a simple sweet shortcrust, such as the one on page 177, works well.

A day ahead, put the cherries in a pan with the alcohol, sugar and lemon zest, bring to a simmer and cook for 5 minutes. Tip into a bowl and leave to infuse overnight. Drain the cherries, reserving the liquor.

To make the pastry, put the flour and cocoa in a food processor and blitz briefly (or sift into a bowl). Add the butter and blitz (or rub in with your fingertips) until the mixture resembles coarse breadcrumbs. Stir in the sugar. Add the egg yolk and just enough milk to bring the mix together in large clumps. Tip on to a lightly floured surface and knead lightly into a ball. Wrap the pastry in cling film and chill for 30 minutes.

Preheat the oven to 180°C/Gas 4. Using a little flour, roll out the pastry quite thinly and use to line a 24cm tart tin, letting the excess hang over the sides. Line with baking parchment and baking beans, stand on a baking sheet and bake for 15 minutes. Remove the paper and beans and bake for 10 minutes more. Trim the excess pastry from the edges.

Heat the cream in a saucepan to a bare simmer, then take off the heat, add the chocolate and leave to melt, stirring gently a few times. Add the vanilla. Whisk a little of the hot chocolate cream into the eggs, then whisk back into the chocolate cream. Add 1 tablespoon of the cherry poaching liquor for an extra kick (save the rest to make cocktails).

Spread the jam on the base of the pastry case, scatter over the drained, infused cherries and pour over the chocolate custard. Bake for about 20 minutes – the centre should still wobble slightly when you take it out of the oven. Leave to cool completely in the tin on a wire rack. Serve cut into small slices, with crème fraîche, if you like.

**Variation** If fresh cherries aren't in season, you can make an equally delicious version with dried cherries. Use 200g and cook as above.

## Serves 10

### For the cherries

350g sweet cherries, stoned

150ml kirsch or brandy

30g caster sugar

A strip of lemon zest

### For the chocolate pastry

170g plain flour

30g cocoa powder

100g butter, chilled and cut into 1cm cubes

2 tablespoons caster or icing sugar

1 free-range egg yolk

About 2–3 tablespoons cold milk (or water)

### For the chocolate filling

250ml double cream

200g dark chocolate (about 70% cocoa solids), chopped

1 teaspoon vanilla extract

2 large free-range eggs, lightly beaten

3–4 tablespoons morello cherry jam

# Peaches and cream
## with meringue and pistachios

**Serves 6**

**For the meringues**

A little sunflower oil, for oiling

2 medium free-range egg whites

100g caster sugar

**For the fruit, cream and pistachios**

75g unsalted pistachio nuts

5–6 ripe peaches or nectarines

2 teaspoons orange flower water (optional)

300ml double cream

35g caster sugar

1 vanilla pod

A very elegant take on the irresistible Eton mess, this dish features a wonderful combination of textures as well as flavours. The orange flower water is not essential – but it helps, along with the pistachios, to take this dish in a delightfully Moorish direction.

For the meringues, preheat the oven to 100°C/Gas ¼. Line a baking sheet with non-stick baking parchment and brush very lightly with oil.

Beat the egg whites in a bowl with a handheld electric whisk, or in a mixer, for several minutes until thick, white and holding firm peaks when you lift up the beaters. Keep beating, gradually adding the sugar a tablespoonful at a time. Stop when all the sugar is incorporated and you have a very thick, glossy meringue that holds firm peaks. Spoon the meringue on to the baking tray in 6 equal-sized oval mounds. Bake for 3 hours, then transfer to a wire rack and leave to cool completely.

Gently toast the pistachios in a dry frying pan over a medium heat for 3–4 minutes, until lightly coloured, then tip into a clean tea towel. Rub the nuts inside the cloth to remove most of the skins. Leave to cool completely, then crush the nuts lightly with the flat of a large knife.

Peel your peaches if you wish (see page 124). Halve and stone the fruit (this is tricky if you've peeled them as they will be slippery but you can simply cut the flesh away from the stones). Now cut the peach flesh into small chunks. If using orange flower water, add it to the peach pieces and toss well. Leave to macerate for half an hour.

Pour the cream into a bowl and add the sugar. Slit open the vanilla pod, scrape out the seeds with the tip of a small, sharp knife and add them to the bowl. Whip until the cream forms soft peaks.

To serve, divide the peaches, meringue and cream between individual bowls and finish with a scattering of pistachios.

**Variations** Replace the peaches with raspberries or strawberries, or tropical fruit such as diced, lime-spritzed mango or papaya, or passion fruit pulp. Toasted flaked almonds are an easy swap for the pistachios.

# Damson ice cream

The flavour of damsons is just superb: they are deeply fruity but their tannins and acidity mingle in a pleasingly complex way with the sweet creaminess of a custard. This is based on a recipe of my Dad's – and it's one of my favourite ice creams.

To make the damson purée, put the damsons into a saucepan with 2 tablespoons water and the 50g sugar. Bring to a simmer and cook gently, stirring regularly, for 8–10 minutes until the fruit has broken down completely and the stones are coming free. Rub the damsons through a sieve into a bowl to give a smooth purée. Leave to cool and then chill.

To make the custard, pour the milk and cream into a saucepan. Heat the mixture to just below boiling, then leave to cool a little. Whisk the egg yolks and sugar together in a bowl, then pour on the hot milk and cream, whisking all the time. Return to the cleaned pan and cook gently, stirring all the time, until the custard thickens. Don't let it boil or it will 'split'. Take off the heat and strain the custard into a clean bowl. Lay a piece of cling film or greaseproof paper over the surface to stop a skin forming. Leave until cold, then chill.

Combine the chilled damson purée and custard, stirring them together until well blended.

Churn the mixture in an ice-cream maker (for this quantity, you'll need one with a 1.5 litre capacity) until soft-set, then transfer to a freezer container and freeze until solid. (Alternatively, freeze in a plastic container for about an hour until solidifying around the sides. Mash the frozen sides into the liquid centre with a fork, and then return to the freezer for another hour. Repeat this at hourly intervals until soft-set and then let the ice cream set solid.)

Transfer the ice cream to the fridge about 30 minutes before serving to soften slightly and make scooping easier. I love to eat this ice cream with a classy biscuit such as shortbread (see page 357), an almond tuile, or even a brandy snap (see page 182).

Serves 8

### For the damson purée

500g damsons

50g sugar

### For the custard

200ml whole milk

300ml double cream

4 large free-range egg yolks

125g caster sugar

# Cherry,
## honey and chocolate dippers

Runny honey

Dark chocolate, coarsely grated or very finely chopped

Ripe cherries, with stalks

**This simple combination is huge fun to eat, and creates some rather sophisticated winey flavours in the mouth. Choose a relatively mild honey so it doesn't overpower the cherries or chocolate.**

Pour some honey into a small dish, teacup or ramekin. Put the grated chocolate into a similar container, wide enough for you to roll each cherry around in the chocolate.

Then simply take a cherry by the stalk, dip it first in the honey, allowing excess to drip off, then coat it generously in the grated chocolate and put it straight in your mouth.

**Variation** Try strawberries instead of cherries – using the green stalky bit to hold on to as you dip and roll. Or, instead of the chocolate, use chopped pistachios or almonds, with a pinch of ground cinnamon or mixed spice. This is particularly good with slices of fresh peach or nectarine. Of course you can make a party piece of it, offering a choice of fruits, and a choice of chocolate or nuts for the final dip and roll.

# Cherry bakewell

I love a classic bakewell tart with its layer of raspberry jam but there's something particularly beguiling about this version, studded with fresh cherries. It's ripe for variations of course, including the raspberry classic, but if you stick with the combination of good jam *and* fresh fruit then you'll have something extra special. The very easy 'pastry', which you press straight into the tin, is really a kind of shortbread – crumbly and delicious. The almond extract gives an intense 'almondy' taste; leave it out if you prefer a mellow flavour.

Preheat the oven to 170°C/Gas 3. Lightly grease a non-stick rectangular baking tin, about 18 x 25cm.

To make the base, cream the butter and sugar together until light and fluffy. Sift the flour and salt together over the mixture and work in to form a crumbly dough. Press this into the base of the tin with your fingertips or the back of a spoon (don't worry if there are a few gaps – it will spread as it cooks). Bake for about 20 minutes until golden brown, then remove. Increase the oven temperature to 180°C/Gas 4.

To make the filling, combine the ground almonds and flour; set aside. Cream the butter and sugar together in a large bowl until very light and fluffy. Gradually beat in the eggs, one at a time, adding a spoonful of the almond and flour mix with each egg. Fold in the remaining almond and flour mix, with the almond extract, if using.

Spread the cherry jam thickly over the cooled base. Spoon on the almond mixture and spread it evenly. Stud the almond mixture with the fresh cherries, pressing them in lightly, then scatter over the flaked almonds. Bake in the oven for 35–40 minutes until golden brown.

Leave the cherry bakewell to cool completely in the tin. Dust with icing sugar if you like, and cut into squares or fingers to serve.

**Variations** You can make mouth-watering versions of this tart using raspberry jam and fresh raspberries, apricot jam and sliced apricots, plum jam and sliced plums, or blueberry jam and whole blueberries.

Makes 8–12 pieces

*For the base*

100g unsalted butter, softened, plus extra for greasing

50g caster sugar

100g plain flour

A pinch of salt

*For the filling*

150g ground almonds

50g plain flour

150g unsalted butter, softened

150g caster sugar

3 medium free-range eggs

A few drops of almond extract (optional)

About ½ x 450g jar morello cherry jam

200g ripe cherries, stoned

15–20g flaked almonds

*To finish*

Icing sugar, to dust (optional)

# Plum and other fridge jams

I'm a big fan of 'fridge jams' – preserves made with roughly half the sugar of conventional jams. They have a lovely, loose, tender set and their fresh, fruity flavour is exquisite. Here I'm sharing a few of my favourites: plum, gooseberry and morello cherry (see below).

Sterilise six 450g jam jars by washing thoroughly in hot soapy water, rinsing well and putting in a low oven (120°C/Gas ½) to dry and heat up.

Halve and stone the plums (or quarter if very large). Put in a preserving pan with 200ml water and the vanilla, if using. Bring to a simmer and cook for about 20 minutes, stirring from time to time, until the plums are very soft. Add the sugar and heat gently, stirring, until fully dissolved.

Bring the jam to a rolling boil, boil hard for just 5–7 minutes, stirring once or twice to ensure the fruit is not sticking, then turn off the heat. You don't need to test for setting point: the jam will be naturally soft-set. Let the jam sit for 5 minutes (to prevent all the fruit floating to the top in the pots) but no longer: it must be potted while still very hot (over 90°C). Pour the hot jam into the hot jars (adding a piece of vanilla pod to each) and seal at once. Label once cool. Store in a cool, dry place for up to a year. Once opened, refrigerate and use within a month.

## Variations

*Gooseberry and elderflower fridge jam* Top and tail 1.5kg gooseberries and place in a preserving pan with the juice of 1 lemon and 750g sugar. Heat slowly, stirring a few times and crushing the fruit a little, until the sugar is dissolved and there is plenty of juice. Tie 6–12 fresh elderflower heads in muslin and push down into the fruit. Turn off the heat and leave to infuse for 30 minutes. Heat to a simmer, discard the elderflower, then bring to a rolling boil. Boil for 5–7 minutes, then pot as above.

*Morello cherry fridge jam* Use 1.5kg morello cherries and just 100ml water. Leave in the stones – they lend a lovely almondy flavour – and add 4–5 star anise, if you like, for a delicate, spicy warmth. Bring slowly to the boil, stirring until the juices run, then cook for about 10 minutes, until the cherries are soft. Add 750g sugar and proceed as above.

### Makes 6 medium jars

1.5kg plums (Victoria is classic and ideal, but any plum will work)

1-2 vanilla pods, cut into 6 pieces in total, i.e. one piece per jar (optional)

750g granulated sugar

I'm absolutely crazy about apples – and if I can persuade you to do nothing else but seek out an orchard, farmers' market or decent greengrocer and try a variety of apple you have never tasted before, then this book will have made its mark. The apple is a miracle of a food, one without rival in the fruit kingdom – or any other kingdom, come to that. There really is no end to what you can do with this world-beating fruit – raw or cooked – in dishes sweet and savoury.

Living the old maxim, I do eat an apple jolly nearly every day, and often several a day – during the apple season anyway. And nowadays I probably cook with them a couple of times a week too. That doesn't mean I'm constantly bombarding my family with apple pies, though they get their fair share – see my Bramley apple pie, and variations on pages 177–8. No, they're also in the firing line for appley salads (try apple, potato and red onion, page 171), appley suppers (like my toad-in-the-hole with apples on page 158, or my apple bubble and squeak on page 168) and even appley seafood – my appley mussels (page 153) is a current family favourite.

Sometimes I need a classic cooker for a recipe, and at other times a dessert apple (what I like to call an 'eater') is my best bet. And sometimes either, or a mix of both, will do. Such is my faith in, and dependence on, the apple, that I make sure I supplement our own homegrown supply with a near constant top-up of other locally grown specimens. Should I ever sense I'm in danger of over-supply, I push a couple of kilos through the juicer. Everybody loves that.

Britain is the best place on earth to grow apples. In truth, they are not *technically* native to these islands – but we did sort of invent them.

It's thought that apples originated in the foothills of the mountains on the border of China and Kazakhstan, then drifted towards Europe via the Silk Road, before coming to us courtesy of the Romans. But it's likely that our monks were the first to sort the saplings and their fruit, reproducing them systematically in pursuit of productivity and flavour. And it was certainly our brilliant Victorian nurserymen who grafted and cross-pollinated their way to an astoundingly diverse legacy of colours, textures, aromas and tastes.

Two thousand varieties of apple have been grown in this country. The names alone are mouth-watering and story-telling, conjuring up the people and places that discovered and championed them: Ribston Pippin, Laxton's Superb, Beauty of Bath, Howgate Wonder, Adams Pearmain, Lord Lambourne, Blenheim Orange... It's a pleasure just to rattle them off, quite another to remember that all are different, all somebody's favourite. Mine is Ashmead's Kernel, which has a nutty snap between the teeth, a luscious crunch, and a Champagne-sherbet sharpness with a touch of honeyed sweetness. I'm also a big fan of Discovery – a great summer apple (ready from early August in a good year), though a lousy keeper. Orleans Reinette is a super-sophisticated aromatic apple that is wonderful on its own or with a wedge of full-flavoured Cheddar. I grow all three of these varieties, and more, at home.

That's not to denigrate the household names of the apple world (or not all of them). For all-round, crowd-pleasing appleyness, it's hard to beat a good old Cox's Orange Pippin. In the kitchen, I would champion the Bramley – that classic 'cooker' that dissolves obligingly when heated into an irresistible golden purée – to the ends of the earth.

Yet, sadly, our demand for apples is now largely met with mass-produced crops, often harvested on the other side of the world, with varieties bred not for taste but for their perfect shape, blemish-free skins and long shelf-life. The Pink Lady, for example, is a recent designer supermarket apple of almost unrealistically pleasing appearance, and negligible character.

The Golden Delicious is not a bad apple if allowed to fully ripen in a sunny orchard, where it will acquire an aromatic note to offset its distinctive sweetness, but several decades of industrial cropping in France and the southern hemisphere have robbed it of its finer qualities. Such apples are the horticultural equivalent of intensively farmed chicken: mass produced to uniform standards, dosed with protective chemicals, harvested too early and shipped too far. In the end they leave a taste in the mouth that, if not actively nasty, is certainly on the dull side. We can do better.

And a resistance corps (core?) is fighting back. Orchards are being revitalised and replanted. At most farmers' markets you can buy apples and juice from named varieties. In the autumn and throughout the winter (many apple varieties keep for months in cold storage) you can order 'tasting crates' of regional British varieties with charming names and equally charming textures and flavours. Enjoy the odd knobbles and blemishes on these fruits as badges of honour – signs that they have escaped the degrading and character-stealing process of industrialised production. The Directory (on pages 402–3) will help you find specialist growers and tap into this flourishing counter-culture.

# Oysters with apple and shallot vinegar

A dab of shallot vinegar is a classic embellishment for oysters, but the addition of apple and tarragon takes the pairing to a whole new level of simple, fresh, refined deliciousness.

To open the oysters, use an oyster knife (which has a guard at the point where the blade meets the handle). Hold an oyster firmly inside a damp tea towel on a steady surface, with the flatter edge of the shell uppermost and the hinge pointing towards you. Protecting your non-knife-wielding hand from the knife and the sharp edges of the oyster shell with the folded tea towel, work the knife between the two halves of the shell, inserting it just to the right or left of the hinge. Twist, prise and lever the shell open, trying not to lose any of the oyster's juices.

Once the shell is open, run the tip of the knife gently under the oyster, severing the muscle that connects it, releasing it from the shell but leaving it in the rounded half-shell with its juices. Repeat with the remaining oysters, discarding the flat halves of the shells.

Arrange the half-shells with the oysters on a tray or large plate. Laying them on crushed ice is traditional, but not essential. However, if there's more than 10 minutes between opening and serving the oysters, keep the plate(s) of opened oysters in the fridge or a very cool larder.

Once you've worked through all the oysters, prepare the vinegar. Put the shallot, tarragon and cider vinegar in a bowl. Peel, quarter and core the apple, then dice into tiny cubes, 2–3mm, and add to the shallot and vinegar. Add a twist or two of black pepper and mix well.

Bring the oysters to the table with the apple dressing and some fresh rye bread and butter. Put a small spoonful of apple on to each oyster before eating.

**Serves 4 as a starter**

16–24 fresh live oysters

1 small or ½ large shallot, finely diced

1 teaspoon finely chopped tarragon

2 tablespoons cider vinegar

1 medium-large tart eating apple (about 150g)

Freshly ground black pepper

# Appley mussels

Serves 2

1kg fresh live mussels

2 crisp, sharp eating apples

A knob of butter

A trickle of olive oil

2 shallots or 1 small onion, finely chopped

1 garlic clove, finely chopped

100ml medium-dry cider

A dash of Calvados or apple brandy (optional)

2 tablespoons crème fraîche or double cream

Freshly ground black pepper

This classic dish from northern France was cooked for me recently by my friend Jerry Skeet, and I loved it. It's a wonderfully simple, quick and delicious supper. Rope-grown mussels are farmed in a very low-impact way, so they're seafood we can tuck into with a clean conscience. I've also made a very good version of this using clams instead of the mussels and pear in place of the apple.

Scrub the mussels thoroughly with a stiff brush under cold running water and pull away the wiry beard from the side of the shell. Discard any mussels with broken shells and any that are open and don't close if you tap them firmly against the side of the sink, as these will be dead.

Peel, quarter and core the apples, then chop into 1–2cm cubes. Heat the butter and olive oil in a large frying pan or wide saucepan (that has a tight-fitting lid). When foaming, add the shallots and cook for a few minutes until starting to soften. Add the garlic and chopped apples and cook for a further 4–5 minutes.

Add the cider, and Calvados if using, and turn up the heat. When the cider is bubbling merrily, add the mussels. Put the tight-fitting lid on the pan and cook for 3–4 minutes, shaking it once or twice, or until all the mussels are open. Discard any that refuse to open up.

Scoop out the mussels with a slotted spoon and transfer to warm bowls. Stir the crème fraîche into the cidery, appley juices in the pan and cook for a minute or two. Taste the juices and add pepper to taste (you're unlikely to need salt). Tip the contents of the pan over the mussels and serve straight away, with bread to help mop up the juices.

**Variation: *Mussels with lime leaves and coconut*** For a very different, highly aromatic take on this dish, add 2–3 shredded fresh kaffir lime leaves, the grated zest of a lime and some chopped red chilli to the pan along with the garlic. Leave out the apples. Use coconut milk rather than cider and Calvados to simmer the mussels. Omit the final spoonful of cream and finish the dish instead with a generous spritz of lime juice and a scattering of chopped coriander.

# Sardines
## with fried
# apples

The combination of fish and fruit is relatively unusual in our culinary culture, yet it can work so well. Apples, for example, are excellent with oily fish. And if you've yet to dip your toe into this particular pairing, this simple recipe is a great place to start.

Quarter the apple and remove the core (either leave the skin on, which I prefer, or peel if you like). Cut each apple quarter into 2 or 3 slices.

Heat the oil and butter in a large frying pan over a medium heat. Add the apple slices and fry gently for 5 minutes or so, turning now and again, until softened. Move the apples to the side of the pan.

Season the sardine fillets all over with salt and pepper, then add them, skin side down, to the frying pan. Cook for about 3 minutes until the flesh is nearly all opaque, then flip them over and cook for another minute or so. By this time the apples should be tender and golden.

Give it all a good squeeze of lemon juice, then transfer to warm serving plates. Tip any pan juices over the fish and add a final seasoning of salt and pepper. Serve with a crisp green salad and some good bread.

**Serves 2**

1 medium eating apple, such as Cox's or Braeburn

1 tablespoon olive, sunflower or rapeseed oil

A small knob of butter

4 sardine fillets

A good squeeze of lemon juice

Sea salt and freshly ground black pepper

# Parsnip and apple cakes

• • • • • • • • • • • • • • • • • • • • • • • • • • • • • • • • • • • • • • • • • • • • • • • • • • • • • • • • • • • • • •

These golden, rosti-like little savoury cakes make a fantastic supper or lunch with some crisp bacon or a fried or poached egg – or indeed both. They're also delicious with pork chops and sausages.

Peel the parsnips, trim both ends and cut into even-sized chunks. Put them into a saucepan and add enough cold water to cover. Salt lightly and bring to the boil. Cook for just 3 minutes, then drain and leave until cool enough to handle.

Coarsely grate the parsnips into a large bowl. Peel the apples and grate them into the bowl with the parsnips. Add the egg, flour and plenty of salt and pepper, and mix well.

You'll need to cook the cakes in batches. Heat a non-stick frying pan over a medium heat and add enough oil to give about a 2mm depth. When it is hot, take a heaped dessertspoonful of the parsnip and apple mixture and drop into the pan, forming it into a rough patty shape with a spatula. Add several more spoonfuls, without overcrowding the pan (you can probably cook 5 or 6 cakes at a time).

Cook for 8–10 minutes, turning carefully once or twice, until golden brown and crisp. You'll need to keep an eye on them – turn the heat down if they look like burning. Serve piping hot.

**Makes 10–12**

300g parsnips

2 medium-large eating apples (about 300g in total), such as Cox's or Russet

1 medium free-range egg, lightly beaten

2 tablespoons plain flour

Sunflower or olive oil, for frying

Sea salt and freshly ground pepper

# Toad-in-the-hole with apples

I've always liked fried apple slices with bangers and roast pork – they are better than apple sauce, in my view. Baking mustardy, sagey apple chunks in your toad-in-the-hole is an original and lovely way to get that brilliant apple and pork combo going.

To make the batter, put the flour into a large bowl with a big pinch of salt and make a well in the centre. In another bowl, beat the whole eggs, egg whites and milk thoroughly together, then pour slowly into the flour well, gradually whisking in the flour until you have a smooth batter. Leave the batter to rest for at least 30 minutes, up to 2 hours.

Preheat the oven to 210°C/Gas 6–7.

Trickle the oil into a large, metal baking dish, about 35 x 25cm. Add the sausages and turn them in the oil. Cook in the oven for 10 minutes.

Meanwhile, peel and core the apples and cut each into 6 or 8 slices, depending on size. Put them into a bowl with the mustard and some salt and pepper and toss to coat evenly.

Take the sausages from the oven, placing the dish on a heatproof surface. Working quickly to keep the heat in the dish, add the mustardy apples, arranging them between the sausages, and tucking a sage leaf under each. Pour over the batter and put the dish back in the oven. Bake for another 20 minutes or until the batter is well risen and golden brown on top.

Serve straight away. This is particularly good with an onion gravy, enriched with a splash of cider.

## Serves 4

150g plain flour

2 large free-range eggs, plus 2 extra egg whites

200ml milk

2 tablespoons olive, rapeseed or sunflower oil

8 large butcher's sausages or 10–12 chipolatas

2 large or 3 medium eating apples

1 teaspoon English mustard (or a milder mustard if you prefer)

8–12 sage leaves

Sea salt and freshly ground black pepper

# Apple bangers

A trickle of olive,
rapeseed or sunflower
oil

4 well-seasoned
butcher's sausages

4 medium-large eating
apples

This is another recipe that celebrates the wonderful affinity between bangers and apples. It's simpler than the toad-in-the-hole on the previous page but, I think you'll agree, very appealing! A couple of these sausage-stuffed baked apples makes a lovely supper, with some mash and a good dollop of mustard. Or you can serve one each as a side dish with roast poultry.

Preheat the oven to 180°C/Gas 4. Line a small roasting dish with baking parchment, or grease it well.

Heat a little oil in a frying pan over a medium heat. Add the sausages and cook them for about 10 minutes, turning frequently, until nicely browned all over (don't worry about cooking them through at this point – they'll finish off in the oven).

Meanwhile, cut a little slice off the base of each apple so they stand steady. Run a small, sharp knife around the equator of each apple, scoring the skin so it won't split as it cooks. Use an apple corer to remove the core of each apple from the top. You'll need to go into the apple with the corer several times, moving it into a slightly different place each time, in order to create a space in the middle large enough to take a sausage.

Stand the apples on the baking sheet. Pick the browned sausages up with a fork and push into the apple cavities, pressing them down so they go right in. Transfer to the oven and bake for about 30 minutes, or until the apples are tender to the point of a sharp knife. Take out one of the sausages and check it's cooked through and piping hot in the centre. Serve without further ado.

# Roast guinea fowl with apples and bay

Free-range guinea fowl can be a delicious bird, the flavour a little richer than chicken but not as gamey as... well, game. However, you can certainly use a chicken or a couple of pheasants for this recipe if you prefer.

Remove the bird from the fridge about an hour before cooking so it comes up to room temperature. Preheat the oven to 210°C/Gas 6–7.

Untruss the bird and put it in a roasting tin. Pull the legs away from the body slightly so hot air can circulate. Push about half of the onion pieces and the lemon half inside the bird, with a couple of bay leaves. Brush the oil all over the bird, or smear with the soft butter. Season the skin with salt and pepper. Roast in the oven for 20 minutes.

Meanwhile, quarter and core the apples, then cut each quarter into a couple of wedges.

Take out the roasting tin and baste the bird. Put the apple wedges and remaining bay leaves and onion in the roasting tin and pour in the wine (but not over the bird). Return to the oven and lower the setting to 180°C/Gas 4. Cook for a further 40–50 minutes (if you have a very small guinea fowl of only 1kg or so, then 30 minutes should do it).

To check that the bird is cooked, plunge a skewer deep into the thickest part of the meat, where the leg joins the body – the juices that run out should be clear with no trace of blood. If there is blood, the meat is not cooked. Return it to the oven and cook for a further 10 minutes, then test again. When nicely done, rest for 10–15 minutes in a warm place – on or beside the cooker if that is convenient.

Tip up the bird so any juices from inside run out into the roasting tin. Transfer the bird to a warm plate or carving tray and carve. Serve with the soft apples and the winey, fruity, savoury juices as a gravy. Simple accompaniments are all you need – roast or mashed potatoes and cabbage or greens.

## Serves 4

1 free-range guinea fowl (1.2–1.5kg) or 1 free-range chicken (1.5–2kg)

1 onion, roughly chopped

½ lemon

At least 8 bay leaves

2–3 tablespoons rapeseed or olive oil, or softened unsalted butter

4 crisp eating apples

A glass of white wine

Sea salt and freshly ground black pepper

# Roast apples, potatoes and carrots

Serves 4–6 as
a side dish

500g potatoes, new
or maincrop

350g eating apples,
such as Cox's

350g onions or shallots,
cut into eighths, root
to tip

350g fairly large
carrots, peeled and
cut into chunks

A few sprigs of thyme

2–3 tablespoons olive
or rapeseed oil

Sea salt and freshly
ground black pepper

With its medley of earthy, sweet and caramelised flavours, this is excellent alongside just about any roast. You can also serve it with a pulsey veg stew for a fantastic meat-free feast. In late summer and early autumn I make it with waxy Pink Fir Apple potatoes and the first sharp, hard eating apples. However, you can cook it right through the year with maincrop spuds, big, chunky 'donkey' carrots and just about any apple you care to choose.

Preheat the oven to 180°C/Gas 4.

If using new potatoes, rub or scrape off their delicate skins under a cold running tap, then cut them, if necessary, into large chunks. If using maincrop spuds, peel and cut them up similarly. Put the potatoes in a pan, cover with water, bring to a boil and simmer for 3–4 minutes.

Meanwhile, quarter and core the apples, then cut each quarter into a couple of wedges – so the apple and potato pieces are a similar size.

Drain the par-boiled potatoes well and tip them into a large roasting dish with the onions, carrots and apples. Add the thyme, trickle over the oil and season well with salt and pepper, then toss the lot together. Roast for 35–45 minutes, stirring a couple of times during cooking, until all the veg are tender and developing some nice golden edges. The apples may collapse a bit, depending on the type, but that's fine – rather nice, in fact. Serve hot, warm or at room temperature.

**Variation:** *Apple and potato mash* This lovely fruity aromatic mash is a different, but equally delicious take on the apple-and-potato idea – great with bangers, chops or fish. Boil 750g maincrop potatoes for about 12–15 minutes until tender. Meanwhile, peel and core 3 medium eating apples, cut into large chunks and add them to the potatoes for the last 5–7 minutes of cooking. Drain well. Melt 50g butter with 1 tablespoon chopped rosemary and plenty of salt and pepper in a pan over a gentle heat. Let bubble for a couple of minutes, then take off the heat and add 50ml milk. Add the potatoes and apples and mash together. Add more salt and pepper if necessary before serving.

# Savoy cabbage with apple and caraway

Apple gives a lovely sweet-sharp note to this fresh, simple side dish. It's ideal alongside a rich roast meat, such as pork, duck or goose.

Trim off the outer leaves of the cabbage, quarter it and remove the tough core. Shred the leaves fairly finely. Put the cabbage leaves into a steamer basket and cook over boiling water for 2–3 minutes until tender but still with a bit of crunch. Meanwhile, peel the apples. When the cabbage is ready, remove from the heat.

Heat the butter in a wide frying pan over a medium heat. Add the caraway seeds and cook gently for a couple of minutes. Add the cooked cabbage to the pan and season with salt and pepper. Grate the apples straight into the pan, tossing or stirring them with the cabbage as you go to prevent browning. Stir over the heat for a couple of minutes, taste and add more salt and pepper as needed, then serve.

**Variation** Try this dish with grated pear in place of the apple and/or spring greens instead of the cabbage. You can also replace the caraway with cumin or fennel seeds.

**Serves 4 as a side dish**

1 smallish Savoy cabbage (about 500g)

2 small-medium eating apples (about 250g in total)

25g butter

1 teaspoon caraway seeds

Sea salt and freshly ground black pepper

# Apple bubble and squeak

I've always loved bubble and squeak and I often tinker with the classic spuds-and-greens combo. Adding some gently fried apple slices is a particularly worthwhile spin. This is delicious just as it is, but equally fine topped with a poached egg (as shown), or grated mature Cheddar. It's also great served with leftovers from a roast chicken, or pork, or some good butcher's bangers.

Heat 2 tablespoons oil in a medium non-stick frying pan over a medium heat. Add the onion and fry for about 10 minutes, until soft and just starting to colour.

Quarter and core the apple, then cut each quarter into 2 or 3 slices and drop them into the pan with the onion. Increase the heat a little and cook for about 5 minutes, stirring once or twice, until the apple starts to soften.

Now add the chopped potato or mash and cook for up to 10 minutes, stirring often, until it starts to colour. You may want to add a little more oil at this stage and you'll probably need to use the edge of a spatula to scrape up some of the lovely crusty bits from the bottom of the pan.

Add the shredded cabbage, mix well and fry for a further 2–3 minutes, until nicely browned with some golden, crispy edges. The finished texture will vary: if you use mash, you can squash the mixture into a rough cake, frying it until golden brown on both sides. If you use chopped cooked spuds, just keep tossing or flipping different parts of it – you'll end up with a looser, hash-like consistency. Both are delicious.

Season your bubble and squeak generously with salt and pepper and serve hot.

**Variation** A teaspoon of curry powder or paste, added once the onions are soft and before the apple slices goes in, turns this into a deliciously spicy dish.

Serves 2

About 2 tablespoons rapeseed, sunflower or olive oil

1 small onion, quartered and sliced

1 medium eating apple (about 120g)

About 250g cooked potato, roughly chopped, or leftover mash

About 100g cooked, shredded cabbage, kale, greens or Brussels sprouts

Sea salt and freshly ground black pepper

# Apple, potato and red onion salad

**Serves 4 as a side dish**

2 crisp medium eating apples, such as Cox's or Worcester Pearmain

About 300g cold, cooked waxy potatoes

½ small red onion or 1 large shallot, finely diced

Sea salt and freshly ground black pepper

*For the dressing*

1½ teaspoons English mustard

2 teaspoons cider vinegar

1 teaspoon caster sugar

65g crème fraîche

*To finish*

A few sprigs of dill or fennel fronds (optional)

I love this crunchy, creamy salad with something proteinaceous on the side, such as some thickly sliced, home-cooked ham or flakes of kipper or smoked mackerel. If you prefer a vegetarian version, you could scatter a few roughly chopped walnuts over it before serving.

For the dressing, put the ingredients into a small jar with some salt and pepper, put the lid on and shake to combine, or whisk together in a jug to emulsify.

Quarter and core the apples. Cut each quarter into a few slices and place in a large bowl. Slice the potatoes slightly more thickly and add to the bowl, along with the onion.

Add the dressing and toss gently before transferring to a serving bowl or individual plates. Finish with a scattering of salt and pepper and, if you like, some fronds of dill or fennel. Serve with brown bread or rye bread and butter.

# Apple snow

This is an old-fashioned pud, but deliciously light and refreshing. If you've got a few Bramleys knocking about and you want something a bit different from a pie or crumble, this is a fab recipe to have up your sleeve.

Peel, quarter and core the apples, and thinly slice them into a saucepan. Add 50g of the sugar, the lemon zest and juice and 50ml water. Bring to a simmer and cook for about 15 minutes, stirring often, until the apples have completely broken down into a pulp. If they are reluctant to do so, you can rub the mixture through a sieve to create a smooth purée. Set aside to cool completely.

Whisk the egg white in a clean bowl until it holds soft peaks, then add the remaining 25g sugar and whisk again until you have a meringue that holds soft peaks. Fold this lightly into the apple purée with a large metal spoon.

Whip the cream until it just holds soft peaks (if it is too stiff, it can be difficult to fold smoothly into the apple). Fold the whipped cream into the apple purée in the same way as the egg white, keeping as much air in the mix as possible.

Spoon into four glasses or sundae dishes and refrigerate for an hour or so before serving. Serve with shortbread if you like – the St Clements shortbread biscuits on page 357 will be perfect.

**Serves 4**

500g cooking apples, ideally Bramleys

75g caster sugar

Finely grated zest and juice of 1 smallish lemon

1 large free-range egg white

150ml double cream

# Bramley apple pie

(continued overleaf)

**Serves 6**

**For the sweet shortcrust pastry**

300g plain flour

50g icing sugar

A pinch of salt

175g cold butter, cut into small dice

1 free-range egg yolk (keep the egg white for the glaze)

About 4 tablespoons cold milk (or water)

**For the filling**

1kg cooking apples, such as Bramleys

150g caster sugar, plus a little extra to finish

2 tablespoons ground almonds (optional)

When it's well made, my favourite apple pie is the straight-up simple one I'm starting with here – just apples, sugar and pastry. But it's nice to ring the changes sometimes (see my suggestions overleaf). I often use a metal or enamel pie dish rather than a ceramic one, as it transmits more heat to the pastry on the base, giving a crisper finish. The ground almonds are not essential but they do soak up some of the apple juices and help to avoid a soggy bottom.

For the filling, peel, quarter and core the apples, then cut into chunky slices (7–10mm at the outer edge) and put into a large saucepan. Add the caster sugar and 2 tablespoons water. Bring to a simmer and cook gently, stirring often, for about 10 minutes, until the apples are tender and starting to break up but not a complete mush. Remove the apple compote from the heat and leave to cool completely.

To make the sweet shortcrust pastry, put the flour, icing sugar and salt in a food processor and blitz briefly to combine. Add the butter and blitz until the mixture resembles breadcrumbs. (Or you can rub the butter into the flour/icing sugar in a bowl, using your fingertips.) Add the egg yolk and just enough milk to bring the mix together into large clumps. Tip on to a lightly floured surface and knead lightly into a ball. Flatten into a disc, wrap in cling film and chill for 30 minutes.

Preheat the oven to 220°C/Gas 7 and put a metal baking sheet inside to heat up.

Cut the pastry into two unequal pieces, roughly two-thirds and one-third. Roll out the larger piece on a lightly floured surface to a round, about 3mm thick. Use this to line a pie dish, about 24cm in diameter and 4cm deep, letting the excess overhang the rim. Scatter the ground almonds, if using, over the base of the pastry. Tip the cooked apple into the pastry-lined dish.

Roll out the remaining pastry, again to a 3mm thickness, for the pie lid. Brush the pastry on the rim of the pie dish with a little water. Place the pastry lid over the apple filling, pressing it down at the edges to seal.

*(continued overleaf)*

# Bramley apple pie, cont...

Trim off the excess pastry around the edge. Brush the top of the pastry with lightly beaten egg white, sprinkle generously with caster sugar and cut a couple of slashes in the top with a sharp knife.

Stand the pie dish on the hot baking tray in the oven and bake for 10 minutes, then lower the oven setting to 180°C/Gas 4 and bake the pie for a further 30 minutes, or until the pastry is a rich golden brown.

Leave the pie to sit for a good 15 minutes before cutting it. Serve with cream or ice cream.

**Variations**
- Stir the grated zest of an orange, or a small lemon, or both, into the cooked apple for a lovely aromatic lift.
- Try introducing the explosive juiciness of whole raisins, or chopped dried apricots, or prunes (about 30g) to the mix. You can, if you like, soak the dried fruit in a little rum or Calvados first.
- A teaspoon of ground cinnamon, or ground mixed spice is lovely too – with or without the dried fruit.
- For a Christmassy apple pie, throw a pinch of ground cloves and a handful of dried cranberries (about 30g) in with the apple.
- In the late summer or autumn, blackberries are, of course, a great addition to an apple pie. Stir a couple of handfuls into the cooked apple before applying the pastry lid.
- For a subtle texture contrast, add a sliced crisp, uncooked Cox apple (or another crisp eating apple) to the cooked Bramley mixture.

# Tarte tatin

Serves 6

**Serves 6**

250g puff pastry (a
ready-rolled sheet of
ready-made all-butter
puff is fine)

Finely grated zest and
juice of ½ lemon (zest
optional)

5 medium-large crisp
eating apples (750–
800g in total), such as
Cox's or Granny Smith

100g caster or
granulated sugar

50g unsalted butter,
cut into about 8 pieces

Finely grated zest of
1 orange (optional)

When it's good, a tarte tatin is divine: buttery pastry soaked in caramelly appley juices, sweet-tart tender fruit – the whole much greater than the summed parts. I make a proper caramel at the start and cook the apples in it to get that lovely, slightly jellied, appley caramel in the finished tart. Granny Smith or Cox are my apples of choice, and I like to include some citrus zest. As to pastry, I use puff – but feel free to go the classic shortcrust route if you prefer (using the sweet shortcrust on page 177). I've deliberately written this recipe in great detail – the idea is that it will enable you to make a tarte tatin as good as – or better than – any you've ever tasted.

If your pastry is not already rolled out, roll it out on a very lightly floured surface to a 4–5mm thickness. Take a 20cm tarte tatin dish or heavy-based ovenproof frying pan (you really need one with a light-coloured base so that you can see the caramel colouring as it cooks). Turn the dish or pan upside down on to the pastry and cut out a circle. Use a sharp fork to prick holes all over the pastry then lay it on a plate and place in the fridge.

Preheat the oven to 220°C/Gas 7. Put the lemon juice in a bowl. Peel the apples, take a small slice off the base of each so they stand steady on a board, then use a corer to remove their cores. Cut each apple in half vertically and transfer to the bowl, turning them in the lemon juice to prevent them browning.

Now do a 'test run': arrange the raw apple halves in the tatin dish or pan, to make sure you have enough of them, and to see how they fit. The apples must go in the pan cut side up, so they will be round side up in the finished upside-down tart. Don't sweat too much about a perfect pattern: it's more important to maximise the amount of apple you get into the dish. You can cut the last apple halves into quarters or smaller pieces to fill the spaces, but try to keep the apples in as large pieces as possible. Remember you'll get a snugger fit all round when the apples are softened from cooking. Now return all the apple pieces to the juice bowl and wipe the pan dry with kitchen paper.

*(continued overleaf)*

# Tarte tatin cont...

Put the sugar into the tatin dish or pan, place over a medium-low heat and let the sugar melt slowly into a caramel. Swirl it around a little to achieve even melting. You can stir it a little too, but be restrained as this can cause the sugar to re-crystallise. By the time all the sugar has melted, some of it will be starting to brown. Keep cooking for a couple of minutes, swirling the pan gently, until all the syrup has turned to a rich, golden brown caramel. Take it as far as you dare, without letting it burn, because the darkness of the caramel is crucial to the flavour of the finished tart. When it is nut-brown, add the butter (it will fizz and bubble). Swirl the pan to help combine the butter and caramel into a bubbling sauce. It may congeal into some sticky, claggy lumps; hold your nerve if it does – just keep stirring steadily and firmly over the heat until the lumps melt back into the caramel.

Now add the apple pieces to the pan (shake off the excess lemon juice, but don't bother to pat dry). Sprinkle the citrus zest, if using, over the apples. Cook for around 10–15 minutes, turning the apples regularly, until they are golden with caramel and fairly tender – they will settle into the pan more obligingly as they cook. Make sure the apples end up rounded side down and fit as snugly in the pan as possible.

Carefully lay the pastry disc over the apples, tucking it down the sides a bit. Bake in the oven for 20 minutes or until the pastry is well puffed up and golden brown. Leave the tart to sit for about 10–15 minutes. Now invert a plate (that is slightly larger than the pan) over the pan and turn them both over to release the tart on to the plate, taking great care because there will be lots of hot, caramelly juices within. If a few pieces of apple stay in the pan, loosen them with a spatula and use to plug the corresponding gap in the tart. Any caramelly juices in the pan can be trickled/scraped over the tart (but avoid anything that's actually burnt on to the pan – it will taste too bitter).

You can serve your tarte tatin warm if you like, but letting it rest for an hour or two completes the caramel-soaking-into-pastry process. Serve plain, or with thick cream, crème fraîche, or vanilla ice cream.

# Apple and chestnut purée with brandy snaps

This lovely, sweet, nutty purée is marbled with a little crème fraîche or yoghurt and served with a crisp brandy snap to make a very smart, retro dessert.

To make the apple and chestnut purée, peel, quarter, core and slice the apples into a saucepan and add the butter, apple juice, sugar and chestnuts. Bring to a simmer and cook gently, stirring often, for about 20 minutes, until the apples are soft. It may take longer, depending on the variety of apple you use. Blitz the mixture to a purée with a handheld stick (or freestanding) blender and leave to cool completely.

For the brandy snaps, preheat the oven to 170°C/Gas 3 and line two large baking sheets with baking parchment. Gently heat the butter, sugar and golden syrup together in a saucepan until the sugar has completely dissolved. Remove from the heat and stir in the flour, then the brandy, to make a smooth batter. Leave to cool for a few minutes, until slightly thickened.

Drop teaspoonfuls of the batter on to the baking sheets, spacing them at least 10cm apart as they will spread a lot. You really only want 4 or 5 per sheet, so you may have to do a second batch. Bake in the oven for about 7–8 minutes until golden brown, then set aside to cool.

Serve the cooled apple and chestnut purée with the brandy snaps, adding a dollop of crème fraîche or yoghurt to each. Finish with a scattering of chestnut pieces, if you like.

**Variations** This luscious purée can be used in lots of other ways. Try it as the filling for a simple sponge, adding a layer of whipped cream to serve it as a pud. Or, for a chestnut and apple 'fumble', swirl with whipped cream or crème fraîche and top with a generous sprinkle of my 'independent crumble' (see page 84).

Serves 4–6

### For the apple and chestnut purée

About 300g eating apples (2 medium)

25g butter

150ml apple juice

25g caster sugar

200g cooked chestnuts, roughly chopped or crumbled

### For the brandy snaps

50g butter, diced

50g caster sugar

50g golden syrup

50g plain flour

1 teaspoon cider brandy

### To serve

4 tablespoons crème fraîche or plain wholemilk yoghurt

A handful of roughly chopped cooked chestnuts (optional)

# Appley
# Chelsea buns

**Makes 12**

250ml whole milk, warmed until tepid

2 teaspoons dried yeast

50g caster sugar

500g strong white bread flour

10g fine sea salt

100g butter, melted

1 medium free-range egg, lightly beaten

*For the filling*

60g butter, 35g of this melted

3 eating apples (about 400g in total)

100g raisins

75g walnuts, roughly chopped

100g caster sugar

1 teaspoon ground cinnamon

*To glaze*

3 tablespoons apricot jam, sieved

**This is my take on the classic Chelsea bun, which is a perfect vehicle for the irresistible combination of apples, dried fruit, nuts and spice.**

In a bowl or jug, whisk the warm milk, yeast and sugar together well and leave for about 15 minutes until the mixture is frothy.

Mix the flour and salt thoroughly in a large bowl. Pour in the yeast mix, melted butter and beaten egg and mix to a rough dough. Turn on to a lightly floured surface and knead for about 10 minutes until smooth and silky. It's a slightly sticky dough, so you may want to flour your hands a little, but try not to add more flour than you have to.

Put the dough in a lightly oiled clean bowl, cover with cling film and leave until doubled in size. This will take at least an hour, but is likely to take more like 2 or 3 hours because the egg and butter in the dough slow down the action of the yeast. Liberally grease a deep rectangular baking tin (I use one 25 x 30cm) with some of the melted butter.

For the filling, peel, core and cut the apples into 5mm–1cm dice. Heat the 25g (non-melted) butter in a large frying pan over a medium heat and cook the apples for 8–10 minutes or until softened. Leave to cool.

Gently tip the risen dough on to a floured surface and roll out lightly to a rectangle about 45 x 30cm, with a longer side towards you. Brush the remaining melted butter over the surface, leaving a 2cm margin free at the furthest edge. Scatter over the apple, raisins and walnuts. Mix the sugar with the cinnamon and sprinkle this over too. Roll up the dough, from the edge closest to you, enclosing the filling (as you would a Swiss roll). Trim the ends to neaten, then cut the roll into 12 equal pieces. Arrange these cut side down in the baking tin. Put the whole tray inside a large, clean plastic bag and leave to prove in a warm place for a good hour, until nicely puffed up. Preheat the oven to 200°C/Gas 6.

Bake for about 25–30 minutes, until the buns are deep golden brown. Warm the jam with a splash of water to loosen it, then brush over the buns while they're still hot. Leave to cool, at least a little, before eating.

# chunky apple
## and marmalade cake

I'm a big fan of this teatime cake, first rustled up by my colleague Nikki Duffy. It has the hearty, substantial charm of a traditional fruit cake, but is lighter in texture and fresher in its fruitiness. The ground almonds are not essential but they do give the cake a particular, yielding moistness.

Preheat the oven to 170°C/Gas 3. Butter a 20cm springform cake tin, line the base with baking parchment and lightly butter the paper.

Warm the whisky in a small pan, then remove from the heat, add the sultanas and leave to soak while you prepare the cake.

Put the ground almonds, if using, flour, baking powder and salt in a large bowl, combine thoroughly and set aside. Peel, quarter and core the apples, then slice thickly.

Beat the butter and brown sugar together thoroughly, ideally in a mixer or using a handheld electric whisk for several minutes, until really light and fluffy. Beat in the eggs, one at a time, adding a spoonful of the flour mix with each, and amalgamating each thoroughly before adding the next. Add the remaining flour and fold it in.

Beat the marmalade to loosen it, then fold into the cake mixture. Fold in the sultanas and whisky, and finally the slices of apple. Spread the mixture evenly in the prepared cake tin and scatter the demerara sugar over the surface. Bake for about 1¼ hours, or until a skewer inserted into the centre comes out clean.

Let the cake cool slightly in the tin for 15 minutes, then turn out and leave to cool completely on a wire rack.

**Variation** This cake is delicious made with dried cherries in place of sultanas – soaked in whisky or added just as they come, as you please.

### Serves 10–12

3 tablespoons whisky

100g sultanas

100g ground almonds (optional)

175g light brown flour (or 225g if not using the ground almonds)

2 teaspoons baking powder

A pinch of salt

3–4 large eating apples (about 500g in total)

200g butter, softened, plus extra for greasing

200g soft dark brown or dark muscovado sugar

3 large free-range eggs

150g thick-cut orange marmalade

25g demerara sugar

These lovely autumn fruits are not close relatives, but there is a physical resemblance and I tend to connect them. Inevitably the pear takes the lead role in this chapter over its quirky cousin the quince (both members of the rose family, like apples, plums and other stone fruits). Whilst we are all familiar with pears, even if we don't always know what to do with them, quinces remain obscure to many cooks. But they have wonderful qualities that are worth exploring.

Voluptuously shaped, perfumed and juicy, a ripe pear epitomises fruity temptation. It is one of my favourite things to eat *au naturel*. (I mean the pear. I don't myself have to be naked when eating it, though the idea is not unappealing in the right circumstances, or indeed the right company.) But pears are not as straightforward as apples. The window of perfection is relatively short. You've got to watch them, and seize your moment.

Like so many fruits, pears are invariably picked under-ripe – but here it's no crime. Most varieties, if left too long on the tree, turn woolly and lose their fragrance. They are at their best when ripened after picking. Even those fruits now helpfully labelled in the supermarket as 'ripe and ready to eat' will almost certainly still be a day or two away from perfect eating. On the other hand, pears that have been picked too hard and green may never ripen properly, so choose ones that are firm, but not rock hard.

It might take more than a week for a pear to ripen at home, and a cool larder is a better environment than a warm kitchen, which can 'rush' them. You can, though, accelerate the process by keeping them in the same fruit bowl as a couple of ripe bananas, which produce ethylene, a natural fruit-ripening gas. As they approach their moment of glory, check them daily with a gentle squeeze. A little give indicates that they are there, or nearly there – but only you will know when they are *exactly* right for you...

Their temperamental ripening habits are no doubt why pears play second fiddle to apples (as well as bananas and oranges) in British fruity culture. But a slightly under-ripe pear, even a pretty hard one, is still a versatile ingredient loaded with potential – provided you are ready to apply some heat to it. Pears respond very well to being poached (page 209), fried (page 197), or even baked on a pizza (page 198).

In fact, one of my missions is to get you cooking with them. You will find they lend their charms to all kinds of unexpected ingredients, including game (page 197) and fish (page 194). They are also outstanding in a salad – particularly a savoury salad. My take on the classic pear, blue cheese and walnut salad (page 192), with its 'double hit' of pear and scattering of raspberries, is one of my favourite recipes in the book.

Ring the changes with your choice of pear variety. The brown-flecked, elongated, often slightly banana-shaped Conference is by far the most common in the UK. Easy to grow and to transport, it's a good all rounder – and delicious when properly ripe – but there are other, sweeter, more floral and interesting pears to be had. Fairly widely available are the comely Comice, pale and interesting Williams, and the perfectly pear-shaped Concorde (actually a cross between Conference and Comice). More unusual varieties can be found at orchards and farmers' markets – Beurre Hardy, so named for its smooth, buttery flesh, is one to look out for.

When it comes to varieties of quince you're unlikely be spoiled for choice, though there are quite a few, all available around October/

November. If you're looking to buy them, try specialist greengrocers and adventurous Italian or Spanish delis, or go online. Chances are you'll just have to take what you find – and take them you should, because they are very rewarding. I have a young quince tree at home, and I can't wait for it to provide enough fruit for me to call off the annual autumnal search for other sources.

Even when ripe, quinces are very hard. The honeyed aroma they release in your kitchen belies the fact that the raw flesh is unyielding and sour. But cooked to tenderness with a fair hit of sugar, they taste amazing – their distinctive tartness offset by floral, muscaty aromas. The texture is special, too, a more granular version of pear. These qualities are fully revealed in the simple poached quince on page 210. But quince also works intriguingly alongside meat – the herby roast quince on page 202 goes brilliantly with roast lamb or pork.

Most quinces have a soft, pale down over their yellow skins, which you must rub off before using. Then, once peeled, cored and sliced, it pays to drop them immediately into a bowl of lemon juice and water, to stop the flesh discolouring. But it's not the end of the world if you do get some browning – when cooked your quince should take on a divine, rosy-amber shade anyway.

Different varieties cook out differently. Some (often the larger, less downy varieties) soften fairly quickly, others (generally the small, hard and furry types) take an hour or more of gentle poaching to become knife-point tender. I prefer the latter type, despite the patience required. They seem to develop a deeper flavour as they cook, and have time to take on that gorgeous, deep, blushing colour. Nothing else looks or tastes quite like it.

# Pear, raspberry, walnut and blue cheese salad

Here, the classic combination of pears, blue cheese and walnuts is enhanced in a particularly lovely way, with raspberries and a clever fruity dressing made from lightly cooked pear pulp and honey.

Preheat the oven to 180°C/Gas 4. Put the walnuts on a baking tray and toast in the oven for 5–8 minutes until fragrant and lightly coloured; check frequently to ensure they don't burn. Tip on to a plate and set aside to cool, then bash the nuts roughly, or simply break them up with your hands.

To make the dressing, peel, core and dice one of the pears. Put it into a small pan with the orange juice and a little splash of water. Bring to a simmer and cook over a medium heat for a few minutes until the pear is beginning to soften. Remove from the heat and push the pear pulp through a sieve into a small bowl. Add the lemon juice, half the thyme leaves, half the honey and all the extra virgin olive oil. Whisk the ingredients together, season with salt and pepper and set aside to cool completely.

Peel, quarter and core the remaining pears, then slice each quarter lengthways in half again. Arrange on a platter or individual plates. Crumble over the cheese and scatter over the raspberries and toasted walnuts. Finish with a few generous dabs of the pear dressing, a spritz more lemon juice, some thyme leaves and a little extra runny honey, if you like.

## Serves 4

100g walnuts

4 ripe pears

Juice of 1 orange

Juice of ½ lemon, plus an extra spritz to serve

1 teaspoon thyme leaves

2 tablespoons runny honey

2 tablespoons extra virgin olive oil

200g blue cheese, such as Dorset Blue Vinney, Cornish Blue, Per Las or Beenleigh Blue

About 150g raspberries

Sea salt and freshly ground black pepper

# Salad of pears, kippers and leaves

I love pears in salads with crunchy, strong-flavoured leaves and salty cheeses – this is a different take on the same idea, with smoky salty fish instead of the cheese.

Heat the butter and oil in a frying pan over a medium heat. Add the kipper fillets and cook for 2–3 minutes on each side, until just done. Leave to cool.

To make the dressing, whisk all the ingredients together in a small bowl with a little salt and pepper.

Pour half of the dressing into another, larger bowl. Peel, quarter and core the pears, then slice each quarter lengthways in half again. Immediately add to the bowl of dressing and toss to coat and prevent the pear slices browning.

Arrange the salad leaves and dressed pear slices on individual plates or a large platter. Take the cooled kipper flesh off its skin, break into small chunks with your fingers and scatter over the salad.

Trickle over some of the remaining dressing (you may not need every last drop), give the salad another squeeze of lemon juice and a final grinding of salt and pepper, and it's ready to serve. Brown bread and butter is a lovely accompaniment.

## Serves 2 as a main course, 4 as a starter

A small knob of butter

1 tablespoon olive or sunflower oil

2–3 kipper fillets (about 200g in total)

2 ripe pears

2–3 good handfuls (about 75g) of slightly bitter and/or peppery leaves, such as rocket, chicory, radicchio and/or cos lettuce

A squeeze of lemon juice

Sea salt and freshly ground black pepper

### For the dressing

1 heaped teaspoon grainy mustard

1 teaspoon runny honey

1 tablespoon lemon juice

3 tablespoons extra virgin olive oil

# Fried pear and venison hotdogs

**Serves 4**

A trickle of rapeseed, sunflower or olive oil

8 venison sausages

2 just-ripe pears

A knob of butter

A little of your favourite mustard (grainy is good)

4 large white rolls, such as ciabatta

Rich venison sausages are set off a treat by slightly caramelised pears and a smear of mustard. But of course, this idea works well with any good bangers, and apples are delicious in place of pears.

Start by cooking the sausages. Heat a trickle of oil in a frying pan over a medium heat. Add the sausages and cook them reasonably gently, turning often, until golden brown all over and cooked through. This will take at least 20 minutes. Alternatively, you can sizzle the sausages for 5 minutes until lightly coloured, then transfer them to a preheated oven at 170°C/Gas 3 for 20 minutes, to cook through.

Meanwhile, peel, quarter and core the pears, then slice each quarter lengthways in half.

Transfer the sausages to a warm dish and set aside in a warm place. If there is a lot of dark residue in the sausage pan, give it a wipe with a bit of kitchen paper, but don't wash it – you want to keep some of those lovely meaty flavours.

Add a knob of butter to the pan and, when melted, add the pears. Cook them over a medium heat for about 5 minutes, turning from time to time, until they are tender and lightly caramelised. Transfer to the dish with the sausages.

Slice open the rolls and dab the bottom cut surface in the pan juices, then spread with a little mustard. Add two sausages to each roll and top with the pear slices, squeeze the rolls shut, then eat.

**Variation** You can make a crusty sandwich version with thick slices of sourdough, slicing the sausages lengthways.

# Fruity pizzas

I'm hoping to persuade you to explore a whole new world of pizzas, using fruit to bring colour, texture and a spectrum of sweet and tart flavours to this familiar favourite. Let's kick off with pear, spinach and blue cheese (illustrated overleaf), a particularly inviting example.

To make the pizza dough, put the two flours in a large bowl with the salt and yeast and mix well. Add the oil and 325ml warm water and mix to a rough dough. Flour your hands a little. Tip out the dough on to a work surface and knead for 5–10 minutes until smooth. This is quite a loose and sticky dough – as it should be – so try not to add too much flour if you can help it. It will become less sticky as you knead.

Trickle a little oil into a clean bowl, add the dough and turn to coat in a light film of oil. Cover with a tea towel and leave in a warm place to rise until doubled in size – at least an hour, probably closer to two.

Preheat the oven to 250°C/Gas 9 if it goes that high, or at least 220°C/Gas 7 and put a baking sheet in to heat up.

For the topping, cook the spinach in a pan with just the water clinging after washing for a minute or two until wilted. Drain in a colander and leave to cool a little. Heat 1 tablespoon olive oil in a frying pan, add the onions and cook gently for 10 minutes or until soft. Squeeze the spinach to remove any water, chop it roughly and mix with the warm onions. Season with salt and pepper. Set aside.

Peel, quarter and core the pears, then cut each quarter across into two pieces. Cut the lower, larger pieces into four and the smaller pieces in two. Put them all in a bowl with 1 tablespoon olive oil, the nutmeg, chilli flakes, if using, and some salt and pepper. Toss well to coat.

Tip the dough on to a lightly floured surface, deflate with your fingers and leave to rest for a few minutes. Cut into 3 or 4 equal portions. Roll out one piece as thinly as you can.

Take the hot baking sheet from the oven, scatter over a little flour, and place the dough base on it. Spread one-third (or one-quarter) of the

## Makes 3–4 pizzas

### For the pizza dough

250g plain white flour, plus extra to dust

250g strong white flour

1½ level teaspoons fine sea salt

1 teaspoon easy-blend (instant) yeast

1 tablespoon rapeseed or olive oil, plus a little extra for oiling

### For the topping

About 500g spinach, any tough stalks removed

2 tablespoons olive oil, plus extra to trickle

2 onions, quartered and finely sliced

2 slightly under-ripe pears

A grating of fresh nutmeg

A pinch of dried chilli flakes (optional)

250g blue cheese

Sea salt and freshly ground black pepper

spinach and onion mixture over the pizza base, top with the same proportion of the pear pieces and crumble over the blue cheese. Trickle with a little more oil and add a grinding of pepper. Bake for 10–12 minutes until blistered, bubbling and browned at the edges. Repeat to make the rest of the pizzas with the remaining dough and topping. Serve at once.

**Variations**

I've had a bunch of fun playing with the fruity pizza theme. Here's the cream of the crop:

*Quince and blue cheese* Use lightly poached slivers of quince (see page 210) as a delicious alternative to the pears.

*Rocket, pear and raspberry* Cook the onions as for the main recipe, but without adding any spinach, and spread over the prepared dough base. Peel, slice and dress the pears as above (I'd definitely include the chilli here too) and add these before baking the pizza as above. Once cooked, scatter a small handful of rocket leaves and some fresh raspberries over each pizza, give it another trickle of extra virgin oil, and serve. (Illustrated on the cover.)

*Beetroot, apple and Cheddar* Peel and thickly slice 200g cooked beetroot (vac-packed or roasted yourself, but not pickled). Arrange over the onion-topped pizza bases, along with 2 peeled, cored and sliced eating apples. Finish with a generous grating of good Cheddar before baking, as above.

*Tomato, strawberry, olive and mozzarella* Scatter 300g halved cherry tomatoes over the onion-topped pizzas. Add 225g halved or thickly sliced strawberries and 100g roughly chopped black olives. Tear up a couple of balls of buffalo mozzarella and distribute over the pizzas, then give them a trickle of olive oil and a grinding of pepper before baking as above. Once cooked, shave a little Parmesan over the pizzas and, if you like, strew with ribbons of basil or coarsely chopped flat-leaf parsley before serving. (Illustrated overleaf.)

# Herby roast quince

Quince is one of the finest fruits to roast, in my opinion. Its firm texture and rich aromatic flavour really lend themselves to this simple method, especially when boosted with generous quantities of fresh herbs.

Preheat the oven to 190°C/Gas 5.

Wash the quinces under a running cold tap, lightly rubbing with your fingers to remove the fine down that clings to their skins. Using a large sharp knife, quarter the quinces. With a smaller knife, remove their cores, then cut each quarter into 2 or 3 wedges.

Put the quince wedges into a roasting tin and scatter over the herbs. Pour over the apple juice, dot with the butter and sprinkle with the sugar and some salt and pepper. Cover the dish with foil and roast for 30–60 minutes, until the fruit is tender (different varieties can vary widely in the time they take to tenderise).

Remove the foil and roast for another 20–30 minutes, until the juices are well reduced and the quince wedges are starting to caramelise. Serve warm.

*Serving your herby roast quince* Cooked like this, quince goes really well with game, lamb or pork. Cut into smaller pieces, the roast quince is also lovely tossed into a salad with some lightly toasted walnuts or hazelnuts, and crumbled or diced blue cheese or goat's cheese.

### Serves 8 as a side dish

About 1kg quinces

Several generous sprigs of thyme

Several generous sprigs of rosemary

6–8 bay leaves

150ml apple juice

15g butter

1 tablespoon caster sugar

Sea salt and freshly ground black pepper

# Mustard pears

**Makes two 1 litre jars**

4 teaspoons yellow
mustard seeds

4 teaspoons black
mustard seeds

2 cinnamon sticks,
broken in half

2 hot red chillies,
roughly sliced

2 thumb-sized pieces
of ginger, sliced

1 litre cider vinegar

Juice of 1 lemon

3kg unripe or just ripe
pears

1kg caster or
granulated sugar

*To finish (optional)*

An extra sprinkling of
yellow mustard seeds

An extra sprinkling of
black mustard seeds

1 cinnamon stick,
broken in half

½ red chilli, sliced

**This lovely, delicately spiced preserve is a nifty way to use up under-ripe pears. Good served with cold meats and leftovers, it looks wonderful in the jar too – a great gift for a foodie friend.**

Sterilise two 1 litre preserving jars, such as Kilner or Le Parfait jars, by washing them thoroughly in hot soapy water, rinsing well, then putting them upside down on a tray in a low oven (at 120°C/Gas ½) to dry out and warm up.

Using a pestle and mortar, roughly crush the mustard seeds, then tip into a large saucepan. Do the same with the cinnamon. Add to the saucepan with the chillies and ginger, then pour in the cider vinegar. Bring to a simmer and simmer very gently for 30–45 minutes.

Meanwhile, put the lemon juice into a large bowl with about 300ml water. Peel, quarter and core the pears, dropping them straight into the lemony water to stop them browning. If some pears are significantly riper than others, put them in a separate bowl.

Strain the spiced vinegar through a sieve and return to the pan. Add the sugar and heat gently until dissolved. Add the pears (under-ripe ones first if they're separate) and poach gently until tender. Ripe pears only need 2–3 minutes, under-ripe pears may take up to 15 minutes.

Transfer the pears carefully to the sterilised jars and immediately pour over the hot liquor, making sure the pears are completely covered and the jar is full to the brim. You can add a sprinkling of mustard seeds, a cinnamon stick and a few fresh chilli slices to each jar at this point too, if you like. Seal the jars straight away and leave to cool.

The pears will be ready to eat in a few days but will taste better if left for a month or two. Once opened, refrigerate and eat within 2 weeks.

*Serving your spiced pears* These are a delicious accompaniment to cold meats such as ham and pork, game pies, pork pies and chunky pork and game pâtés and terrines. Also good with rabbit rillettes (see page 27), cold roast venison and sausages – hot or cold.

# Pears poached with cider and bay

**Serves 4**

4 pears

75g caster sugar

2–3 wide strips of lemon zest

4–5 bay leaves, torn in half

300ml medium dry cider, or perry

**This elegant autumn dessert is a good one to make in advance. Of course, poaching the pears in perry makes even more sense than poaching them in cider but a good perry (as opposed to more commercial types of 'pear cider') is hard to come by – a good quality cider will do very nicely.**

Peel the pears, but leave them whole, ideally with the stalk on. Put them into a saucepan in which they fit fairly snugly in one layer. Add the sugar, lemon zest and bay. Pour over the cider or perry, then add enough water to just cover the pears.

Bring to a simmer, lower the heat, cover and simmer gently until the pears are tender right through. The time this takes can vary greatly depending on the ripeness of the pears – it could be just 5 minutes for ripe pears, or as long as 20 minutes for very firm fruit – so keep checking them with the tip of a small, sharp knife.

When the pears are done, remove them from the pan with a slotted spoon and place in a dish. Turn up the heat under the pan and boil the liquor until reduced down by at least half and lightly syrupy. Pour this reduced liquor back over the poached pears. Leave to cool completely, then chill.

Serve the chilled pears with their sweet fragrant juice spooned over. They're very good just as they come, but a spoonful of crème fraîche, or even a scoop of best vanilla ice cream, is a lovely enrichment.

# Poached quince

This is my default method for cooking quinces for a range of sweet dishes. Poached until completely tender and yielding, they are luscious, full flavoured and have their own delectable syrup.

Peel, quarter and core the quinces, then cut each quarter lengthways into 3 or 4 slices. Put the quince slices into a saucepan with the sugar, lemon juice and enough water to just cover the fruit. Bring to a simmer, then turn the heat right down and poach, uncovered, at a very gentle, tremulous simmer.

You want to poach the fruit for as long as you can – up to 1½ hours – in order to get butter-soft quince slices in a rose-hued, syrupy liquor. If your quinces cook much more quickly and are in danger of collapsing (some varieties are inclined to do so) don't worry; take them out when tender, then boil down the liquor until syrupy before re-combining with the fruit.

Leave the quinces to cool in their syrup, then place in the fridge until ready to eat. They'll keep, immersed in their syrup, for a week.

*Serving your poached quince* You can eat poached quinces warm, but I prefer them chilled from the fridge. They can be enjoyed just as they are, or with a scoop of ice cream or crème fraîche. They also make a great fool, when combined with a little whipped cream and yoghurt, or if you add some 'independent crumble' to the mix, a fumble (see page 84). And they are delicious with a simple rice pudding, served hot or chilled. For breakfast, try poached quince with muesli and yoghurt.

Serves 6

500g quinces

75g caster sugar

Juice of 1 lemon

# Pear and vanilla crisp

## Serves 4

1 vanilla pod

35g caster sugar

4 firm pears (about 700g)

### For the crisp topping

100g coarse, fairly fresh breadcrumbs

25g caster sugar

50g butter, melted

**This is a very simple, breadcrumb-topped alternative to a crumble or pie, deliciously sweet and fragrant.**

Preheat the oven to 200°C/Gas 6. For the crisp topping, combine the breadcrumbs, sugar and butter and set aside.

Slit the vanilla pod open and scrape out the seeds with the tip of a small, sharp knife into a bowl. Add the sugar and mix the seeds with it (don't worry if some of them remain clumped together).

Peel the pears. Cut a slice off the base of each so they stand upright on a board, then cut slices, 3–4mm thick, working from one side of the pear towards the core. When you reach the core, turn the pear and slice it from the other side. Then slice the two remaining thinner sides of the pear.

Arrange a third of the pear slices in a fairly shallow oven dish, about 25 x 18cm. Sprinkle a third of the vanilla sugar over them. Repeat with the remaining pears and sugar, then scatter the topping over the surface. Bake for 20–30 minutes, until the pears are bubbling and the breadcrumb topping is golden brown and crisp.

Leave the pudding to stand for 10 minutes or so, then serve hot, with whipped cream or vanilla ice cream.

# Pear and frangipane toffee tart

This is such a winning flavour combination and the tart looks really impressive. It also works well with apples.

To make the pastry, put the flour, icing sugar and salt in a food processor and blitz briefly to combine. Add the butter and blitz until the mixture resembles breadcrumbs. (Or you can rub the butter into the flour/icing sugar in a bowl, using your fingertips.) Add the egg yolk and enough milk to bring the dough together in large clumps. Tip on to a lightly floured surface and knead lightly into a ball. Wrap in cling film and chill for 30 minutes.

Preheat the oven to 200°C/Gas 6 and grease a large baking tray or line with baking parchment.

Peel, quarter and core the pears, then slice each quarter lengthways in two. Heat the butter and brown sugar together in a frying pan over a medium heat and, when bubbling, add the pears. Cook gently for a few minutes, until the pears are just tender and bubbling in a toffeeish sauce. Drain the pears in a sieve over a bowl, retaining all the sauce. Allow to cool. Set the sauce aside.

For the frangipane, cream the butter and sugar together in a bowl until fluffy. Add the egg, flour, ground almonds and vanilla and beat well until evenly combined.

Roll out the pastry into a rough rectangle, no thinner than 4mm, and trim to about 30 x 25cm. Place on the prepared baking tray. Spread the frangipane mixture over the pastry, leaving a slight border around the edge. Arrange the cooked pears over the frangipane, then sprinkle with the demerara sugar and flaked almonds. Bake for 20 minutes until the pastry is golden brown at the edges.

Allow the tart to cool for 10 minutes or so before serving. Meanwhile, warm the toffee sauce through, stirring well to re-emulsify if it has separated slightly. Serve slices of the warm tart, with pouring cream and a generous trickle of the warm toffee sauce.

Serves 8–10

### For the sweet shortcrust pastry

250g plain flour

25g icing sugar

A pinch of salt

150g cold unsalted butter, cut into cubes

1 free-range egg yolk, beaten

About 50ml cold milk (or water)

### For the pears

4 barely-ripe pears

50g butter

2 tablespoons soft brown sugar

1 tablespoon demerara sugar

1 tablespoon flaked almonds

### For the frangipane

75g butter, softened

75g caster sugar

1 large free-range egg, lightly beaten

20g plain flour

75g ground almonds

A dash of vanilla extract

# Steamed quince pudding

This zesty alternative to a classic steamed treacle pudding is a great way to use quinces.

For the quince purée, wash the fruit under a running cold tap, then chop, including the skin and core, into 1–2cm pieces. Place in a saucepan with the lemon zest and juice, 2 tablespoons water, the star anise and 100g sugar. Bring to a simmer, cover and cook gently until the quince is very soft and pulpy – up to an hour. Allow to cool slightly.

Tip the contents of the pan into a sieve over a bowl and work the fruit through. You should end up with 150–200ml quince purée. Taste and add more sugar if necessary. It should be lovely and sweet, with the muscaty tartness of the quince shining through. Leave to cool.

Generously butter an 850ml–1 litre pudding basin. Cut a double layer of foil or baking parchment and butter this too.

To make the sponge, put the butter and sugar in a large bowl. Slit open the vanilla pod, scrape out the seeds and add these to the bowl. Beat together for several minutes until very light, pale and fluffy, using a handheld electric whisk if you like. Beat in the eggs, one at a time, adding a spoonful of flour with each, then fold in the remaining flour.

Put the cooled quince purée into the pudding basin, then gently spoon the sponge mixture on top, covering it as best you can. Tie the foil or parchment, buttered side down, over the top of the basin. Put a trivet or upturned small heatproof plate in a large saucepan and stand the basin on it. Pour in boiling water to come about halfway up the side of the basin, then put the lid on and bring to a gentle simmer. Steam for 1½ hours, topping up the boiling water as necessary.

Remove the foil or paper cover and run a knife around the side of the pudding to loosen it. Invert a plate on top, then turn the plate and basin over to unmould the pudding on to the plate. The quince purée will now be on the top; if there's any left in the pudding bowl, scrape it out and dollop it on the sponge. Serve with cold double cream.

## Serves 4–6

### For the quince purée

1 large or 2 small quinces (250–300g in total)

Finely pared zest (in strips) and juice of 1 lemon

1 star anise

About 100g caster sugar

### For the sponge

100g unsalted butter, softened, plus extra for greasing

100g caster sugar

1 vanilla pod

2 medium free-range eggs

100g self-raising flour, sifted

# Chocolate pear cake

This is a chocolatey variation on the classic River Cottage apple and almond cake. And, since pears and chocolate go *so* well together, I couldn't resist adding a simple chocolate sauce as well.

Preheat the oven to 170°C/Gas 3.

Peel, quarter and core the pears. Melt the butter in a frying pan over a medium heat. Add the brown sugar and orange zest and stir until the sugar has dissolved. Add the pears and cook them gently for a few minutes, turning frequently, until completely tender. Set aside.

Butter a 20cm springform cake tin and line with baking parchment. Combine the ground almonds, flour and cocoa powder and set aside.

Beat the butter and sugar together with a handheld electric whisk or in a mixer for several minutes until very light and fluffy. Beat in the eggs, one at a time, adding a spoonful of the almond mix with each. Fold in the remaining almond mix, with a large metal spoon or spatula, then stir in a little milk to get a mixture with a soft dropping consistency.

Spread this cake mixture in the prepared tin and arrange the pears on top, finishing them off with any buttery, sugary juices still in the pan. Bake for about 45 minutes, or until a skewer inserted into the centre of the sponge comes out clean. Leave to cool slightly in the tin.

To make the sauce, break up the chocolate into small pieces and put into a heatproof bowl with the cream, sugar and 2 tablespoons water. Set over a pan of just-simmering water, making sure the water doesn't touch the base of the bowl and leave to melt, stirring once or twice. When melted, stir until smooth to give a glossy sauce with a thick pouring consistency; if necessary, stir in a tiny splash of hot water.

Serve slices of the cake, ideally still warm from the oven, with the hot or warm chocolate sauce.

Serves 4–6

### For the pears

4 just-ripe pears

35g butter

2 tablespoons soft brown sugar

Finely grated zest of 1 orange

### For the cake

150g butter, softened, plus extra for greasing

100g ground almonds

100g self-raising flour

25g cocoa powder

150g caster sugar

2 large free-range eggs

A splash of milk

### For the chocolate sauce

75g dark chocolate (about 70% cocoa solids, broken into small pieces

75ml double cream

25g caster sugar

Now let's celebrate uncultivated fruit – the wild bounty that flourishes in woodland, heathland and waste ground up and down the land. This is the democratic fruit harvest – quite literally free for all.

There isn't much to match the satisfaction of eating food you've found yourself – perhaps only food you've *grown* yourself can compete. And hedgerow fruits are the first step on a journey that might take you on to foraging wild greens and leaves, to fungi or seaweed. But even if your wild food adventures remain at the blackberrying level, they are always worthwhile. They tune you in to shifting seasons, awaken dormant instincts of self-reliance and reconnect you to the landscape.

Traditional hedgerow fruit recipes are often very simple, and I don't feel inclined to tinker with them much. Most wild fruits are less versatile than cultivated types – there aren't a million ways with a sloe – but that is part of their charm. Filling your hat with rosehips or haws, and knocking out a big batch of rosehip syrup (page 230), hedgerow jelly (page 224) or sloe vodka (page 228) is not something you are going to do more than once or twice in a season.

But the creative endeavour doesn't end there – in fact, it's where the fun begins. These classic hedgerow concoctions will prove wild and willing accomplices in your culinary experiments. So how about squid with rosehip hot 'n' sour dipping sauce (page 230), a vegetable stir-fry with haw'sin' sauce (page 233), or a sloe vodka sorbet (page 237)? Why not sweeten the gravy for your roast lamb with half a teaspoon of homemade hedgerow jelly? How about rosehip syrup on your breakfast porridge, yoghurt or pancakes? Or a grown-up pud of vanilla ice cream with a shot of blackberry whisky (page 228) poured over it?

Coming into season first – usually in August – blackberries are juicy harbingers of a hedgerow harvest that can take you right through to Christmas, when the last of the rosehips – though mottled with brown patches and a little shrivelled – will still make you a fabulous syrup. Blackberries feature heavily in my recipes because they are so abundant and so immediately scoffable. They are pretty much the only wild fruit you'll want to eat raw, and their juicy sweetness makes them more versatile than other wild fruits.

The harder hedgerow fruits like haws, hips and sloes need to be softened through juxtaposition with other ingredients; whereas, as far as I'm concerned, the purer the flavour of blackberry the better. And so my mission is often to make something as blackberryish as possible. And I believe you'll find that mission accomplished in my blackberry jelly (the wobbly pudding kind, not the preserve) on page 238, and my blackberry-soaked cake on page 247.

Even if you live in a city, you will discover wild fruits worth picking within walking distance of your door. Rowan (or mountain ash), for instance, is a lovely tree with bright orange-red berries. It grows wild on heaths and hillsides, but is also a popular municipal planting, often seen in streets and parks. Hawthorn is widespread; its small scarlet berries (haws) pepper canal paths and scrubland, and are easy to spot and to pick in quantity (mind the thorns, though). Elder, with its messy little wine-dark berries, is also plentiful, as are plump, purple sloes and glossy, crimson rosehips.

Crab apples should be grabbed whenever you see them; they are incredibly useful in making preserves – a stand-alone crab apple jelly or a mixed up, multi-fruit hedgerow jelly (page 224). True crabs are most often found in old hedgerows, whereas apples growing wild near roads and gardens are likely to have sprung up from discarded domestic fruit (but small and tart as they usually are, they may still be pressed into service as if they were crabs). There are also cultivated, ornamental varieties – you might have one in your garden. The fruit is often a bit small and fiddly, but they can be used.

Truly wild crab apples are roughly golf-ball sized, green or almost golden, and often pitted and marked. If you bite into one, it should pucker you up with its appley tartness – that's what you're after. Underlying that austere first impression is a deep apple flavour, and some very useful pectin, waiting to be released by cooking. Both can contribute to the truly wild version of the autumn pudding on page 244.

Aside from stout footwear and gloves, you need no special equipment to gather these fruits – except perhaps secateurs for rosehips, and you may wish you'd brought a stepladder when you see hundreds of crab apples hovering just out of reach. Avoid foraging in field margins where chemical sprays may have penetrated. And, axiomatically, always pick above the height at which an Alsatian cocks its leg.

Otherwise, just make sure you know what you're harvesting, wash it thoroughly and be prepared to be flexible when you get your treasure to the kitchen. These fruits vary greatly in flavour, acidity and sweetness – not to mention their abundance or scarcity in any given year. Many hedgerow recipes, mine included, take account of this, allowing for mixtures of different fruits and for substitutions of one for another.

All of which ensures that, though you may be following time-honoured tradition, what you end up with will always be unique – your very own vintage.

HEDGEROW Fruit

# Hedgerow
## jellies

Hedgerow berries make a wonderful preserve for both sweet and savoury uses. I like to use at least two of them – often blackberries plus elderberries or haws, though rowanberries make a classic jelly on their own. In all cases these wild fruits are low in pectin, so it makes sense to combine them with apples in order to get a good set.

Roughly chop the apples (no need to peel or core). Put into a preserving pan with the berries and add enough water to almost cover the fruit. Bring to a simmer and cook gently until all the fruit is soft and pulpy.

Tip the mixture into a jelly bag (or muslin-lined sieve) suspended over a bowl and leave to drip for several hours or overnight.

Prepare 6–8 small (250–300g) jars by washing thoroughly in hot soapy water, rinsing well, then putting them upside down in a low oven (at 120°C/Gas ½) to dry out and heat up. Put a saucer in the fridge to chill.

Measure the juice and pour into the cleaned preserving pan. For every 600ml fruit juice, add 450g sugar. Bring slowly to the boil, stirring to dissolve the sugar, then bring to a rolling boil. Let the mixture boil hard for 8 minutes, then turn off the heat and test for setting point: drip a little of the jelly on to the cold saucer, refrigerate for a couple of minutes, then push the jelly with your fingertip. If it has formed a skin that wrinkles with the push, setting point has been reached. If it hasn't, boil the jelly for another 2–3 minutes then test again. If unsure, err on the side of caution: a lightly set jelly is far nicer than a solid one.

Once setting point is reached, pour the jelly into the hot, sterilised jars. Seal straight away. Label when cool, then store in a cool, dark place and use within a year. Refrigerate after opening.

*Using your hedgerow jelly* Serve with game, such as venison and hare, and full flavoured meats like lamb. It's also good partnered with rich terrines and pâtés, especially if game or liver is included, and strong salty cheeses. And don't neglect its potential as a breakfast or teatime preserve – on hot buttered toast, scones or crumpets.

**Makes 6–8 small jars**

1kg crab apples or cooking apples

1kg blackberries, haws, sloes, elderberries or rowanberries, or a mix

About 750g–1kg granulated sugar

# sloe syrup

Sloes are a wonderful and often abundant hedgerow fruit, but they are almost exclusively used to make hedgerow liqueurs – either sloe gin or sloe vodka. Lovely as these are, their alcoholic kick dominates, so we rarely get a chance to explore sloes outside of that context. This simple and versatile syrup is intended to put that right.

Sterilise a few bottles or jars and screwtops or stoppers by washing them thoroughly in hot soapy water, rinsing well, then putting them on a tray in a low oven (at 120°C/Gas ½) to dry out and heat up.

Put the sloes in a saucepan with the lemon juice and 750ml water (it should just cover the fruit). Bring to the boil, lower the heat and simmer for about 10 minutes until all the skins have burst and the fruit is simmering in a deep purple juice.

Tip the sloes and their juice into a muslin-lined sieve or colander, or a jelly bag. Leave until the juices have stopped dripping through – up to an hour. Do not squeeze the fruit in the muslin because you may get too much tannin from the fruit skins coming through.

Measure the juice into a large, clean pan (you may find a film has formed on top of the juice – don't worry, it will dissolve as the syrup cooks). For every 100ml juice, add 100g sugar. Stir over a low heat until the sugar has completely dissolved, then bring to the boil and boil hard for 3 minutes. You will probably get some pink scum coming to the surface – skim this off as best you can but don't worry about it too much, any remainder should disperse as the syrup boils.

Immediately funnel the sloe syrup into the prepared bottles or jars and seal straight away. Use within 6 months and refrigerate once opened.

*Using your sloe syrup* It's delicious on pancakes, with vanilla ice cream, rice pudding or a tart apple compote. Or to make a refreshing non-alcoholic drink: in a glass, mix the juice of an orange with 50ml sloe syrup, add a few ice cubes and top up with soda. The same drink, with a large measure of vodka, is as good as any sloe gin cocktail.

**Makes about 1 litre**

1kg sloes, washed and picked over

Juice of 1 lemon

About 800g granulated or caster sugar

# Sloe or damson vodka

This liqueur is one of my favourite ways to enjoy the flavour of sloes, and it's excellent with damsons too. You can use the same recipe to make sloe or damson gin but I prefer the neutrality of vodka, which allows the full flavour of the fruit to shine. My recipe contains a lot less sugar than is customary, which leads, I think, to a better flavour. However, it does take longer to mature. I wouldn't drink this until at least 2 years after bottling. And if you can leave it 3 years, you'll be rewarded with a far mellower and more sophisticated liqueur. If you don't think you can wait that long, and you want to drink the vodka within a year, double the sugar to 500g.

Sterilise a large Kilner jar, demi-john or similar container and lid or stopper, by washing thoroughly in hot soapy water, rinsing well, then putting in a low oven (at 120°C/Gas ½) for 20 minutes to dry. Let cool.

You first need to break the skins of the fruit: either prick each sloe or damson several times with a pin or give them a *very* quick blitz in a food processor (which is easier), just enough to break the skins. Either way, transfer the fruit to the sterilised jar. Add the sugar, pour in the vodka, seal and leave in a cool place away from direct sunlight.

Every week or two, turn the jar on its head and back again. After 6 months, strain the liquid through several layers of muslin, or a clean cotton tea towel. Don't discard the pulp – you can use it to make some boozy fruit chocolates (see page 250). Sterilise two 75cl bottles (as above) and let cool. Bottle the strained liqueur and seal tightly. Leave for at least 2 years (see above), or longer... if you have the patience.

**Variation:** *Blackberry whisky* This is one of the finest of all hedgerow liqueurs but it does need ageing to reach its full potential. The quantities are different but the method is the same. Give 2kg blackberries a shake or stir to bruise them a bit and let the juice start to run (there's no need to prick or blitz them), then put into a large sterilised jar with 200g caster sugar and 1 litre whisky. Proceed and bottle as above. Leave for at least 3 years... if you can. Delicious trickled over vanilla ice cream.

**Makes two 75cl bottles**

1kg sloes or damsons

250g granulated or caster sugar

1 litre vodka

# Rosehip syrup

Rosehips are, of course, a fruit – the same family as apples in fact – and this classic autumn hedgerow syrup has a unique and lovely flavour: warm, floral and fruity. This method is the simplest and best I've found for making rosehip syrup. Double-straining ensures that the tiny, irritant hairs found inside rosehips are removed.

Sterilise a couple of bottles and vinegar-proof screwtops or stoppers by washing thoroughly in hot soapy water, rinsing well, then putting them on a tray in a low oven (at 120°C/Gas ½) to dry out and heat up.

Roughly chop the rosehips in a food processor in batches, then transfer to a large saucepan and add 1.25 litres water. Bring to the boil, then turn the heat down and simmer for around 15 minutes. Strain through a double layer of muslin, letting the pulp sit for a good half hour so that all the juice passes through. Wash out the muslin, or cut a fresh piece, fold to double it and pass the strained juice through it again.

Measure the rosehip juice into a large saucepan. For every 500ml, add 325g sugar. Heat slowly, stirring, until the sugar has dissolved, then bring to the boil and boil for 3 minutes, skimming off any scum if necessary. Decant immediately into the prepared bottles and seal.

Label when the bottles have cooled completely. Use within 4 months and refrigerate once opened.

*Using your rosehip syrup* Try it for breakfast trickled over porridge, pancakes, drop scones or eggy bread; use it to sweeten plain yoghurt (with some chopped apple if you like); or for a delicious pud, trickle it on to hot or cold rice pudding or good vanilla ice cream.

**Variation:** *Rosehip hot 'n' sour dipping sauce* Warm 100ml rosehip syrup with 1 garlic clove and ½ fairly hot red chilli, both finely chopped. Simmer for 3–4 minutes, then leave to cool. This fragrant, spicy-sweet sauce is great as a dip for seafood tempura, goujons of crumbed fish, fried squid rings or fishcakes. It's also a lovely dressing for freshly picked white crab meat, which I like to scatter with coriander leaves.

**Makes about 1 litre**

1kg rosehips, trimmed and washed

About 500g granulated sugar

# Haw 'sin' sauce

**Makes a 330ml bottle**

500g haw berries, thoroughly washed

300ml cider vinegar

4–5 garlic cloves, peeled and smashed

1–2 bay leaves

170g granulated sugar

2 star anise

1 cinnamon stick

3 whole cloves

A pinch of cayenne pepper

Sea salt and freshly ground black pepper

**Haws are even more plentiful than blackberries and just as easy to pick. Though they're too hard and bitter to eat straight off the bush, they give a delightful fruity flavour to hedgerow jellies and wines. They can also be used to make this delicious sweet-sour sauce/ ketchup, which is based on a recipe from my friend Pam Corbin.**

Sterilise a 330ml bottle and a vinegar-proof screwtop or stopper by washing thoroughly in hot soapy water, rinsing well then putting in a low oven (at 120°C/Gas ½) to dry out and heat up.

Put the haw berries in a saucepan with the cider vinegar, garlic, bay and 300ml water. Bring to the boil, reduce the heat and simmer for about 30 minutes, until the berries will have turned a dull brown and their skins have split to reveal their yellow flesh. Discard the bay. Rub the fruit and garlic through a sieve into a clean pan, leaving the skins and pips behind. You will probably need to do this in batches.

Add the sugar, spices and some salt and pepper to the purée in the pan. Heat gently, stirring, until the sugar has dissolved, then bring to the boil and simmer for 5 minutes, stirring often to ensure it doesn't stick to the base of the pan. Fish out the whole spices. Taste a little of the sauce and add more salt or cayenne if you think it needs it.

While still piping hot, funnel the sauce into the hot, clean bottle and seal straight away. The sauce improves on keeping, so leave it for a few weeks before opening. Use within a year and refrigerate once open.

*Using your haw'sin' sauce* You can use this spicy, fruity sweet-sour sauce, rather like the Chinese hoisin sauce it is cheekily based on – as a dipping sauce, especially for chicken, duck or pork. You could even serve it with crispy duck pancakes. It's also great as a change from ketchup or brown sauce in a hot bacon – or cold ham – sandwich. And it goes brilliantly in a spicy vegetable stir-fry – try using it generously to flavour a combination of celeriac and/or carrot julienne, sliced red onion and mushrooms spiked with ginger, garlic and a pinch of dried chilli flakes.

# Rosehip and apple sorbet

**Serves 8**

About 1kg crab apples or cooking apples, such as Bramleys

200–400ml rosehip syrup (see page 230)

A little sugar syrup (see variation) or icing sugar (if needed)

1–2 crisp eating apples, to serve (optional)

**This is a wonderful and unusual way to use rosehip syrup, giving you a delicate and refreshing sorbet with a subtle, fruity, floral hip flavour. If you're able to forage a good haul of crab apples, they work a treat here. And do try the sloe vodka variation – it's excellent.**

Cut the apples into chunks (no need to peel or core). Put into a heavy-based saucepan and add 150ml water for crab apples, 250ml if using cooking apples. Bring to a simmer and cook, stirring often, for about 15 minutes until the apples are reduced to a pulp. Some crab apple varieties may take longer – add a splash more water if you need to, but you are aiming to create a thick purée. Tip into a sieve over a bowl and rub through with a wooden spoon to remove the skins and pips.

Weigh the purée: you should have about 800g, though crab apples may give you less. For every 400g purée, stir in 200ml rosehip syrup, then taste. The purée needs to be quite sweet, as it will taste less so when frozen, so add a little more syrup if needed. (If you run out of rosehip syrup, add a little sugar syrup or icing sugar.) Leave to cool, then chill.

Churn in an ice-cream maker (you'll need one with a 1.5 litre capacity) until semi-set, then transfer to a freezer container and freeze until firm. (Alternatively, freeze in a plastic container for about an hour until solidifying around the sides. Mash the frozen sides into the liquid centre with a fork, then return to the freezer for another hour. Repeat this at hourly intervals until soft-set and then let the sorbet set solid.)

Transfer the sorbet to the fridge about 30 minutes before serving to soften slightly. Serve scooped into bowls, with apple slices if you like.

**Variations** Instead of rosehip syrup, you can add a slug of blackcurrant liqueur (see page 62) or sloe or damson vodka or gin (see page 228). First you will need to sweeten the apple purée with a sugar syrup: dissolve 125g sugar in 150ml water, then boil for 5 minutes. Weigh your hot, sieved apple purée. If you have around 800g, add all the hot sugar syrup; if you have less, adjust the quantity to taste. Leave until cold, then stir in the liqueur (75ml for 800g purée) before churning.

# Blackberry jelly

As you can see, this is a pudding jelly – not a jammy jelly. Made with pure blackberry juice, it looks amazing, has an intense flavour and is wonderfully wobbly. Cold cream really sets it off perfectly.

Put the blackberries, lemon juice and 75ml water in a large saucepan. Bring to a simmer and cook for 5–10 minutes until the fruit is soft and has released lots of juice. Tip the contents of the pan into a sieve set over a large bowl and let the juices drain through. Stir and press the berries to extract maximum juice but don't actually rub them through the sieve – you want the juice to remain thin and smooth.

Following the guidelines on the pack, calculate the quantity of gelatine needed to set 750ml liquid. Although you'll only have 500ml liquid, you need a little more gelatine than normal because the acid in the fruit juice affects its setting power. Put the gelatine leaves in a small bowl of cold water to soak for about 10 minutes until soft and floppy.

Measure out 500ml of the hot juice, whisk in 50g icing sugar and taste the liquid. It should be sweet, but with the tartness of the blackberries and lemon coming through. Add a little more icing sugar if necessary.

Drain the soaked gelatine leaves and squeeze out excess water, then add them to the hot juice and stir until completely dissolved. (If the juice has cooled down, heat it again gently before adding the gelatine, but don't let it boil or it will be too hot.)

Very lightly oil 4 darioles or similar moulds, using a few drops of oil on a wad of kitchen paper. Pour the warm blackberry liquid into the moulds and leave to cool, then refrigerate for at least 6 hours, until set.

To turn the jellies out, first use the tip of a small, sharp knife to release the edge of the jelly where it meets the side of its mould. Invert the mould on to a plate. If the jelly won't come out, sit the mould briefly – just for a few seconds – in a bowl of warm water to barely soften the outside. Then invert it on to the plate again. Serve the jellies with a scattering of fresh blackberries, and a jug of double cream if you like.

**Serves 4**

1kg blackberries, plus an extra handful to serve

75ml lemon juice

About 50g icing sugar

Enough sheets of leaf gelatine to set 750ml liquid

A few drops of sunflower oil

# Blackberry
## crème brûlée

How do you beat a classic crème brûlée, with its thick, creamy, vanilla-perfumed custard and burnt sugar top? Well, I'm not sure you can actually, but you can make something equally fabulous by adding soft berries, which release their sharp juices into the custard as you eat. The beauty of this recipe is that it works just as well – arguably even better – if you start with frozen berries. They collapse slightly as they thaw in the custard, marbling it with their juices.

Put the cream into a saucepan. Slit open the vanilla pod, scrape out the seeds with the tip of a small, sharp knife and add them to the cream, with the pod. Slowly bring the cream to just below boiling point, then take off the heat and set aside for a few minutes to infuse.

Divide the berries evenly between 6 ramekins or other heatproof dishes, 125ml capacity.

Whisk the egg yolks and caster sugar together in a bowl until well combined, then pour on the hot cream, whisking all the time. Return the mixture to the pan and heat gently, stirring all the time, until the custard thickens. You can take it to the point when it *just* starts to bubble at the edges, but don't actually let it boil. As soon as you have a nice thick custard, remove from the heat and immediately strain through a fine sieve into a jug.

Carefully pour the custard over the berries in the dishes. It should be thick enough to stop the berries rising to the surface, but if any start to lift, poke them back down! Leave to cool completely, then chill.

Preheat the grill to very high (unless you have a cook's blowtorch). Sprinkle a thin, even layer of brown sugar over the top of the custards – they should be set firmly enough for you to be able to pick them up and shake them gently to distribute the sugar evenly. Place under the grill until the sugar is golden brown and bubbling. Or, use a blowtorch to melt and caramelise the sugar. Either way, leave the brûlées to cool, then put them in the fridge to chill until needed, but you should serve them within a few hours or the caramel can start to soften.

**Serves 6**

500ml double cream

1 vanilla pod

150g fresh or frozen blackberries (or you can use raspberries, alpine strawberries or blueberries)

6 medium free-range egg yolks

100g caster sugar

1–2 tablespoons soft brown sugar

# Blackberry and apple clafoutis

## Serves 6

3 medium eating apples (about 350g in total)

25g butter

25g caster sugar

Finely grated zest of 1 smallish lemon

100g blackberries

### For the batter

50g plain flour

A pinch of salt

25g caster sugar

2 medium free-range eggs

200ml whole milk

### To finish

Icing sugar, to dust

**Clafoutis is a traditional French batter pudding, classically made with cherries (see the variation below), but ripe for adaptation with other fruits. This is a favourite variation of mine.**

Preheat the oven to 190°C/Gas 5.

Peel, quarter and core the apples, then cut each quarter in half. Melt the butter and pour into a 25cm diameter ceramic oven dish. Add the apples, sugar and lemon zest and toss together in the dish. Use a pastry brush to brush the buttery mix all over the inside of the dish, right up to the rim. Roast the apples in the oven for about 15 minutes until tender and bubbling.

Meanwhile, to make the batter, sift the flour and salt into a large bowl and stir in the sugar. Make a well in the centre. Beat the eggs lightly in another bowl, then pour into the flour and whisk in, gradually incorporating the flour from the sides. Gradually whisk in the milk to make a smooth batter.

Take the apples out of the oven and scatter the blackberries evenly over them, then pour over the batter. Bake for 35 minutes, or until the clafoutis is puffed up and golden brown. Leave to cool slightly, or completely. The batter will collapse back down as it cools, and the correct finished texture is tender, but fairly solid – not airy.

Clafoutis is best eaten warm or at room temperature, rather than hot. Serve it dusted with icing sugar, with a jug of cold cream on the side.

### Variations

You can also make clafoutis with chunks of lightly cooked, drained rhubarb, or raw blueberries, or booze-soaked prunes or dried apricots.

*Cherry clafoutis* Make the batter as above, using 50g sugar. Heat the baking dish in the oven for 5 minutes, add the butter and put it back in the oven until melted and bubbling, then brush it all over the inside of the dish. Add 500g whole cherries (leave the stones in), pour over the batter and bake as above.

# Autumn
# pudding

**This is an autumnal version of the classic berry-filled, bread-lined summer pudding and the flavour is excellent. For even more of a wild hedgerow affair, you can use crab apples (see the variation below).**

Peel, quarter and core the apples, then chop into roughly 2cm pieces. Melt the butter in a saucepan. Add the apples, sugar and apple juice and heat gently, stirring often, to dissolve the sugar. Cook gently for about 5 minutes, then add the blackberries and continue to heat for just long enough to get their juices running – you want to keep their fresh flavour. Taste and add more sugar if needed. Leave to cool a little.

Lightly butter a 1 litre pudding basin and line with the slices of bread: start with a small, squarish piece to cover the base of the basin, then cut long, wedge-shaped pieces of bread to line the sides from the base to the top, so that the joins run from top to bottom, not around the middle. Cut small slivers of bread to plug any gaps, if necessary.

Spoon the warm fruit and its juice into the bread-lined basin. The aim is for the juice to completely soak the bread so, if it looks like it's not penetrating completely, I sometimes ease the bread away from the side of the basin in a few places and trickle some juice down the outside. When you've filled the pudding, cut some more bread to form a neat 'lid' and position to completely cover the fruit. Stand the pudding basin on a plate to catch any overflowing juice. Put a saucer on top of the pudding and place a weight on top to compress the pud. Once it has cooled, refrigerate for at least 12 hours, ideally 24.

To serve, use a thin-bladed knife to release the bread from the sides of the basin. Put a plate on top of the basin, then invert the whole thing on to the plate. Serve in slices, with a jug of double cream.

**Variation** For a true hedgerow pudding, use crab apples in place of the eaters, upping the sugar to 200g. Peel, quarter and core the crab apples (fiddly, but worth it), then chop roughly. Proceed as above, testing the cooked fruit mixture for sweetness – crab apples can be very sharp, so you may need to add more sugar.

---

**Serves 6–8**

500g crisp eating apples, such as Cox's

25g butter, plus extra for greasing

150g caster sugar

100ml apple juice

500g blackberries (or a mix of blackberries and autumn raspberries)

250–300g slightly stale white bread, sliced fairly thinly, crusts removed

# Blackberry-soaked cake

## Serves 8

125g butter, softened, plus extra for greasing

100g caster sugar

2 large free-range eggs

200g self-raising flour

A splash of milk (no more than 50ml)

### For the blackberry syrup

500g blackberries

A good squeeze of lemon juice

25–50g caster sugar

This is a spectacular recipe for a good haul of blackberries. There's a lovely contrast, both visual and textural, between the pale, fluffy sponge and its dark, juice-soaked purple top.

Preheat the oven to 180°C/Gas 4. Butter a 24–25cm ceramic flan dish.

Beat the butter and sugar together for several minutes until very light and fluffy, ideally in a mixer or with a handheld electric whisk. Beat in the eggs, one at a time, adding a spoonful of the flour with each. Add the rest of the flour and fold in lightly with a large metal spoon, adding a splash of milk towards the end to obtain a good dropping consistency. Spread the mixture in the prepared dish. Bake for about 25 minutes until golden; a skewer inserted into the centre should come out clean.

Meanwhile, put the blackberries in a saucepan with the lemon juice and 2–3 tablespoons water. Bring to a simmer and cook gently for about 5 minutes until the fruit is soft and has released lots of juice. Tip into a sieve over a bowl and stir and press the blackberries to extract as much juice as possible. Stir 25g of the sugar into the warm strained juice, then taste: it should be lightly sweetened but with a pleasant tartness (as the sponge is also sweet). Add more sugar only if needed.

As soon as the cake comes out of the oven, make lots of deep holes all over the surface with a fine skewer. Carefully pour on the blackberry syrup, covering the whole cake and letting it seep down the sides. It may seem too much syrup but don't worry – it will all be soaked up! Leave for at least 20 minutes to allow the juices to seep in.

You can serve the cake while it's still warm, or wait until it is cold. You can even refrigerate it overnight and serve it chilled the next day. Either way, a little lightly whipped cream is a lovely accompaniment.

**Variations** You can replace the blackberries with raspberries. Or use cooked rhubarb – simmer in 150ml freshly squeezed orange juice, with up to 50g sugar, then strain the fruit to get the syrup for soaking the cake. Serve the leftover pulp for breakfast, with yoghurt.

# Blackberry, apple and orange smoothie

To enjoy the goodness from a handful of early autumn blackberries, I often whip up a quick smoothie. I like to use frozen berries, which gives a nicely chilled drink, but you could refrigerate the ingredients instead for an hour or so before you start – or just add an ice cube or two to the blender.

Peel, core and chop the apple into 5–6mm chunks. Put these into a blender with the blackberries and the juice of 1 (or 2 small) oranges, plus a little honey or sugar if you like. Process until you have a smooth, drinkable purée. You can add the juice of another orange if needed, and pulse again.

Pour your smoothie into a glass and drink straight away. If left to stand it may start to separate, but you can re-combine it with a good swizzle from a fork.

**Variation** Raspberries – either instead of or combined with the blackberries – also work very well here.

**Serves 1**

1 medium eating apple, such as a Cox's

75g blackberries (ideally frozen)

Juice of 1–2 medium-large oranges (or 2–3 small ones)

½–1 teaspoon honey or sugar (optional)

# Boozy fruit chocolates

This is a brilliant way to use some of the spent fruit from the sloe or damson vodka recipe on page 228. You can also make it with dried fruit that you've soaked in your favourite tipple overnight.

If you are using sloes or damsons left over from sloe or damson vodka-making, after straining off the vodka, remove the stones/pips from some of the fruit. With sloes, this is a bit fiddly, as you have to scrape the flesh away from the stones – a small, sharp knife is the best tool for the job. Damsons are much easier – you can just squeeze the stones out. You need about 50g de-stoned/de-pipped fruit pulp.

If you are using dried fruit, put it to soak in the alcohol for 24 hours, until plumped up. Drain off any excess liquid (and drink it, of course).

Line a baking tray with baking parchment. Break the dark chocolate into small pieces and put it into a large bowl. Set over a pan of just-simmering water, making sure the water doesn't touch the base of the bowl, and leave to melt gently, stirring once or twice.

Remove from the heat and leave the chocolate to cool in the bowl until barely tepid, then gently stir in the 50g boozy fruit pulp or the drained, soaked dried fruit (this can sometimes make the chocolate look slightly grainy, but don't worry).

Spread the mixture in a thin layer over the lined baking tray. Leave in the fridge or a cool larder until cold and set, then cut or break into pieces. The chocolates will keep in a plastic container in the fridge for a week or two.

Serve the chocolates just as they are or sprinkled lightly with sugar. A glass of your vintage sloe or damson vodka is the perfect complement.

**Serves 8–10 as an after-dinner nibble**

Boozy hedgerow fruit pulp (see page 228)
OR
50g dried fruit, such as sultanas, raisins or dried cherries, plus 3 tablespoons brandy, rum or whisky

200g dark chocolate (at least 70% cocoa solids)

Caster sugar, to sprinkle (optional)

The fruits in this chapter are a cosmopolitan bunch, corralled together not in botanical kinship, but due to their ancient links with the Middle East and the Mediterranean. Their sultry origins may in part explain why some of these fruits are heavy with associations of erotic sensuality and indulgence – though clearly their sheer naked loveliness, inside and out, has also had a say in the matter. Who can break open a ripe fig and keep their thoughts entirely pure? The fig leaf's symbolic modesty surely arose as an antidote to its uniquely seductive flower-fruit. Some believe that the pomegranate, rather than the apple, is the true forbidden fruit of Eden, while grapes epitomise the Roman orgy.

Any of these fruity beauties could tempt me off the straight and narrow – so much so that I've tried to grow most of them at home in the West Country, with varying degrees of success. I can expect a good bowlful of homegrown figs most years and I've got a decent crop of dessert grapes flourishing in my greenhouse. But I've given up dabbling with melons, as it were, and the kiwis seem to have given up on me. There's no question that all these fruits crave sunnier climes. Being an eternal optimist, I'll continue to do my best to coax sweet and fragrant examples off my vines and trees, whatever the Devon weather. But I'm enough of a realist to accept that for the most intense flavour and chin-dripping juiciness we must look to imports.

None of these fruits are hard to find, indeed grapes have become a stalwart of the British fruit bowl – so easy to eat that in my house a plump bunch will be reduced to a stalky skeleton less than an hour after appearing. But as a delicate, vulnerable crop, grapes are commonly treated with a wide range of agricultural chemicals – they often turn up on 'fruits with the most pesticide residue' lists. So, for me, it's got to be organic (or homegrown) every time. Assuming I can save a few from the ravening hordes, I like to fling them into savoury salads – see my Coronation chicken on page 270. They are also the vital finishing touch of a lovely Mediterranean soup called ajo blanco (page 260) that I urge you to try.

Another fabulous salad fruit is the melon. The partnership of a silky, perfumed slice with salty slivers of air-dried ham is almost a cliché, for good reason – it's delicious. I like to think my bruschetta on page 259 is a pretty nifty and original take on it. To ensure that your melon is ripe press it at the flower end (i.e. the 'bottom', if you take the stalky end as the top) where it should give a little. Smell it too: if it doesn't have at least some melony bouquet it isn't right, and never will be. Best not to buy. Watermelons are the exception – even a ripe one gives off scarcely any scent, which makes buying a whole one something of a lottery. If buying a cut slice, simply look for the deepest crimson you can find.

For full flavour and complex aromatics the orange-fleshed Charentais is hard to beat, though the green-tinged opalescent-fleshed Galia, when fully ripe, is lovely too. On a hot day, spare a slice for the lovely cooling melon milkshake on page 283. A fridge-chilled, fully ripe, crimson-fleshed watermelon is also a refreshing treat, but I would only ever serve it straight up, or as a thirst-quenching smoothie.

Pomegranates are a gift to the cook. Indeed, I almost invariably deploy them as an ingredient, rather than a stand-alone, and usually in a savoury context. A scattering of their jewel-like seeds adds a tart juicy crunch to my aromatic noodly salad (page 262), and finishes off a roast chicken (page 272) in the most agreeable way. Kids seem to love these dishes – perhaps because, as my friend Nikki says, 'adding pomegranate seeds is like turning on the Christmas tree lights'.

The kiwi is an unassuming little fruit that nonetheless packs a powerful punch of flavour and goodness – gram for gram it has ten times more vitamin C than a lemon. Often described as tropical, it is technically *sub*tropical and Italy is now the world's biggest producer. Slice through that dull fuzzy skin, and its neon-green flesh – the source of its sherbety sweet-sour flavour – is revealed. Kiwi's a winner in juices and smoothies, and I hope you'll love it in the quirky, herby fruit salad on page 276. It also contains generous amounts of the enzyme actinidain, which can be used to great effect to tenderise cuttlefish and squid (see page 264). Kiwis ripen really nicely at home – buy them when firm, and let them soften for up to ten days in the fruit bowl.

And finally to figs. I just love them. But I have to accept that the figs we get here – imported or homegrown – are never quite so arousing as those eaten on Mediterranean shores. Figs will only ripen on the tree, and a truly ripe fig just won't cope with the journey north. Even so, buy the best you can. Look for plump flesh that gives willingly when lightly squeezed. If it's already cracking open at the base, revealing a little of the pink pleasure that lies within, it pretty much wants to be eaten.

And we can still do some lovely things to less than perfectly ripe figs in the kitchen. A little heat, a little honey, and we're back in business. My baked figs with honey, ricotta and almonds on page 279 are properly lascivious – warm, welcoming and just a little bit wicked.

FIGS, MELONS, GRAPES & more

# Fig and celery bruschetta

If you happen to have some really flavoursome, ripe figs, you can use them raw for this dish, just cutting them into pieces and tossing with the celery, then trickling the honey over the finished bruschetta. However, figs that are a little under-ripe, or not oozing with fragrant flavour, benefit hugely from being cooked gently with a touch of honey first. I like this with a mild cheese such as ricotta, but you could use a punchy blue instead.

Cut each fig from stem to base into 8 wedges (or into 6 pieces if they are not large). To cook the figs, heat the olive oil and butter in a frying pan over a medium-low heat. When the butter is melted, add the honey and a few thyme leaves, if using. Add the figs and cook gently, turning the pieces over in the honeyed juices, for about 5 minutes, until they are softened and releasing their juices. Set aside.

Slice the celery thinly, on the bias, and put into a bowl with a trickle of extra virgin olive oil, some salt and pepper and a squeeze of lemon juice. Toss together well.

Toast the bread. While still hot, rub each slice with the cut garlic clove, if you like, then trickle with a touch of olive oil.

Pile the celery on to the hot toast slices, then add the fig wedges and trickle over any juices from the pan. Crumble a little cheese over each bruschetta. Finish with a trickle of extra virgin olive oil, a scattering of thyme leaves, if you have them, and an extra grinding of salt and pepper. Serve straight away.

## Serves 4

4 large (or 6 medium) figs

1 tablespoon olive oil

A nut of butter

2 teaspoons runny honey

A sprig of thyme, leaves only (optional)

6–8 tender, inner celery stalks

Extra virgin olive oil, to trickle

A squeeze of lemon juice

4 large slices of sourdough, or other good robust bread

1 garlic clove, halved (optional)

75–100g ricotta or other soft, mild cheese such as a mild goat's cheese or mozzarella, or a blue cheese

Sea salt and freshly ground black pepper

# Melon, ham and rosemary bruschetta

**Serves 4**

½ large, ripe honeydew, Charentais or Galia melon (700–800g)

About 4 tablespoons extra virgin olive oil

Juice of ½ lemon

1 teaspoon chopped rosemary

A handful of peppery salad leaves, such as rocket and/or mizuna

A pinch of dried chilli flakes (optional)

4 large slices of sourdough or other good robust bread

1 garlic clove, halved

3–4 large, very thin slices of air-dried ham (about 50g), such as prosciutto

Sea salt and freshly ground black pepper

**A classic duo since it first graced tables in the seventies, melon and Parma ham has become something of a cliché that, although tasty, doesn't exactly inspire. But marinate the fruit briefly with lemon, rosemary, chilli and olive oil, then serve it with some really good air-dried ham on garlicky, oily toast, and you'll have a lively dish to get excited about.**

Scoop out the seeds from the melon half with a teaspoon, then slice the fruit into slim wedges (1–1.5cm thick at the outside edge). Use a small sharp knife to cut away the skin, keeping the outside edge a smooth curve if you can. Cut each wedge across in half.

Place the melon pieces in a bowl, add 2 tablespoons of the extra virgin olive oil, the lemon juice, rosemary, salad leaves, chilli flakes, if using, and a twist of salt and pepper. Toss gently to combine.

Toast the bread on both sides – either in a toaster or in a ridged cast-iron grill pan, which will give you a lovely toasty flavour and attractive scorch lines on the bread. Either way, rub the toasts lightly with the cut garlic clove and trickle with some more olive oil.

Roughly tear the air-dried ham and arrange on the garlicky toasts. Pile the melon mixture on top and finish with a trickle of the oily, rosemary-spiked melon juices and a grinding of pepper.

**Variations** Other fruits work well with air-dried ham – the best, in my view, being pears and figs. In both cases they need to be ripe, tender, sweet and full flavoured. Simply marinate quarters of fig, or thick long slices of peeled pear, as above. Mini version of these bruschettas make fantastic canapés.

# Ajo blanco

Ajo blanco (literally 'white garlic') is a classic Spanish almond soup, served chilled and garnished with grapes. Also described as a white gazpacho, it makes a punchy, refreshing starter to a summer meal. You can save time and use ready-blanched almonds, but blanching them yourself gives you the edge on flavour.

Put the almonds into a bowl, cover with boiling water and leave for 5 minutes, then scoop a few out with a slotted spoon. The dark brown skins should have loosened enough for you to slip them off quite easily. If not, leave them in the water a little longer. Skin all the almonds and place in a blender.

Tear the bread into chunks and soak them in cold water to cover for a couple of minutes, then lift from the water and add to the blender. Add the garlic, olive oil, vinegar, 1 teaspoon salt and a little pepper. Pour in enough cold water to cover all the ingredients and blend until smooth, adding more water as necessary to create a soup with the consistency of double cream.

Transfer the soup to a bowl or jug, cover and refrigerate for an hour or so until thoroughly chilled.

Once chilled, you might want to add a little more water if the soup has thickened significantly. Taste it and add more salt or vinegar if needed. Serve in bowls, with the halved grapes floating on top. Finish with a trickle more extra virgin oil and a sprinkling of pepper.

**Variations** Grapes are not the only Mediterranean fruit that can be used as the garnish for this soup. Slices of ripe fig are also perfect, as are little cubes of melon. In the absence of such sun-kissed delights, slices of sweet crisp apple work well too.

### Serves 4

200g whole almonds (skin on)

75g slightly stale, crustless robust white bread, such as sourdough

3 garlic cloves, peeled and halved

100ml extra virgin olive oil, plus extra to serve

2 tablespoons sherry vinegar or balsamic vinegar

Sea salt and freshly ground black pepper

20–24 seedless white grapes, halved, to finish

# Pomegranate,
## grapefruit and noodle salad

This is inspired by a recipe shown to me by the wonderful vegetarian chef David Bailey. It's an invigorating assembly, giving you mouthfuls of explosive and juicy Asian flavours. You can buy crisp-fried shallots in jars, or deep-fry a few thinly sliced shallots yourself.

Peel and segment the grapefruit (see page 329), cut each segment into 3 or 4 chunks and place in a large bowl; squeeze the juice from the membrane into a small bowl and save for the dressing.

To make the dressing, put the ingredients into a food processor with 2 tablespoons grapefruit juice and whiz together. Strain through a fine sieve, pressing the solid ingredients with the back of a spoon to extract the maximum flavour. Taste the dressing and adjust the seasoning if required; you may also want an extra splash of grapefruit juice.

Bring a pan of lightly salted water to the boil. Add the noodles and simmer for 3 minutes (or according to pack instructions) until tender. Drain and refresh under cold water, then drain thoroughly and toss with a splash of oil to stop them sticking together. Use a pair of scissors to cut the noodles into manageable lengths. Set aside in a bowl.

Halve the pomegranate around its equator and hold one half, cut side down, over the bowl of grapefruit. Gently whack the outside of the fruit with a wooden spoon until the juicy seeds fall out into the bowl. A twist and a squeeze between whacks will help release reluctant seeds.

Roughly chop the coriander and mint leaves. Cut the spring onions on the diagonal into 1cm slices and add to the fruit with the herbs, half the peanuts and a pinch of salt. Toss gently, then add the noodles and gently tumble (with your hands, or two forks). Trickle over two-thirds of the dressing and carefully but thoroughly tumble to combine.

Arrange the salad over one large platter or in individual bowls. Scatter over the remaining peanuts and whack over the seeds from the other pomegranate half. Top with the crispy shallots and a few toasted coconut shavings. Finally, trickle over the remaining dressing to serve.

**Serves 4**

2 grapefruit

100g fine rice noodles

A splash of sunflower oil

1 pomegranate

A small bunch of coriander

A small bunch of mint

4 spring onions

75g roasted peanuts, roughly chopped

1 tablespoon crispy fried shallots

A small handful of toasted shaved coconut

Salt

### For the dressing

4 teaspoons caster sugar

2 lime leaves (optional)

1 lemongrass stalk, tough outer layers removed, finely sliced

1 hot red chilli, deseeded and finely chopped

1 large shallot, chopped

1 garlic clove, chopped

A finger-sized piece of ginger, grated

2 tablespoons tamari or soy sauce

# Barbecued cuttlefish with kiwi

Cuttlefish flesh is cleverly tenderised by the powerful enzyme actinidain in kiwi fruit (this works with large squid too). It can then be cooked very quickly on a barbecue or in a hot grill pan, becoming lovely and succulent, without any hint of rubberiness. With their juicy acidity, a few extra kiwi fruit – dressed with oil and seasoned – work very well as an accompaniment.

Open up the cuttlefish bodies (if they are not already opened), slicing the 'cone' or 'tube' down one side so it opens into a triangular sheet. Score the inside surface of the cuttlefish flesh in a diamond pattern with a serrated, not-too-sharp knife, at 5mm intervals, but don't go all the way through the flesh. Then slice the body into pieces or strips, roughly finger length. Cut the tentacles into 2 or 3 pieces each. Place all the prepared cuttlefish in a bowl.

Peel two of the kiwi fruit and grate the flesh coarsely over the cuttlefish. Add 1 tablespoon extra virgin olive oil, the garlic, chilli flakes and lemon zest. Stir well, then cover and leave to marinate in the fridge for at least 2 hours, or up to 24.

Shortly before you're ready to serve, peel the remaining kiwi fruit and slice them thickly into rounds. Toss in a little lemon juice, olive oil, salt and pepper, and set aside.

If you plan to cook the cuttlefish over the barbecue, make sure it is very hot, the flames have died down and the coals are coated in a layer of white ash. Alternatively, if you're cooking indoors, heat a ridged cast-iron grill pan over a high heat until smoking hot.

Wipe the excess marinade from the cuttlefish and then place on the barbecue grid, or in the pan. Cook for about 1 minute each side only, until opaque and marked with grill lines.

Divide the cuttlefish between individual bowls. Add the dressed kiwi slices and serve straight away. A white bean or chickpea salad and some fresh flatbreads or pitta breads are ideal accompaniments.

**Serves 4**

2 medium cuttlefish 'tubes', cleaned and ready to cook, plus tentacles if available (about 750g in total)

4–5 medium-large ripe kiwi fruit

About 2 tablespoons extra virgin olive oil

2 garlic cloves, thinly sliced

A pinch of dried chilli flakes

Finely grated zest of 1 lemon, plus a good squeeze of the juice

Sea salt and freshly ground black pepper

# Marinated *lamb* and **fig** kebabs

This is a very simple way to produce some really gorgeous tasty kebabs. Best on the barbecue of course – but also delicious cooked indoors on a searing hot cast-iron grill pan. You'll need eight long wooden or metal skewers.

Put the lamb cubes in a bowl with the onion and garlic. Spoon over the extra virgin olive oil and mix well. Cover and leave to marinate in the fridge for 2–3 hours.

If you're using wooden skewers, soak them in cold water for at least 30 minutes ahead of cooking (to stop them catching under the grill).

Thread the marinated lamb cubes and fig pieces alternately on to the skewers and season well with salt and pepper.

If you are cooking on a barbecue, make sure it is very hot, the flames have died down and the coals are coated in a layer of white ash. Alternatively, heat a ridged cast-iron grill pan until smoking hot, or your overhead grill to high.

Cook the kebabs for 4–6 minutes on each side, so that both meat and figs are nicely charred – go for a shorter cooking time if you like your lamb pink. Transfer the lamb to a warm plate or board and leave to rest in a warm place for 5 minutes.

Scatter the chopped mint over the kebabs, squeeze over a little lemon juice and finish with a final trickle of olive oil – and a little honey too if you like. Serve at once.

These kebabs are delicious served with lightly grilled flatbreads and thick wholemilk yoghurt. If you want some greens too, wilted spinach dressed with olive oil and a squeeze of lemon is particularly good.

**Serves 4**

About 500g leg of lamb, cut into large cubes

1 small red onion or 2 shallots, finely chopped

1 garlic clove, crushed or finely grated

3–4 tablespoons extra virgin olive oil, plus a little extra to serve

6 figs, quartered

A handful of mint leaves, chopped

½ lemon

A scrap of runny honey (optional)

Sea salt and freshly ground black pepper

# Roast bacon and figs

## Serves 4–6

A piece of unsmoked streaky bacon, with rind (800g–1kg)

1 onion, halved

1 carrot, thickly sliced

1 celery stalk, thickly sliced

2–4 bay leaves

A few parsley stalks (optional)

10–12 figs

35g soft brown sugar

2 heaped teaspoons English mustard

A bunch of thyme

Sea salt and freshly ground black pepper

**The combination of salty, tender bacon and sweet roasted figs is hard to resist. Not all butchers stock streaky bacon in the piece, though you should be able to order it in advance. If you can't get hold of any, it's very easy to cure some pork belly at home yourself (see below). Alternatively, you can use a joint of unsmoked gammon.**

Place the bacon in a large saucepan. Add the onion, carrot, celery, bay and parsley stalks, if using. Cover with water and bring to a simmer. Skim off any froth or scum from the surface, then put the lid on and simmer gently for 2–3 hours or until the meat is tender but not falling apart, topping up with boiling water as necessary during cooking.

Remove the bacon from the pan, reserving the liquor (which is now a tasty stock) and leave to cool a little. Preheat the oven to 200°C/Gas 6.

Cut the skin from the bacon, then score the fat lightly with a sharp knife. Place the bacon in a roasting tin and arrange the figs around it. Mix the brown sugar and mustard to a paste and spread over the scored fat. Tuck some thyme sprigs under the meat and add a few tablespoons of the stock to the pan. Roast for about 20 minutes, until the glaze is well browned, but keep checking to make sure it doesn't burn. Remove from the oven and set aside to rest for 20 minutes or so.

Serve thick slices of the glazed bacon with the soft, juicy figs. A sharply dressed green salad and mash or plain boiled spuds are excellent accompaniments. Don't discard the leftover bacon stock – it makes a flavourful base for a hearty split pea or lentil soup.

*To make your own home-cured chunk of bacon* You need a 1kg piece of pork belly, boned-out but with the skin still on. Combine 50g fine sea salt, 25g soft brown sugar, 1 teaspoon finely ground black pepper, 3 shredded bay leaves and 12 lightly crushed juniper berries. Put this mixture into a plastic tub, add the pork belly and rub the cure all over the meat and skin. Cover and refrigerate for 48 hours, turning the meat once or twice. Remove the bacon from its salty bath, rinse it well and proceed with the recipe as above.

# Coronation **chicken** with **grapes** and almonds

This is my take on a classic Coronation chicken – with grapes for a burst of sweetness and the added crunch of celery and almonds. It's great for a special summer weekend lunch or a picnic. To save time, you could just use 100g good quality ready-made mayonnaise but, of course, it is better to make your own.

Start with the mayonnaise. Crush the garlic with a pinch of salt and combine in a bowl with the egg yolks, mustard, cider vinegar and some pepper. Start whisking in the oils, a few drops at a time to start with, then in small dashes, whisking in each addition to amalgamate. Stop when you have a glossy, wobbly mayonnaise. Check the seasoning and add more salt, pepper, mustard or vinegar if you like.

Measure 100g of the mayonnaise (refrigerate the rest for other uses) and combine thoroughly with the yoghurt, curry paste and chutney. Cut or tear the chicken into bite-sized pieces and fold through the dressing, with the grapes and celery. Taste and add lemon juice, salt and pepper as needed.

Spread the salad out on a large serving platter and finish with celery leaves or torn parsley and a scattering of toasted almond flakes. Serve a green salad and some good bread on the side, or with the classic rice salad accompaniment.

**Variations** I sometimes ring the changes radically and use blueberries or stoned apricots or cherries in place of the grapes. Alternatively, you can make this into a sort of curried chicken Waldorf by adding slices of apple to the grapes and using roughly broken walnuts instead of the flaked almonds.

**Serves 4**

100ml plain wholemilk yoghurt

1 tablespoon medium hot curry paste, such as Madras or Korma

1 tablespoon mango (or other fruity) chutney

About 400g cold roast chicken

100g grapes, halved (deseeded if necessary)

2–3 inner celery stalks, sliced

A spritz of lemon juice

Sea salt and freshly ground black pepper

*For the mayonnaise*

½ small garlic clove

2 large free-range egg yolks

½ teaspoon English mustard

1 teaspoon cider vinegar

175ml sunflower oil

75ml extra virgin olive or rapeseed oil

*To finish*

Celery leaves or parsley

Toasted flaked almonds

# Roast chicken with pomegranate

Pomegranate seeds have a fresh-scented juice bubble around a pleasingly crunchy little 'nut' and they are a gorgeous way to dress tender roasted meats, especially lamb and chicken.

Take the chicken from the fridge about an hour before cooking so it comes to room temperature. Preheat the oven to 210°C/Gas 6–7.

In a small bowl, work the butter with the lemon zest, chopped thyme, 1 tablespoon extra virgin olive oil and a good twist of salt and pepper.

Untruss the bird and put it into a smallish roasting dish. Pull the legs away from the body slightly so hot air can circulate. Carefully release the skin over the breast at the neck end with your fingers and spread most of the flavoured butter under the skin, smearing the rest over it. Season the skin with salt and pepper.

Roast the bird in the oven for 20 minutes, then take it out and baste with the buttery juices. Lower the setting to 180°C/Gas 4 and return the chicken to the oven. Roast for a further 40–50 minutes.

To check if the bird is cooked, pull at the leg. It should come away from the body with relative ease, and the juices between the leg and breast should be clear. If the leg is reluctant, and the juices still pink, give it another 10 minutes, then test again. When you're happy your bird is nicely done, rest it for 10–15 minutes in a warm place – on or beside the cooker if that is convenient.

Meanwhile, in a bowl, mix the yoghurt with the lemon juice, garlic, chilli flakes, if using, and the remaining olive oil. Season with a pinch of salt and some pepper.

Cut the chicken into chunky pieces and arrange on a warm serving dish or plates. Spoon over the yoghurt, scatter over the pomegranate seeds and trickle over the warm roasting juices. Serve at once. This is particularly good with rice or couscous, and a bitter leaf salad.

**Variation** You could use a pheasant (or two) instead of the chicken.

## Serves 4–6

1 free-range chicken (1.75–2kg)

30g butter, softened

Finely grated zest and juice of 1 lemon

A small bunch of thyme, leaves only, roughly chopped

2 tablespoons extra virgin olive oil

200ml plain wholemilk yoghurt

A scrap of crushed or finely grated garlic (about ¼ clove)

A pinch of dried chilli flakes (optional)

2 pomegranates, seeds extracted (as described on page 262)

Sea salt and freshly ground black pepper

# Kiwi and apple with tarragon

The thing I love about this unusual but super-simple salad is its versatility. Kiwi and apple have enough acidity to make this a savoury dish – an intriguing first course, or palate-cleansing middle course. But tweak the dressing a little (see the variation) and you have a sweet fruit salad instead – perfect as a light dessert. The same combination makes a pretty zingy drink too (see below).

Stand an apple on a board, stalk upwards. Take a sharp knife and slice thin rounds from one side of the apple, cutting top to tail and working inwards until you get to the core. Now turn the apple around and again slice thin rounds back to the core. Slice the remaining sides, which will, if you've understood me correctly, be rectangles. Repeat with the other apple. (Or, quarter, core and slice the apples in the conventional way, if you prefer.) Lay the apple slices over 4 large plates.

Top and tail the kiwi fruit, then put them, base down, on a board and slice the skin off in strips. Slice the peeled kiwis into thin rounds and arrange them over the apple slices.

Scatter over the chopped tarragon, add a good squeeze of lemon juice, a trickle of extra virgin olive oil and some salt and pepper. Serve straight away.

## Variations

To make this an entirely sweet salad, leave out the olive oil, salt and pepper. Squeeze the lemon juice over the fruit and then sprinkle with a little sugar or trickle over some mild-flavoured honey. Tarragon will still be delicious in this sweet version of the dish, but you could use shredded mint or basil instead.

*Kiwi, apple and tarragon juice* For a refreshing drink, feed 2 peeled and roughly chopped large kiwi fruit into a juicer with the leaves from a large sprig of tarragon, followed by 2 quartered small eating apples. If you don't have a juicer, you can make a very good smoothie version by blitzing the kiwi fruit and tarragon in a blender with 125–150ml freshly pressed, cloudy apple juice. Drink quickly before it separates.

## Serves 4 as a starter or side dish

2 crisp, tart eating apples, such as Cox's, Ashmead's Kernel or Egremont Russet

2 fat, firm kiwi fruit (not too ripe)

About 1 teaspoon chopped tarragon

A squeeze of lemon juice

Extra virgin olive oil, to trickle

Sea salt and freshly ground black pepper

# Honey and cardamom poached figs

**Serves 4–6**

2 oranges

100g caster sugar

2 tablespoons well-flavoured honey

20 cardamom pods, bashed

500g figs, halved or quartered, depending on their size

Toasted flaked almonds, to serve (optional)

Fresh figs bought (or grown) in the UK are not always ripe, juicy and sweet enough to really enjoy raw, but it doesn't take much to turn them into a sexy, fragrant pud, as this recipe (and the variation below) demonstrates.

Finely pare the zest from the oranges, using a vegetable peeler or one of those zesters that removes the zest in long strips.

Squeeze the juice from the oranges into a measuring jug and make up to 200ml with water. Pour this into a saucepan and add the orange zest, sugar, honey and cardamom. Bring slowly to a simmer, stirring to dissolve the sugar and honey.

Add the figs to the syrup and simmer gently for about 10 minutes, turning gently occasionally, until the fruit is tender and has turned the syrup a rosy red colour (under-ripe figs may take a bit longer). Leave to cool completely.

Finish with a scattering of toasted almond flakes, if you like, and serve with crème fraîche or yoghurt.

**Variation:** *Honey baked figs with ricotta* Halve the figs and put them cut side up in a small baking dish. Trickle over 1 tablespoon honey, dot with 20g butter and scatter over 50g roughly chopped almonds. Bake in a preheated oven at 190°C/Gas 5 for 15–20 minutes or until the figs are soft and the almonds nicely toasted. Spoon dollops of ricotta on top of the hot figs, then trickle over a little more honey and serve.

# Melon and pineapple with ginger

Fresh root ginger gives a lovely heat to this juicy salad. Make sure you use ripe, fragrant pineapple and melon – Galia and Charentais are particularly fine melon varieties.

Remove the seeds from the melon. Cut the flesh into slices, then into bite-sized pieces, cutting away the skin as you go.

Cut the pineapple flesh across into slices, about 1cm thick. Quarter the slices and remove the core and any remnants of 'eyes' from the outside. Cut the pineapple into bite-sized pieces.

Grate the ginger finely, then extract the juice from it. You can do this by simply squeezing the pulp in your hands over a bowl. Alternatively, grate the ginger into a fine sieve and press with a spoon to extract the juice into the bowl. Either way, you need about 25ml ginger juice.

Divide the melon and pineapple between individual bowls and toss to combine. Stir the orange zest and juice into the ginger juice. Trickle this zingy dressing over the fruit and serve straight away.

## Serves 4

500g ripe melon (about ½ medium Galia or Charentais)

500g ripe, peeled pineapple flesh (from 1 medium pineapple)

A large piece of ginger (about 75g)

Finely grated zest and juice of 1 small or ½ large orange

# Melon shakes

Melon flesh has a high water content, so it's ideal for thirst-quenching drinks – either on its own or in combination with other fruits.

## Melon milkshake

**Serves 2**

½ ripe medium Galia, Charentais or honeydew melon (500–600g), chilled

200ml cold whole milk

This may sound unlikely but it's a revelation – wonderfully fragrant and satisfying. Use fridge-cold milk and chill your melon first – for maximum refreshment.

Scoop out the seeds from the melon, then scoop the flesh off the skin in chunks, dropping it into a blender as you go. Add the milk and whiz until smooth. Drink straight away.

## Melon and orange smoothie

**Serves 2**

1 small-medium Galia, Charentais or honeydew melon, or a large wedge of watermelon (about 1kg), chilled

150ml freshly squeezed orange or clementine juice

A sprig of mint (optional)

1 or 2 ice cubes

Here's a sharper, tangier combination.

Scoop the seeds out of the melon, then scoop the flesh off the skin in chunks, dropping it into a blender as you go. Add the orange juice, mint, if using, and an ice cube or two, and whiz until smooth. Drink straight away.

**Variations** Add a ripe (but not over-ripe) banana to the blender for a sweeter, thicker, banana-y version of this smoothie – or the melon milkshake above.

Fan as I am of all that's local and homegrown, I also think there's a time and a place for the tropical. It would be ludicrously hair-shirted to deny myself the pleasure of sun-drenched fruits from exotic climes. And if I tried to ban bananas from the family fruit bowl there would be mutiny…

But some caveats apply. Long distance travel doesn't always agree with these fruits. I adore a properly ripe mango, but that's not an easy thing to find in the UK. It is far too easy to shell out on expensive fruit like mangoes, papayas and passion fruit only to wish you really hadn't bothered, so I'll come to my tropical shopping tips in a moment.

But first let's focus on the banana, an immigrant which, like oranges and lemons, is so much part of our culture that it's an honorary native. And that's in large part because it *does* travel well. Picked green and shipped in bunches by the ton, bananas are ripened in controlled conditions when they reach their destination. They are usually taken to the point of just-turning-yellow, when they will be distributed to our shops. Here we will find them in varying stages of ripeness – and simply finish the job when we get them home. Their sweetness intensifies and their aroma deepens as they move through that familiar spectrum of green to yellow to speckled to brown to black – a transformation that takes about 10–14 days in a warm kitchen. No doubt you know at exactly what point *you* personally like to intercept the process.

But don't forget that bananas are brilliant in recipes, too. However ripe they are, there's always something you can do with them. On the soft side and speckled with brown, they're just what you need for a banana cake (try my chocolate version on page 316), or a cool yoghurty thickie (page 394), or an amazingly easy banana ice cream (page 306).

Just ripe, they're perfect for a banana split – the fastest indulgent pud (page 314). A bit green and under-ripe, they can be cooked – in savoury dishes as well as sweet. Check out my banana kedgeree on page 290.

And if you like this idea, you must also try plantains – bananas' chunkier, starchier cousins. They are almost inedible when raw. Cooked, however, they make an intriguing alternative to spuds. I love them doused in spicy, meaty pan juices – as in my pork with plantain and Szechuan pepper on page 295. They also make a great snack or side veg when simply spiced and fried (page 300). Sometimes you can find plantains in supermarkets, but markets and shops that cater to African, West Indian and South American cooks are your best bet.

In fact ethnic markets are my favoured haunts for buying most tropical fruits. This is because they are being traded by those in the know, who won't tolerate the second rate. Supermarkets are getting better at handling tropical fruit, but they are not there yet. Mangoes are a case in point. The large, greenish-red-skinned Keitt mangoes dominate the supermarket supply. But picked too hard and green, and stored too long in chillers, they often simply refuse to ripen. Market stalls and ethnic grocers are more likely to sell a wider variety of mangoes, and to be offering properly ripened fruit. (The best way to judge a mango's ripeness is to squeeze it gently: it should give a little at the stalk end.) Look out especially for the small golden-skinned Alphonso variety, mostly from India and available in late spring/early summer – they are the chin-dripping joy that a mango ought to be.

Papayas (also called pawpaws) grow almost effortlessly all over the tropics, and globetrotters will no doubt have discovered they make a delicious and reliable breakfast – famously calming for a travel-troubled tummy. These days papayas are available all year round in the UK. But they are fragile and hard to transport – bruising while they're still green will mean they rot before they ripen. Skin colour gives an indication of ripeness. Of the several types of papaya you may find in the shops, most are ripe when more or less completely yellow, but some may be ripe when still mottled green and yellow. A little give when lightly squeezed promises that the pinky orange flesh within will be tender and perfumed.

Passion fruit, on the other hand, can be tricky to judge, since their hard carapace doesn't give much away, and different varieties have different coloured skins. Generally, the wrinklier the skins the riper the fruit, and the sweeter the crunchy-seeded fragrant pulp within. But in really shrivelled specimens, the contents can taste woozily over-ripe.

Saving the most flamboyant tropical treat of all for last, we arrive at the pineapple. Tropical kitsch they may be – think Carmen Miranda's hat – but they are no less delicious for that. As for judging ripeness: look for a golden tone to the skin, with green-ness absent or minimal, particularly at the base (i.e. not the green frondy end). Your best tool is your nose: give the bottom a sniff. A sweet pineappley fragrance is a good indicator that your fruit will deliver its promise.

To find any of these tropical wonders at optimum ripeness, and to consume them just as they are, guarantees you a treat. But I'm also proposing that you start shuffling their luscious textures and heady aromas with all kinds of other ingredients, in surprising recipes like fried fish with pineapple salsa (page 292), seared scallops with mango salsa (page 288) and the BLP (bacon, lettuce, pineapple sandwich) on page 297. Get your gnashers around one of these and you're almost on holiday.

TROPICAL FAVOURITES

# Seared scallops with mango salsa

Mostly I like to contrast sweet-fleshed scallops with salty, spicy things like bacon or chorizo. But sometimes one kind of sweet with another (that has some balancing acidity) is a pleasing route to go down. This colourful dish makes a stunning starter or light meal. I like to use passion fruit juice to season the mango – it's got a nice, acidic tang and keeps the whole thing very tropical – but a good squeeze of lime or lemon juice works equally well.

To make the salsa, peel the mango with a potato peeler, then slice off the two 'cheeks' from either side of the stone. (You don't need the rest of the mango flesh, so slice it off to use for a fruit salad or smoothie – or just eat it!) Chop the mango cheeks into roughly 5mm dice and place in a bowl.

Halve the passion fruit and scoop out the pulp and seeds into a sieve over the bowl of mango. Rub the seeds in the sieve with the back of a wooden spoon to release as much juice as possible on to the mango. (Alternatively, use the lime or lemon juice.)

Add the chopped onion, chilli and coriander to the mango with some salt and pepper and mix well. Taste and adjust the seasoning if necessary. Set aside.

To cook the scallops, heat a large heavy-based frying pan over a high heat until really hot. (If you don't have a large pan, cook the scallops in two batches – you don't want to crowd the pan.) Lightly oil the scallops on both sides and season them well with salt and pepper. Carefully place them in the hot dry pan and cook, without moving, for 1–1½ minutes, until they have a good, golden brown crust underneath. Turn them over and cook for a minute on the other side.

Transfer the seared scallops to plates and serve with the mango salsa, and some peppery green leaves, if you like.

Serves 4 as a starter or light lunch

A trickle of rapeseed or sunflower oil

12 diver-caught scallops, cleaned, with corals attached (if plump and bright)

Sea salt and freshly ground black pepper

*For the mango salsa*

1 large mango (about 400g)

2 passion fruit (or juice of ½ lime or ½ small lemon)

1 small red onion, very finely chopped

½ fairly mild red chilli, deseeded and finely chopped (or a pinch of dried chilli flakes)

About 1 tablespoon chopped coriander

# Banana
## kedgeree

I often put dried fruit (usually sultanas or chopped apricots) in my kedgerees – the sweetness is a lovely touch. Banana is also delicious with the flavours of curry spices and smoked fish. I love the nutty bite of wholegrain rice in this dish, but you can use white basmati if you prefer, reducing the liquid and cooking time accordingly.

Rinse and drain the rice.

Put the smoked fish in a large saucepan, cutting it into pieces to fit the pan if necessary. Pour over the milk and 300ml water. Cover and bring to a gentle simmer. Turn off the heat and leave the fish to cook in the residual heat for 2–3 minutes; it should be nicely cooked and coming easily off its skin. Scoop the fish out of the pan and set aside. Reserve the poaching liquid (for cooking the rice).

Heat the 1 tablespoon oil and a knob of butter in a large saucepan over a medium-low heat. Add the onion and sweat for 10–12 minutes until soft. Add the garlic and cook for another couple of minutes, then add the curry powder. Stir well and cook for a couple more minutes.

Add the rice to the pan, stir and cook for a couple of minutes. Pour in the reserved fish poaching liquid. Bring to a simmer, cover and cook over a low heat for 30 minutes. Gently stir the rice, replace the lid and turn off the heat. Leave the rice to finish cooking in the residual heat for 10 minutes or so, while you prepare the bananas.

Heat another knob of butter and a little trickle of oil in a non-stick frying pan over a medium heat. Peel the bananas and cut them in half lengthways, then cut across into roughly 5mm–1cm slices. Add the bananas to the frying pan and cook, turning once or twice, for about 5 minutes, until nicely coloured and caramelised. Take off the heat.

Flake the smoked fish off its skin, checking for any bones as you go. Add to the cooked rice with the bananas and stir together carefully. Season with pepper (and salt if necessary), scatter over a little torn coriander or parsley if you like, give it a squeeze of lemon, and serve.

**Serves 4**

200g wholegrain basmati rice

500g smoked haddock or kipper fillet

300ml whole milk

1 tablespoon rapeseed or sunflower oil, plus an extra trickle

2 knobs of butter

1 large onion, finely sliced

1 garlic clove, sliced

1 tablespoon mild or medium curry powder

2 fairly large under-ripe or just-ripe bananas (about 200g each)

A handful of coriander or parsley (optional)

A squeeze of lemon juice

Freshly ground black pepper (and salt if required)

# Fried fish with pineapple salsa

Inspired by a memorable dish I once ate in a beach cafe in Thailand, this fresh and fruity salsa is exquisite with a whole fish that's been rubbed with aromatics and soy and fried until crispy. The saltiness of the soy and pungency of the garlic and ginger combine beautifully with the flavours of the salsa. You do need a pretty large frying pan to tackle a whole fish. If that daunts you, the salsa is also delicious with a grilled, barbecued or baked fish (see the variation below).

To make the salsa, cut the pineapple flesh into roughly 5mm chunks. Combine with the garlic, chilli, lime zest, a squeeze of lime juice and the coriander. Taste and add salt and pepper, plus a little more lime juice if needed. Cover and set aside, while you cook the fish.

Make several diagonal slashes on both sides of the fish, without going right through to the bone. Mix the garlic and ginger with enough soy sauce to make a wet paste. Rub this over the fish, working it into the slashes and the belly cavity. Tuck a bay leaf into a few of the slashes. Season the fish with salt and pepper.

Heat the sunflower oil in a large, non-stick frying pan over a medium heat. Add the fish and fry for 5–6 minutes each side, until cooked through to the bone, turning the heat up towards the end to help crisp the skin.

Serve the fried fish straight away with the pineapple salsa, some plain boiled rice and steamed greens.

**Variation** To oven-cook your fish, preheat the oven to 190°C/Gas 5. Slash the fish, rub in the aromatic flavouring paste and season, as above. Place in an oiled baking dish and trickle over a little more oil. Bake for 20–25 minutes or until the fish is cooked through.

## Serves 2

1 gurnard, black bream, sea bass, grey mullet, or trout (about 1kg), or 2 smaller fish, gutted and descaled

2 garlic cloves, grated

A thumb-sized piece of ginger, grated

A dash of soy sauce

A few bay leaves

2 tablespoons sunflower oil

Sea salt and freshly ground black pepper

### For the salsa

200g peeled and cored ripe pineapple

½ small garlic clove, very finely chopped

½ medium-hot red chilli, deseeded and finely chopped

Finely grated zest of 1 lime, plus a spritz of juice

1 tablespoon chopped coriander

# Pork with plantain
## and Szechuan pepper

**Serves 2**

1 large plantain, or under-ripe banana (about 250g)

About 400g outdoor-reared pork tenderloin (fillet), trimmed

1 tablespoon olive, rapeseed or sunflower oil

A knob of butter

2 teaspoons Szechuan pepper, roughly crushed with a pestle and mortar

2 garlic cloves, thinly sliced

Sea salt and freshly ground black pepper

I am not one for overselling my recipes, but as this is a bit unusual, I'm ready to promise you that it is just *so* delicious: tender pork and sweet caramelised plantain brought together with the mouth-tingling flavour of Szechuan pepper. The sticky, garlicky, buttery, spicy juices that you scrape from the base of the pan have to be tasted to be believed. You can certainly make a lovely version of this dish with good old black pepper, but the distinctive clovey-citrus tang of the Szechuan pepper is very special.

Peel the plantain or banana. To peel the plantain, trim off either end, then slit the peel lengthways into strips. If the plantains are ripe, you should be able to pull away most of the peel with your hands. If they're a tad under-ripe, you will find it easier to use the knife to slice off the peel strips. Cut the peeled plantain or banana on the diagonal into thickish slices: 7–8mm is about right. Season with a little salt.

Slice the pork into medallions, 2–3cm thick and season lightly with salt. Heat a large frying pan over a medium heat and add the oil. When hot, add the pork and fry for 3–4 minutes, then turn the pieces over and add the plantain or banana to the pan. Cook for another 3–4 minutes, turning the fruit once or twice during this time, until the pork is just cooked. (Check that one medallion is done all the way through and no longer pink – or just a faint blushing pink.)

Add the butter, Szechuan pepper and garlic to the pan. Toss or stir the ingredients for a couple of minutes as the butter melts and the pepper 'wakes up' in the pan juices.

Give it all a final stir, and transfer to warm plates. Be sure to scrape up all the pan juices, and trickle over the meat. Serve, with plain rice and a simple green salad or wilted greens. You may well want to wipe the pan clean with a scrap of bread and scoff that too.

# The BLP

**Per person**

A trickle of sunflower oil

2–3 rashers of good bacon (back or streaky, smoked or unsmoked, as you prefer)

2 slices of good white bread

Butter, for spreading

A little of your favourite mustard

1–2 slices of peeled ripe pineapple, 1.5–2cm thick

A couple of radicchio, chicory or romaine lettuce leaves

Freshly ground black pepper

If you think it sounds odd to augment a bacon sarnie with pineapple, think again. Bacon goes with tomato – a fragrant, sweet-tart fruit – so it should work with a tropical candidate too. And gammon and pineapple is a tried and trusted pairing. A couple of crisp, delicately bitter leaves and a smudge of mustard give the perfect edge to the salty-sweet combination.

Heat the oil in a non-stick frying pan over a medium heat. Add the bacon rashers and fry, turning once or twice, until done to your liking. Butter one piece of bread and put the hot bacon on it.

Rub the second piece of bread around the frying pan to absorb some of the bacon fat, then spread it with a little mustard.

Add the pineapple to the hot pan and fry for a couple of minutes each side, until golden and hot.

Put the hot pineapple on top of the bacon and give it a few twists of pepper. Add the salad leaves and top with the mustardy piece of bread. Leave it a minute or two for the pineapple to cool a little, then tuck in.

**Variation** For a more substantial, main meal dish based on the pork and pineapple combo: fry a pork chop, then sear a couple of slices of pineapple in the fat left in the pan. Use a splash of cider, white wine or just plain water to deglaze the pan. Combine these pan juices with a little mustard, olive oil and salt and pepper to make a simple warm dressing for some salad leaves to serve alongside.

# Pineapple, Cheddar and radicchio salad

Remember cheese and pineapple squares on sticks? If not, then you must be at least 10 years younger than me. Some claim to have reviled this seventies 'finger buffet' classic even at the time, though I suspect them of retrospective food snobbery. I'll admit I found it pleasant enough, even made with mediocre Cheddar and tinned pineapple. But revisit the notion with a bit of post-modern culinary nous – fresh ripe fruit, top-drawer mature Cheddar, a bitter leaf to offset the tangy fruit and creamy cheese, a simple well-seasoned dressing – and you have a fresh and rather classy salad. With crusty bread it is a lively take on the ploughman's lunch. As a side dish, it's splendid alongside a good bit of ham or a pork pie.

Thinly slice the pineapple, remove the core and cut into bite-sized pieces. Put these into a large bowl.

Trim the radicchio or chicory and shred the leaves fairly coarsely. Add to the pineapple. Add 1 tablespoon extra virgin olive oil and some salt and pepper and toss together thoroughly. Arrange over a serving plate or divide between individual bowls.

Slice the cheese thinly, or shave with a potato peeler, then tear or break each slice into flakes, scattering them evenly over the pineapple and radicchio. Squeeze over the lemon juice, give the salad another trickle of olive oil and another grinding of black pepper, and serve.

**Serves 2 as a lunch, 3–4 as a side dish**

¼–⅓ large ripe pineapple, peeled (about 300g peeled weight)

1 radicchio or 2 heads of white chicory

1 tablespoon extra virgin olive oil, plus extra to trickle

100g crumbly, nutty, mature Cheddar

Juice of ½ lemon

Sea salt and freshly ground black pepper

# Fried spiced
# plantain

This is a delicious side dish to chicken or fish. But the plantain slices are also lovely to enjoy on their own, with a cold beer or a glass of white wine, as a 'bar snack'. Ideally, you need ripe or medium-ripe plantains that have yellowish skins patched with black. If they are under-ripe and green, they will be dry. If very ripe (mostly black) they may go a bit mushy and absorb a lot of oil.

Peel the plantains. To do this, first trim off either end, then slit the peel lengthways into strips. If the plantains are ripe, you should be able to pull away most of the peel with your hands. If they're a tad under-ripe, you will find it easiest to continue using the knife to slice off the peel strips. Cut the peeled plantains on the diagonal into fairly thick slices (7–8mm).

Heat 1 tablespoon sunflower oil and a knob of butter in a wide frying pan over a medium heat. Fry a batch of plantain slices, in a single layer, for around 3–4 minutes, until golden brown on both sides. Watch carefully and turn them often because they can burn easily. Transfer to a plate lined with kitchen paper while you cook the remainder, adding more oil and butter to the pan as necessary.

Return all the plantain slices to the pan. Add another knob of butter, the garlic, some chilli flakes or cayenne and plenty of salt and pepper and cook for another couple of minutes, tossing the lot together. Serve hot, with a squeeze of lemon if you like.

Serves 4

About 750g fairly ripe plantains

2–3 tablespoons sunflower oil

A few knobs of butter

1 garlic clove, finely chopped

Dried chilli flakes or cayenne pepper, to sprinkle

A squeeze of lemon juice (optional)

Sea salt and freshly ground black pepper

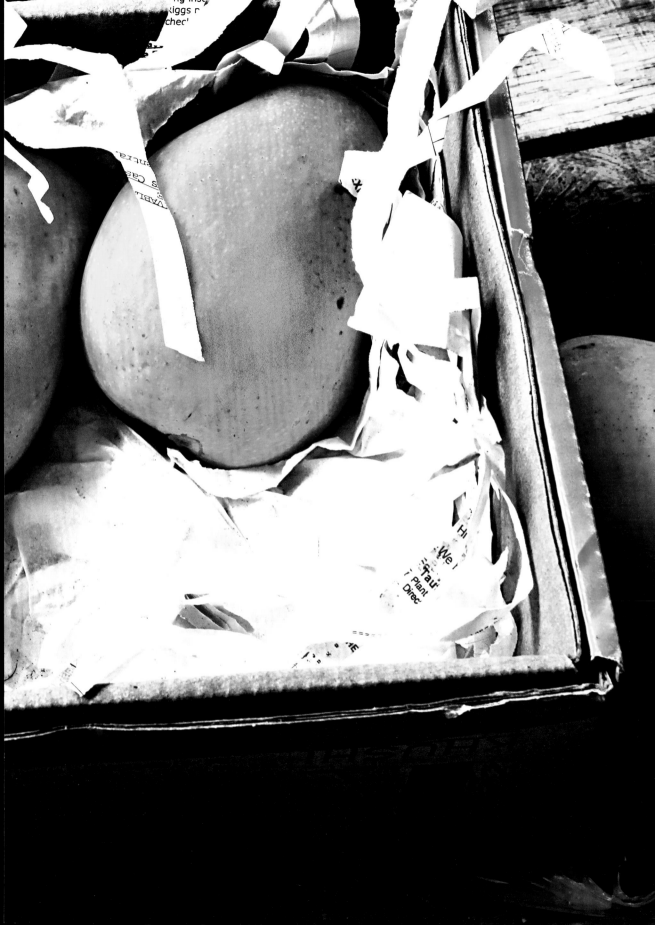

# Barbecued
## pineapple

**Serves 4**

1 pineapple, about
1.5kg

*For the dry marinade*

2 teaspoons fennel
seeds

A pinch of dried chilli
flakes

2 teaspoons demerara
sugar

1 teaspoon coriander
seeds

Finely grated zest of
1 lime

*To serve*

Lime juice

Shredded mint

**Some fruits have an amazing affinity with the grill, and pineapple is definitely one of them. Dust it in a dry marinade of spices and lime zest, then char-stripe it on the grill and you get a warm, fragrant, sweet, caramelised delight. A barbecue is not essential – a ridged grill pan on the stovetop works just as well.**

For the dry marinade, grind all the ingredients together as finely as you can using a pestle and mortar or a spice grinder.

Cut the top and base off the pineapple, then stand it on a board and slice off the skin. Turn the fruit on its side and cut into 1–1.5cm thick slices (2 per person). Lay these on a plate and scatter with the dry marinade, patting it on so each piece is well coated. Leave for about 30 minutes (after which time, the pineapple will taste pretty amazing already, before you even get round to grilling it).

Working in batches, cook the pineapple on the barbecue or in the pan, turning each slice from time to time to get plenty of colour on each side – this can take up to 12 minutes. Transfer to a large plate.

Finish with a squeeze of lime juice and some shredded mint. I like to serve something creamy on the side, such as ice cream, crème fraîche, yoghurt or the chilled coconut rice pudding on page 312. The spiced pineapple goes well with meat too, in a savoury context.

**Variation: *Barbecued tropical fruit salad*** Mango and banana also barbecue well to make a tempting warm fruit salad with pineapple. Cut 4 slices of pineapple, as above; peel 1 large mango and slice away the flesh from either side of the stone in two thick 'cheeks', plus the side bits; peel 2 slightly under-ripe bananas and halve lengthways. Brush all the fruit very lightly with sunflower oil and grill on a barbecue or ridged pan. The pineapple will take longest, then the mango, while the banana needs only 2–3 minutes each side. As each piece of fruit is cooked, transfer it to a large plate, squeeze over some lime juice and sprinkle with soft brown sugar. Keep going, stacking the fruit if necessary, until all the fruit is cooked and dressed with lime and sugar. Serve warm.

# Easy banana ice cream

This luscious frozen pud lies somewhere between an ice cream and a sorbet. Amazingly simple, it's one of my favourite ways of dealing with slightly over-ripe bananas. You want to get them at the stage when the skins are very well speckled but ideally still more yellow than brown.

Break the banana flesh into chunks and put into a blender with the crème fraîche, lemon zest and juice, and 1 tablespoon sugar. Blitz, then taste and add more sugar if needed. You want the mixture to taste fractionally over-sweet, as it will seem less sweet when frozen.

Churn the mixture in an ice-cream maker until soft-set, then transfer to a freezer container and freeze until solid. (Alternatively, freeze in a plastic container for about an hour until solidifying around the sides. Mash the frozen sides into the liquid centre with a fork, and return to the freezer for another hour. Repeat this at hourly intervals until soft-set and then let the ice cream freeze solid.)

Transfer the ice cream to the fridge about 30 minutes before serving, to soften a little. It is delicious with a few fresh strawberries sliced on top; or a tart purée of crushed, sieved strawberries, sweetened with a little icing sugar.

**Variation** For an indulgent banoffee sundae, serve the banana ice cream topped with a toffee sauce: gently melt 100g creamy toffees in a pan with a little milk (or use the butterscotch sauce on page 314). Finish with some fresh banana slices.

## Serves 3–4

250–300g very ripe banana flesh (2 large or 3 medium bananas)

200g crème fraîche or plain wholemilk yoghurt

Finely grated zest of ½ and juice of 1 lemon

Up to 4 tablespoons caster sugar

### To serve (optional)

A handful (or two) of strawberries

A little icing sugar

# Papaya citrus salad

If I have a ripe papaya to hand, and not much time, I just split it open, deseed it, spritz it generously with lime juice then tuck in, scooping the rosy flesh from the skin with a spoon. It's a fruit experience that's pretty hard to beat. If you're feeding friends, this lovely fragrant salad is a slightly more developed version of the idea.

Finely grate the zest from two of the limes into a small saucepan and squeeze their juice into a small measuring jug. You should have about 50ml – make it up with a splash of water, or a squeeze of lemon or orange juice if necessary.

Pour the lime juice into the pan with the zest. Add the sugar and heat gently, stirring, until the sugar has dissolved, then increase the heat. Once boiling, boil the syrup for just 1 minute, then take off the heat and leave to cool completely.

Shortly before you want to serve, peel each papaya, using a vegetable peeler. Top and tail the papayas, quarter them lengthways, then scoop out and discard the black seeds. Slice each quarter across into pieces about 1cm thick. Put these in a large bowl.

You now need to segment the grapefruit, orange(s) and remaining 2 limes. Do them all the same way: cut a slice off the top and base of each fruit and stand them on a board. Use a sharp knife to cut down through the peel and pith, slicing it away completely, in sections, so you have a whole, peeled citrus fruit with no white pith left at all. Now slice the segments of fruit out from between the membranes, working over the bowl of papaya and dropping the segments directly into it. You can squeeze any juice from the membrane 'cores' into the bowl too.

Now gently stir the cooled lime syrup into the papaya and citrus fruit salad, and it's ready to serve.

Serves 4–6

4 limes

50g caster sugar

2 medium or 1 large papaya (about 1kg)

1 pink grapefruit

1 large or 2 small oranges

# Passion fruit syllabub

**Serves 8**

A glass (150ml) of
dryish white wine
(not dessert wine)

100g caster sugar

8 ripe passion fruit

350ml double cream

**This luscious but simple pud is based on a recipe made by pub landlord Donal Falvey for a pudding competition featured in a River Cottage show a few years back. I was very impressed by it at the time (it beat my own entry) and I've made it several times since – it always goes down an absolute storm.**

Put the wine in a small pan and add the sugar. Heat gently, stirring, just until the sugar has dissolved (no need to boil), then remove from the heat and leave to cool completely.

Cut the passion fruit in half and scoop out the pulp and seeds from the halves into a small bowl.

Whip the cream until it holds soft peaks. Carefully fold in the cooled sweetened wine, a small splash at a time, then fold in three-quarters of the passion fruit pulp and seeds.

Spoon the syllabub into individual glasses and top with the remaining passion fruit. Serve immediately, or chill in the fridge and serve within the hour – if you leave it too long, the liquid will start to separate out.

# Coconut rice pudding with rum pineapple

This is basically a pina colada pud: good old rice pudding given a makeover and taken out for a night on the town.

Rinse the pudding rice in a sieve under a running cold tap.

Pour the coconut milk and whole milk into a large saucepan and add the sugar. Snip the vanilla pod, if using, into a few pieces and add these to the pan. Bring slowly to a simmer, stirring to dissolve the sugar and amalgamate the coconut milk.

Add the rice and cook gently over a very low heat, barely allowing it to simmer and stirring often, until the rice is swollen and tender and the mixture has the texture of a very loose risotto. This should take about 45 minutes. It will thicken more as it cools.

Remove the pieces of vanilla pod, if using. Transfer the rice pudding to a dish and leave to cool completely, stirring it now and then to prevent a skin forming. When cold, cover and chill in the fridge for at least a couple of hours.

Meanwhile, cut the pineapple into bite-sized chunks, discarding the core. Combine the pineapple, rum and brown sugar in a bowl, cover and leave to macerate in the fridge until ready to serve.

Serve the rice pudding in bowls with a generous spoonful of the pineapple and its rummy juices.

## Variations
For a lighter, less rich and slightly less coconutty version of this pud, you can cook the rice with just 1 tin of coconut milk and 600ml whole or semi-skimmed milk.

Try topping your coconut rice pudding with other tropical fruits, such as lime-spritzed mango, or passion fruit pulp. Or serve it with the barbecued pineapple or tropical fruit salad on page 305.

### Serves 6

80g pudding rice

2 x 400ml tins coconut milk

200ml whole milk

60g caster sugar

½ vanilla pod (optional)

### For the rum-macerated pineapple

500g peeled ripe pineapple

4 tablespoons dark rum

2 tablespoons soft dark brown sugar

# Nutty toffee
## banana split

This is a fun toffeeish take on the classic banana split: sweet and indulgent, but made a touch more sophisticated with the saltiness of the peanuts and (if you like the idea) a pinch of aromatic cumin in the sauce.

Start with the butterscotch sauce. Put the brown sugar, butter, cream, cumin, if using, and salt in a small saucepan. Slowly bring to a bubbling simmer, stirring as you do. Simmer for 1 minute, then take off the heat and set aside to cool a little. You can serve the sauce warm or at room temperature, but not scalding hot.

When you're ready to eat, peel the bananas and slice them lengthways in half, from tip to tail. Place two banana halves in each serving bowl with a generous scoop of your chosen ice cream, a scattering of peanuts and a generous spoonful of the butterscotch sauce.

**Variation:** *Quick raspberry jam and cream banana split* This is my Dad's favourite standby pud, when he feels there's still a sweet space left after supper. Split a banana lengthways, dab with raspberry jam and pour over double cream (or spoon over wholemilk yoghurt, for a marginally less greedy version).

Serves 2

2 ripe bananas (not over-ripe)

2 scoops of homemade or good-quality vanilla ice cream, or easy banana ice cream (see page 306)

40g salted roasted peanuts

### For the butterscotch sauce

50g soft dark brown sugar

20g butter

100ml double cream

A large pinch of toasted crushed cumin seeds (optional)

A pinch of salt

# Banana, chocolate and cardamom loaf

This is a classic banana cake to which I've added chocolate and cardamom for a luxurious, sophisticated twist. Without them, it stands as a top, plain banana cake – lovely and rich and tender. As with any banana loaf, it pays to use really ripe fruit, the skins well patched with brown and the flesh nice and soft – it will lend much more flavour and sweetness to the finished cake.

Preheat the oven to 180°C/Gas 4. Grease and line a 1kg loaf tin, about 11 x 22cm.

Extract the seeds from the cardamom pods and crush them, using a pestle and mortar, to a coarse powder.

In a large bowl, thoroughly beat together the oil, brown sugar, vanilla extract and eggs (if you're using coconut oil, beat it with the sugar first, until smooth, then add the eggs).

In a separate bowl, mash the bananas. Add the yoghurt and ground cardamom and mix well. Stir this mixture thoroughly into the oil and egg mixture.

Sift the flour with the bicarbonate of soda, baking powder and salt over the banana mixture. Add half the chopped chocolate and fold it all together lightly but thoroughly.

Pour the mixture into the prepared loaf tin. Sprinkle the remaining chocolate over the surface, followed by the demerara sugar. Bake for 50–55 minutes or until the cake is springy to the touch and a skewer inserted into the centre comes out clean.

Leave the cake to cool in the tin for at least 10 minutes, then transfer to a wire rack and leave to cool completely before slicing.

**Makes 8–10 slices**

100ml sunflower, rapeseed or coconut oil, plus extra for greasing

About 12 cardamom pods (or ½ teaspoon ground cardamom)

175g light brown sugar

1 teaspoon vanilla extract

2 medium free-range eggs

300g peeled ripe banana flesh (about 3 medium bananas)

75g plain wholemilk yoghurt

200g light brown plain flour or spelt flour

1 teaspoon bicarbonate of soda

1 teaspoon baking powder

A pinch of salt

100g dark chocolate (about 70% cocoa solids), chopped

2 tablespoons demerara sugar, or extra soft brown sugar, to finish

# Mango lassi

Serves 2

1 large, ripe mango
or 2 smaller ones (such
as Alphonso), ideally
chilled for an hour or so

150ml plain wholemilk
yoghurt

A couple of pinches of
sea salt

A pinch of ground
cardamom (optional)

A lassi is a traditional Indian yoghurt drink. The basic version is just yoghurt, thinned with water and seasoned with a little sea salt – surprisingly refreshing and nourishing in the heat, and of course the salt replaces that lost through sweating. There are all kinds of fruity lassi recipes too, some sweet, some spiced, some salty. My mango version is a mingling of these different approaches. You can sweeten it up and leave out the salt if you like (see the variation below). But unless you are avoiding salt, I'd encourage you to try this version first. The salt-with-fruit thing is under-explored in our culture, and is a pleasing revelation for the uninitiated.

Slice off the 'cheeks' from the mango, by cutting either side of the flat stone. Score the flesh into a criss-cross pattern, going right down to the skin, then turn the skin inwards, so the flesh side opens up like a hedgehog. Slice the cubes of flesh off the skin. Cut the remaining peel away from the rest of the mango and slice the flesh off the stone.

(Alternatively, you can simply peel the mango with a potato peeler and slice away the flesh back to the stone – but you might have to go over the skin with the peeler a couple of times to get through the stringy strands just beneath the skin. 'Hedgehogging' is a good way to avoid that – and very satisfying.)

Put all the mango flesh in a blender. Add the yoghurt, 100ml ice-cold water, the salt, and cardamom, if using. Whiz up to a frothy purée, pour into tall glasses and serve.

**Variation** For a sweet mango lassi, omit the salt and, depending on the ripeness of your mango, add up to 1 tablespoon caster sugar to the blender before puréeing.

# Papaya smoothie

This simple, intensely fruity smoothie plays on the glorious marriage of papaya and lime (see also the salad on page 308). You don't get a huge glassful from the flesh of a papaya but it's intense, fragrant and invigorating – perfect for a special breakfast or brunch. Chill the papaya in the fridge shortly before using.

Halve the papaya and scoop out all the little black seeds, using a teaspoon; discard these. Now scoop all the rosy-coral flesh out of the papaya skin, again with a teaspoon, and drop it into a blender (or jug).

Add the orange juice and the juice of ½ lime and blitz (or use a hand-held stick blender in the jug) until smooth. Taste and add more lime juice if you like. Pour into a glass and drink straight away.

**Variations** The base of freshly squeezed orange and lime, or lemon if you like, is a good one for other tropical fruit smoothies too. So feel free to swap the papaya flesh for mango, guava, pineapple – or indeed any combination thereof.

### Per person

1 medium or ½ large ripe papaya (about 500g)

Juice of 1 orange

Juice of ½–1 lime

Without citrus fruits in my kitchen I'd be lost. They are exotic, of course, yet so much part of the family that they feel like honorary natives. Their scope and sheer usefulness extend way beyond this chapter – they probably appear in more of my recipes than any other kind of fruit.

Lemon juice is one of my staple seasonings – being lemonless is almost as unthinkable to me as lacking garlic, or even pepper. It's hard to over-emphasise its value. There's something about that tangy, almost painfully sharp juice that whips other ingredients into shape and pulls them into focus. We know how magical it is with fish. But even a simple fruit salad of sliced banana and apple is transformed by a few drops (and a good squeeze of orange juice does no harm either).

As can happen with things you use all the time and almost take for granted, it's easy to forget the full range of possibilities that these ingredients hold. So I hope it may prove a revelation to explore my citrus-centric recipes, to invite these bright, thick-skinned fruits to step out of the background and into the limelight (of course).

Oranges – and their little brethren, tangy tangerines and delectable, fragrant clementines – are most often juiced or just torn apart to be eaten *au naturel*, but they have so much more potential. It's really worth sharpening your orange-segmenting skills (the drill is described on page 330). Okay, it's a bit of a fiddle. But freed from peel, pith and membrane, orange pieces are ready to combine with other ingredients in all kinds of unexpected ways (try blackcurrants and oranges with mint sugar, page 44). And when you can segment an orange, you can segment a grapefruit, a lime or a lemon, paving the way for these fruits to explode into your cooking in ways you simply hadn't imagined before.

To the cook, the zest is every bit as precious as the juice or flesh. Full of aromatic oils, this is where the intense scent of these fruits is to be found, and it's where the differences between them are most striking. (Try the salted chocolate lime mousse and the orange variations on page 348 – it's the zest that sets them so intriguingly apart.)

Citrus juice delivers acidity, but has a much more muted flavour than the zest. Small amounts of juice added to a savoury dish won't necessarily make it taste citrussy at all, just brighter and fresher. In most of the recipes in this chapter, both the zest and the juice are used to get not just the juicy fruit itself, but the high aromatic notes that also give each citrus fruit its unique character.

To make a cake, mousse, syrup or sorbet taste *properly* lemony, limey or orangey, some zest is pretty much essential. But zesting has to be done right. In order to remove that lovely outer rind without picking up the bitter white pith beneath, grate it with a sharp, fine grater (a Microplane or similar). One pass of the grater, then turn the fruit a few degrees, and grate again. Don't rub away at the same spot, or you'll pick up that dreaded pith. Alternatively, for bigger strips of zest, pare it off with a small, sharp knife or a potato peeler. Trying to zest citrus with a blunt tool is a futile task.

Frustratingly for the zester, it's standard commercial practice to coat citrus fruits with a transparent 'wax' that prolongs their shelf life and makes them more shiny. Some waxes are based on polyethylene, some on shellac, and some contain both. Such coatings are meant to be harmless, but just reading those words makes me want to take evasive action. So I choose unwaxed fruit if at all possible; organic citrus fruits are always unwaxed. If you can only get waxed fruit – and with limes and grapefruits, that may be the case – then submerge them in a bowl of very hot water for a minute. This loosens the waxy oil, which can then be removed altogether with a thorough wipe from a cotton cloth.

Though a lot of the citrus fruit we eat in the UK is produced in southern Europe, Spain in particular, our summer supply comes largely from Africa, where working conditions are often poorly regulated and fair prices may not be guaranteed. So I'm a big fan of the Fairtrade label – a supply chain which happily is very often coupled with organic farming methods. It can only add to the feel-good factor of buying exotic fruit to know that the land it comes from, and those working it, are being treated with respect.

While all citrus fruits have their own distinct characteristics, they are a friendly bunch who'll cover for one another surprisingly well. If I don't have any limes, for instance, I'll spritz my papaya with lemon. It's not *the same*, but it's still good. And on the rare occasions when I have run out of lemons, I've found orange or grapefruit juice to be an intriguing alternative in dishes, both sweet and savoury. Lemon is the obvious citrus partner to fish but orange works well too. Try the simple steam-braised fish with orange on page 339, or serve my orange, fennel and celeriac salad (page 330) with grilled sardines and you'll see what I mean. Or, for another surprising collision, see how well grapefruit works with olives and onions (page 329), or lemon in a pudding cake with potatoes (page 358)!

We may think we know our citrus fruits inside out. The truth is, we've hardly scratched their zesty surface.

CITRUS FRUIT

# Grilled orange,
## carrot and halloumi

This robust yet refreshing salad is inspired by chef Sophie Wright, who cooked a similar dish on one of my shows. To make it easier, you could just cook the halloumi and carrot, and add the orange slices to the salad raw, but they are delicious grilled.

Peel the carrots, cut them lengthways into slices about 5mm thick and put them into a large bowl.

Slice all the peel and pith away from the oranges: to do this, cut a slice off the base and stand the orange on a board. Then use a sharp knife to cut down through the peel and pith, slicing it away completely, in sections, so you have a whole orange with no white pith left at all. Slice the oranges across into rounds, 6–7mm thick. Add them to the carrots with 2 tablespoons extra virgin olive oil and some salt and pepper and toss gently.

Heat a ridged cast-iron grill pan (or another heavy-based frying pan) over a high heat. Lay half the carrot slices in the pan and cook for about 5 minutes, turning once or twice, until marked with grill lines and reasonably tender, with a bit of crunch left. Transfer to a bowl. Repeat with the remaining carrots.

Add the orange slices to the hot pan and cook for 3–4 minutes, turning once, then transfer to the bowl with the carrot. Don't worry if the orange pieces stick to the pan slightly or break up a little – just use a spatula to scrape up any sticky bits and add them to the bowl.

Add the cider vinegar to the carrots and oranges, along with any juices left from their original bowl, and toss together gently.

Toss the halloumi with another trickle of olive oil and cook in the grill pan for a couple of minutes each side, until soft and nicely marked.

Arrange the salad leaves, carrots, oranges and halloumi on a large platter or individual plates and trickle over any juices from the bowl. Add a squeeze of lemon juice, a trickle more olive oil and a twist more black pepper, and it's ready to serve.

**Serves 4 as a starter, 2–3 as a lunch**

250g carrots

2 medium oranges

3–4 tablespoons extra virgin olive oil

About ½ teaspoon cider vinegar

250g packet halloumi, sliced

4 handfuls of mixed leaves, such as rocket, spinach and flat-leaf parsley

A squeeze of lemon juice

Sea salt and freshly ground black pepper

# Grapefruit,
## olives, red onion and basil

**Serves 4 as a starter**

2 grapefruit (any kind)

1 small red onion

2 tablespoons extra virgin olive oil

50g full-flavoured black olives, such as kalamata, stoned

A handful of basil leaves, torn or shredded if large

Sea salt and freshly ground black pepper

**The striking contrast of juicy sweet-sharp grapefruit flesh with salty olives is further enhanced with tangy red onions and fragrant fresh basil leaves.**

Slice all the peel and pith away from the grapefruit: to do this, cut a slice off the base and stand the grapefruit on a board. Then use a sharp knife to cut down through the peel and pith, slicing it away completely, in sections, so you have a whole grapefruit with no white pith left at all. Now slice the segments of grapefruit out from between the membranes, working over a large serving bowl and dropping the segments into it.

Squeeze the juice from the grapefruit membranes into a small bowl. Finely chop the red onion and add to the grapefruit juice, along with the extra virgin olive oil and some salt and pepper. Toss to mix.

Roughly tear or chop the olives and scatter them over the grapefruit. Strew the basil over and then trickle over the oniony dressing. Serve straight away.

**Variations** You can substitute oranges for the grapefruit here, and mint or coriander for the basil. And in any version of the salad, a sliced avocado is a good addition that makes it a little more substantial.

# Orange, fennel and celeriac

A fine example of just how delicious it can be to tumble together some raw fruits, roots and nuts. Crisp, crunchy aromatic and juicy, this is a perfect autumn or winter salad. Hold the cashews and it's a delicious accompaniment to grilled or barbecued fish.

If using the cashew nuts, toast them in a dry frying pan over a medium heat for a few minutes until lightly coloured. Tip out on to a plate and set aside.

For the dressing, whisk the extra virgin olive oil and cider vinegar together in a large bowl and add some salt and pepper.

Peel the celeriac and cut it into thin matchsticks. Immediately add to the dressing and toss to combine, to stop it browning.

Trim the fennel and remove any tough outer layers, reserving any green frondy bits. Cut the fennel bulb in half and slice each half as thinly as possible (you can even 'shave' it with a vegetable peeler). Add to the celeriac.

Slice all the peel and pith away from the orange: to do this, cut a slice off the base and stand the orange on a board. Then use a sharp knife to cut down through the peel and pith, slicing it away completely, in sections, so you have a whole orange with no white pith left at all. Working over the bowl of celeriac and fennel, slice out the orange segments, letting them drop into the bowl. Squeeze any juice out of the remaining orange membranes into the bowl.

Divide the dressed celeriac, fennel and orange between individual bowls or arrange on a large platter. Scatter over the toasted cashew nuts, if using, and any reserved fennel fronds, add a grinding of pepper and serve.

**Variations** You can use carrots or even young parsnips here instead of the celeriac. And, although I think all of these root vegetables will look and taste best when cut into thin matchsticks, you could grate them coarsely if you're in a hurry.

## Serves 4

75g raw cashew nuts (optional)

2 tablespoons extra virgin olive oil

2 teaspoons cider vinegar

250g celeriac

1 large fennel bulb

1 large orange

Sea salt and freshly ground black pepper

# Brussels sprout, clementine and chestnut salad

**Serves 4 as a starter**

160g fresh chestnuts in shells, or 125g cooked vacuum-packed chestnuts

1 tablespoon extra virgin olive oil, plus extra to trickle

2 bay leaves, torn (optional)

About 150g small, firm Brussels sprouts

2 clementines or tangerines

Juice of ½ lemon

Sea salt and freshly ground black pepper

**Taking three classic festive ingredients and using them in a rather unexpected way, this is a lovely, quick Christmas salad. It makes a wonderfully crisp and refreshing starter to a rich meal.**

If you are using fresh chestnuts, preheat the oven to 220°C/Gas 7. Cut a slit down the flat side of each shell. Place the chestnuts in an oven dish and roast in the oven for 8–10 minutes until lightly charred. Leave them until cool enough to handle, then peel away the shells and thin inner husk.

Whether you are using freshly roasted or pre-cooked chestnuts, crumble them into pieces.

Place a small frying pan over a medium heat, add 1 tablespoon extra virgin olive oil and the chestnut pieces, followed by a generous pinch of salt, some pepper and the bay leaves, if using. Toss the nuts in the hot pan for a few minutes, coating them in the seasoned oil. Turn off the heat and leave the nuts in the pan while you prepare the rest of the salad.

Trim the Brussels sprouts and remove any tough or discoloured outer leaves, then slice the sprouts thinly from top to base. Arrange over four serving plates.

Peel the clementines and separate the segments, removing as much of the stringy white pith as you have the patience for. Cut each segment almost in half by slicing from the inner edge to the wide outer edge, without going quite all the way through, then open up the segment like a butterfly (see photograph).

Arrange the clementine butterflies over the sprouts, scatter over the salty roasted chestnuts and trickle over a little more extra virgin olive oil. Season the salad generously with lemon juice and salt and pepper, then serve.

# Preserved lemons

Makes 1 large jar

14–16 unwaxed lemons

About 8 tablespoons
coarse sea salt

Salt-pickled lemons are a traditional ingredient in Middle Eastern and North African cooking. They have a unique sour-salty flavour, which is wonderful with spicy foods. This method is based on one from the brilliant cook and food writer, Claudia Roden.

Sterilise a large preserving jar, such as a Le Parfait or Kilner jar, and its lid, by washing in very hot, soapy water, rinsing well then putting in a low oven (at 120°C/Gas ½) for 20 minutes to dry out. Leave to cool.

Cut 8 lemons almost into quarters, top to toe but not right through, so the fruit is still joined at the base and the top. Pack sea salt into the cuts – about 1 level tablespoon for each lemon. Squash the salt-packed lemons into the sterilised preserving jar. In order to maximise your lemon-packing, you might want to cut one or two lemons fully in half so they fit into any smaller gaps. Seal the jar and leave the lemons for a couple of days. By this point you'll see that the salt has drawn out a lot of lemon juice.

Squeeze enough juice from the remaining lemons to fully submerge the fruit in the jar (6 or 7 lemons should do it but you may need one more). Seal again and store for at least 1 month before using, turning the jar upside down and back again every now and then.

Once opened, keep the jar of lemons in the fridge. If you ensure that the lemons are completely covered by the salty liquid, they should keep well for up to a year. They will slowly change colour, from yellow to golden brown. In a Moroccan market, you will be asked what colour, or what age, lemons you would like; many consider the older ones more subtly flavoured and they are sometimes more expensive.

*Using your preserved lemons* Usually, just the tender rind (peel and pith) is used in cooking. The flesh is scraped away and discarded, then the peel is chopped into dice, or thicker strips, and added to tagines, salads and other delightful dishes. It's a vital element in the lovely lamb breast dish on page 372. But the fleshy pulp isn't always thrown away – you can add it to soups and dips, as in the soup overleaf.

# Spicy **potato** soup with preserved lemon

**This is a thoroughly warming soup with some gentle spicing and a bitter-sharp note from the preserved lemon (you can preserve your own lemons following the recipe on page 334).**

Heat the olive oil in a large saucepan over a medium heat. Add the onion, garlic and chilli and sauté gently for about 10 minutes until softened. Stir in the cumin, coriander and paprika and cook gently for a few more minutes.

Meanwhile, scoop out the pulp from the preserved lemon and discard any pips; set the rind aside. Peel the potatoes and cut into large chunks (you'll need to scoop them out of the soup later). Add the lemon pulp and potatoes to the onion and pour on the stock. Bring to a simmer, then cover and cook for about 20 minutes, or until the potatoes are completely tender.

Scoop out the pieces of potato and place them in a colander. Purée the rest of the soup in a blender until smooth, then return to the pan. Pass the potatoes through a ricer, or rub through a sieve, back into the soup and stir to combine (if you purée potatoes in a blender, they tend to go a bit gluey). This is meant to be a thick soup but add a little more stock or water if it seems overly so. Taste and add more salt and pepper as needed and reheat gently if necessary.

Chop the preserved lemon rind into little dice. Ladle the soup into warm bowls and top each portion with a scattering of diced preserved lemon rind and a dollop of yoghurt. Add a dusting of paprika and a grinding of pepper. Finish with a trickle of extra virgin olive oil.

**Variations** This soup also works very well with parsnips instead of potatoes (and parsnips can be puréed along with the rest of the soup, rather than being mashed separately). Or you might prefer to use a combination of the two.

## Serves 4

2 tablespoons olive oil

1 onion, roughly chopped

2 garlic cloves, roughly chopped

1 medium-hot red chilli, deseeded and sliced

1 teaspoon ground cumin

1 teaspoon ground coriander

½ teaspoon sweet smoked paprika

½ large preserved lemon (see page 334)

500g floury potatoes, such as King Edward

About 750ml light vegetable or chicken stock

Sea salt and freshly ground black pepper

### To finish

A little paprika, to dust

4 good tablespoons plain wholemilk yoghurt

Extra virgin olive oil, to trickle

# Steam-braised fish with orange

**Serves 2**

1 large or 2 small oranges

1 tablespoon olive oil

A knob of butter

1 garlic clove, finely sliced

A sprig of thyme (optional)

1 bay leaf (optional)

2 robust fish fillets (200–250g each), such as sea bass, black bream or grey mullet, skinned

1 teaspoon baby capers, rinsed and drained

Sea salt and freshly ground black pepper

Steam-braising is one of my favourite quick methods for cooking fish – it's very simple and automatically creates a little pool of tasty juice in the pan. Orange, a little more subtle than lemon, makes a warm and winning companion to fish, and capers provide a spark of salty-sharp flavour.

Finely grate the zest from about half the orange (if large, or a whole orange if small) and set aside. Slice all the peel and pith away from the orange(s): to do this, cut a slice off the base and stand the orange on a board. Then use a sharp knife to cut down through the peel and pith, slicing it away completely, in sections, so you have a whole orange with no white pith left at all. Now slice the segments of orange out from between the membranes, working over a bowl and dropping the segments into it. Squeeze the juice from the remaining orange membranes into the bowl too.

Put the olive oil and butter in a wide, deep frying pan (ideally non-stick) along with 2 tablespoons water, the garlic, thyme and/or bay, if using, and grated orange zest. Strain the juice from the bowl of orange segments into the pan too. Bring to a simmer over a gentle heat.

Season the fish fillets with salt and pepper and lay them skinned side down in the pan. Cover and cook for 5–8 minutes, depending on the thickness of the fish, until opaque all the way through. Spoon the hot, aromatic pan juices over the fish every now and again to speed the cooking. If you do this frequently, there's no need to turn the fish.

Lift the fish fillets carefully on to warmed plates. If you find there is quite a bit of liquid in the pan, turn up the heat and boil the juices for a minute or two to reduce them slightly. Add the orange segments and capers at the last minute, warming them briefly in the juices (you don't want to cook them). Taste and add more salt and pepper if needed.

Spoon the juices over and around the fish, and arrange the orange pieces alongside. Serve straight away with green beans or broccoli and new potatoes, mash or plain boiled rice.

# Oranges in mulled wine syrup

The combination of citrus, spices and wine is much enjoyed as a hot drink at Christmas time, but I like the blend even better like this, served cool as a spicy fruit salad, with luscious slices of orange to sink your teeth into.

Pare 3 or 4 thin strips of zest from one of the oranges (making sure you leave all the bitter white pith behind).

Put the wine and sugar in a saucepan. Heat gently, stirring, until the sugar has dissolved, then add the orange zest, cinnamon, cloves, star anise, allspice berries and peppercorns. Bring to a simmer and allow to bubble gently for about 10 minutes until the wine is reduced by about half and lightly syrupy. Leave to cool completely.

Slice all the peel and pith away from all the oranges: to do this, cut a slice off the base and stand the orange on a board. Then use a sharp knife to cut down through the peel and pith, slicing it away completely, in sections, so you have a whole orange with no white pith left at all. Slice the oranges horizontally into rounds around 3mm thick. Place in a large bowl, along with any juice.

Pour the mulled wine syrup over the orange slices. Cover and leave to macerate in the fridge for at least a few hours (up to 24) to allow the flavours to develop.

Take out of the fridge half an hour or so before serving to bring to room temperature. The oranges and their spicy liquor are delicious just as they are – but a little ginger biscuit on the side is rather good.

**Variation: *Dried figs in spiced wine*** Use the same ingredients as above, but up the wine to 500ml and substitute 250g dried figs for the oranges. Trim the tough little stalk ends off the figs, then put them in a pan with the wine, sugar and spices. Bring to a simmer, stirring to dissolve the sugar, then simmer gently for around 30 minutes, or until the figs are tender. Transfer to a bowl, leave to cool in the syrup, then chill. Serve with a spoonful of thick yoghurt or crème fraîche.

## Serves 4

5 medium oranges

250ml red wine

50g caster sugar

1 cinnamon stick, broken in half

2 cloves

1–2 star anise

3 allspice berries

6 black peppercorns

# Lemon and mint sorbet

**Serves 8**

Finely grated zest of
1 lemon

225g caster sugar

A bunch of mint (about
30g), leaves only

300ml freshly squeezed
lemon juice (from 8–10
lemons, depending on
size)

*To serve (optional)*

200g strawberries,
thickly sliced and/or
raspberries

25g caster sugar

A squeeze of lemon
juice

This is a beautifully refreshing sorbet. Very lemony and not too sweet, it makes a perfect palate cleanser between courses, but also works wonderfully as a summer dessert with berries such as strawberries or raspberries. The variations below are all lovely too.

Put the lemon zest and sugar in a saucepan with 300ml water and the mint leaves. Bring to a simmer, stirring to dissolve the sugar, then remove from the heat and leave to cool completely.

Stir in the lemon juice, then strain through a fine sieve, pressing the mint leaves with the back of a spoon to extract maximum flavour. Chill.

Churn the liquid in an ice-cream machine until thick and soft-set, then transfer to the freezer to set solid. (Or, freeze in a plastic container for about an hour until solidifying around the sides. Mash the frozen sorbet into the liquid centre with a fork, then return to the freezer. Repeat at hourly intervals until soft-set, then allow to freeze solid.)

If you're serving the sorbet with berries, place them in a bowl and sprinkle with the sugar and a squeeze of lemon. Stir gently so the juices run and leave to macerate for about half an hour before serving.

Transfer the sorbet to the fridge about 20 minutes before serving, to allow it to soften a little. Serve scooped into bowls, with the macerated berries if serving.

### Variations
*Watermint sorbet* Wild watermint is a more zingy and pepperminty alternative to spearmint (which is almost certainly what you'll get if you buy mint in a shop). If you grow your own peppermint, try that too.

*Blackcurrant leaf sorbet* Replace the mint with young blackcurrant leaves (about 30g), picked in spring or early summer before the hard green berries have formed. This sorbet has a lovely muscat aroma.

*Lemon verbena sorbet* Use lemon verbena leaves, fresh or dried, in place of the mint. Outstandingly refreshing.

# Tangerine carpaccio with marrons glacés and chocolate

This recipe takes three Christmas classics – tangerines, chestnuts and chocolate – and transforms them into a fancy fruit salad. A lovely alternative to heavier festive puds, it's fun, easy, stunning and delicious.

Break up the chocolate into small pieces and put into a heatproof bowl over a pan of just-simmering water, making sure the water doesn't touch the base of the bowl. Leave to melt, stirring once or twice, then take off the heat.

Meanwhile, peel the tangerines. Then, using a small knife to help you, remove as much of the white pith and membrane as possible. Use a large, sharp knife to slice the tangerines across into rounds about 5mm thick. Reserve the small endy bits.

Arrange the tangerine slices evenly over each plate and crumble the marrons glacés over them. Now trickle the molten chocolate over the cool fruit, where it will quickly set into gorgeous whirls and ribbons. Squeeze the juice from the reserved fruit end bits over the plate, and it's ready to serve. This is delicious with a glass of chilled Champagne.

**Per person**

2–3 squares of dark chocolate (about 70% cocoa solids)

2 tangerines or clementines, chilled

1 large marron glacé

# Salted chocolate lime mousse

This is a great take on a classic chocolate mousse. The lime works brilliantly with a good dark chocolate and the addition of a little flaky salt emphasises the fruity richness. You can of course leave the salt out, but I'd urge you to give it a try.

Break up the chocolate into small pieces and put into a heatproof bowl over a pan of just-simmering water, making sure the water doesn't touch the base of the bowl. Leave it to slowly melt, stirring once or twice, then take off the heat and allow to cool slightly.

Put the egg yolks and sugar in a bowl with the lime zest and juice and whisk with an electric whisk for a couple of minutes until foamy and slightly lighter in colour. Whip the cream in another bowl until it just holds soft peaks, then gently stir into the lime and egg yolk mixture. If necessary, give it an extra brief whisk to amalgamate.

Whisk the egg whites in a clean bowl with a tiny pinch of fine sea salt until they hold soft peaks.

Fold the melted chocolate into the egg yolk and cream mixture until evenly combined. Add the whisked egg white and fold in carefully. Lastly, gently fold in the ½ teaspoon sea salt flakes.

Divide between glasses or bowls and refrigerate for at least 2 hours.

Just before serving, sprinkle a little flaky salt over the surface of each mousse. It's also very good with some freshly shaved coconut on top.

## Variations

*Chocolate orange mousse* For this lovely classic pairing, replace the lime with the grated zest of 1 large orange and 2 tablespoons of its juice, and leave out the salt (except the tiny pinch in the egg whites).

*Boozy chocolate orange mousse* For a more grown-up version of the above – a bit more pirate, a bit less Terry's chocolate orange – add a shot of rum (or whisky, or brandy) and the grated zest of an orange, and leave out the juice.

**Serves 4**

100g dark chocolate (about 70% cocoa solids)

2 medium free-range eggs, separated

40g caster sugar

Finely grated zest and juice (about 50ml) of 2 small-medium limes

100ml double cream

A pinch of fine sea salt

½ teaspoon flaky sea salt

### To finish

A little more flaky salt

A little fresh coconut, shaved with a peeler or coarsely grated (optional)

# Orange mousse with caramelised oranges

A gorgeous pud for citrus lovers – and a good one to make ahead of time. The caramelised oranges are also great served on their own, or with a chocolate mousse or crème brûlée.

Finely grate the zest of all 3 oranges into a large bowl. Add the cream cheese and 50g of the sugar and beat until soft and well combined.

Using an electric whisk, beat the egg whites in a large clean bowl until they form soft peaks. Gradually whisk in 50g of the sugar, a spoonful at a time, to give a smooth glossy meringue. Fold this into the cream cheese lightly but thoroughly. Lightly whip the cream until soft peaks form, and fold this in too. Spoon the mousse into glasses or sundae dishes and chill for several hours or overnight.

Meanwhile, prepare the oranges. Slice all the peel and pith away from all 3 oranges: to do this, cut a slice off the base and stand the orange on a board. Then use a sharp knife to cut down through the peel and pith, slicing it away completely, in sections, so you have a whole orange with no white pith left at all. Now slice the segments out from between the membranes, working over a bowl to catch the segments along with any juice. Strain off the juice into another bowl and squeeze in as much as you can from the membranes – you need at least 50ml juice and up to 100ml. (If there isn't enough, squeeze another orange.)

Put the remaining 100g sugar and 50ml water in a small heavy-based pan (ideally stainless steel rather than black-based, so you can see the colour of the caramel). Heat gently, stirring, until the sugar has fully dissolved. Bring to the boil and boil hard for a few minutes to a golden brown caramel. Immediately take it off the heat and carefully pour in the reserved orange juice (it will boil violently). Stir the caramel and orange juice together into a smooth syrup, putting it back on the heat if necessary to melt any lumps. Let cool slightly for 10 minutes, then pour the syrup over the orange segments. Allow to cool and then chill.

When you're ready to serve, spoon the caramelised oranges and their bittersweet juices on top of the orange mousse.

**Serves 4**

3 large oranges

200g cream cheese

200g caster sugar

2 large free-range egg whites

200ml double cream

# Lemon tart

**Serves 12**

## For the sweet shortcrust pastry

200g plain flour

35g icing sugar

A pinch of salt

125g cold unsalted butter, cut into cubes

1 free-range egg yolk

About 2–3 tablespoons cold milk (or water)

## For the filling

4–6 medium-large juicy lemons

4 large free-range eggs, plus 4 extra egg yolks

250g caster sugar

150ml double cream

## To finish

Icing sugar, to dust

**This is my version of the classic *tarte au citron*. I've recently discovered the filling makes a nifty, no-stir, 'fridge' lemon curd (see below).**

To make the sweet shortcrust pastry, put the flour, icing sugar and salt in a food processor and blitz briefly (or sift into a bowl). Add the butter and blitz (or rub in with your fingertips) until the mixture resembles breadcrumbs. Add the egg yolk and just enough milk to bring the mix together into large clumps. Tip on to a lightly floured surface, knead lightly into a ball and flatten. Wrap in cling film and chill for 30 minutes.

For the filling, finely grate the zest of 3 lemons. Squeeze the juice from these lemons and strain into a measuring jug. Juice as many more as you need to get 175–200ml. Whisk the eggs, egg yolks and sugar in a bowl until well blended, then stir in the lemon zest and juice. Let stand for 10 minutes, then whisk once more. Leave for another 10 minutes.

Preheat the oven to 180°C/Gas 4. Roll out the pastry fairly thinly and use to line a 24cm loose-based tart tin, letting the excess hang over the sides. Prick the base with a fork. Line with baking parchment and baking beans (or dried beans), stand the tin on a baking sheet and bake for 15 minutes. Remove the paper and beans and bake for a further 10 minutes, or until the pastry looks cooked and is lightly golden. Trim the excess pastry from the sides. Lower the oven setting to 150°C/Gas 2.

Strain the filling into a clean bowl, skim off any surface froth, and stir in the cream until well combined. Carefully pour into the tart case. Bake for 30–35 minutes, or until the filling is barely set, with a slight wobble in the centre. Leave to cool completely before serving. Unmould the tart on to a board and dust with icing sugar to serve.

**Variation: *Lemon curd*** Make the lemon filling as above, pour into four 200–250ml sterilised jam jars and seal tightly with lids. Stand the jars on a folded cloth in a large, deep pan, making sure they're not touching each other or the side of the pan. Cover with cold water. Bring to a low simmer and simmer very gently for 30 minutes. Let cool in the water. Refrigerate and use within 2 weeks. Once opened, use within a week.

# Orange, honey and cardamom pannacotta

I love a good pannacotta, and I enjoy experimenting with the classic recipe, sharpening it with a little yoghurt and flavouring it in various ways. In the winter, blood oranges – with their dramatic colour and tart flavour – are very effective here.

**To achieve the perfect just-set pannacotta consistency, you'll need less gelatine than you would for, say, a jelly. I haven't specified the number of gelatine leaves here because different brands vary. But if you use the number that the pack states will set 600ml of liquid (as opposed to the litre or so of liquid in the recipe), you'll be spot on.**

Finely grate the zest of 1 or 2 of the oranges into a saucepan. Add the milk, cream, sugar, honey and bashed cardamom pods and bring to a simmer, stirring to dissolve the sugar. Remove from the heat.

Meanwhile, calculate how many gelatine leaves you need to set 600ml liquid. Place them in a shallow bowl of cold water to soak for about 10 minutes, to soften.

Drain the soaked gelatine leaves and squeeze to remove excess water, then add them to the hot, infused cream and stir gently until dissolved. Leave to cool to room temperature, then stir in the yoghurt. Strain the mixture through a fine sieve into a jug.

Pour the pannacotta mixture into 8 dariole moulds or small cups and put in the fridge for at least 4 hours, to set.

Meanwhile, slice all the peel and pith from the oranges and slice out the segments from between the membranes (see page 330) into a bowl to catch any juice as well as the segments. Set aside until you are ready to serve.

To serve the pannacottas, dip the moulds in warm water very briefly to loosen. Carefully turn out the pannacottas into glass bowls or on to plates. Serve with the orange segments, spooning any juice over them.

## Serves 8

4 large or 6 small oranges (ideally blood oranges)

200ml whole milk

500ml double cream

50g caster sugar

3 tablespoons honey

10 cardamom pods, bashed

Enough sheets of leaf gelatine to set 600ml liquid

300ml plain wholemilk yoghurt

# St Clements shortbread biscuits

**Makes 12–15**

100g unsalted butter, well softened

Finely grated zest of 2 large lemons, plus a squeeze of juice

Finely grated zest of 2 large oranges

50g caster sugar, plus a little extra to dust

50g cornflour or rice flour

100g plain flour

A pinch of salt

**A delicate, crisp, crumbly sweet shortbread biscuit is the perfect accompaniment to many fruity salads and creamy puds – especially ice creams, pannacottas, mousses and fools. Enhanced with orange and lemon zest, these biscuits have a lovely, aromatic note. If you want a classic plain version, simply leave out the citrus. There are all kinds of intriguing ways to flavour a good shortbread – I've given a couple more of my favourites below.**

Preheat the oven to 160°C/Gas 3. Line two baking sheets with baking parchment or a silicone liner.

Beat the soft butter, citrus zests and sugar together in a bowl until thoroughly blended. Sift the cornflour, flour and salt over the buttery mixture and mix together with a wooden spoon to form a crumbly dough, adding a squeeze of juice from the lemon to help bring it together. Gather the dough into a ball with your hands.

Roll out the dough on a floured surface, sprinkling it lightly with flour to stop it sticking to the rolling pin or the work surface, until 3–4mm thick. Use a cutter of your choice to cut out shapes and transfer to the prepared baking sheets. Re-roll the dough once to get more shapes, but no more than that or you will start to overwork it and it can become greasy and/or tough.

Bake for 15–20 minutes, until the shortbread biscuits are pale golden. Sprinkle each biscuit, while still hot, with a pinch more sugar. Leave for a few minutes, then transfer to a wire rack to cool and crisp up.

## Variations
*Lavender and lemon shortbread biscuits* Leave out the orange zest and add 1 teaspoon finely chopped fresh lavender leaves or buds with the lemon zest. Especially good with raspberry or strawberry dishes.

*Caraway shortbread biscuits* Omit the orange zest. Add 1 teaspoon lightly bashed caraway seeds (with or without the grated lemon zest) for a lightly spicy flavour.

# Potato lemon drizzle cake

This deliciously rich yet gluten-free cake is a great way to use up leftover boiled spuds – and well worth boiling up some spuds for specially. You can get away with making it with leftover mash too, as long as you haven't over-seasoned it with salt, though a little pepper doesn't hurt at all.

Preheat the oven to 180°C/Gas 4. Butter a 23cm springform cake tin and line with baking parchment. Lightly butter the paper.

Beat the butter and sugar together until really pale and fluffy, ideally in a mixer or using a handheld electric whisk for about 5 minutes. Beat in the eggs, one at a time, adding a spoonful of ground almonds with each.

Stir the baking powder into the remaining ground almonds, then fold into the whisked mixture. Push the cold potato through a ricer into the mixture (or rub it through a sieve), add the lemon zest and fold in lightly but thoroughly.

Spoon the mixture into the lined cake tin and bake for 30–40 minutes, or until a skewer inserted into the centre comes out clean. Check after 25 minutes to make sure it is not colouring too much and cover the tin lightly with foil if it appears to be.

Leaving the hot cake in its tin, pierce it all over with a skewer. Combine the lemon juice and caster sugar for the topping and, before the sugar has had a chance to dissolve too much, pour all over the cake. Leave to cool completely before serving.

Serve straight up for tea or, with cream or crème fraîche – and perhaps a few sliced strawberries or a handful of raspberries – for pud.

### Serves 10–12

175g unsalted butter, softened, plus extra for greasing

200g caster sugar

4 large free-range eggs

200g ground almonds

2 teaspoons gluten-free baking powder

250g cold, plain boiled potato (ideally a really floury type such as King Edward)

Finely grated zest of 3 medium lemons

### *For the topping*

Juice of 2 medium lemons, strained

75g caster sugar

# Lemonade

This is the ultimate summer cooler, with a delicate, refreshing sourness. Just double up the quantities if you're quenching a crowd. And be gung-ho with the scented variations.

**Makes about 1.2 litres**

5–6 medium-large lemons

75g caster or granulated sugar

Pare the zest from two of the lemons, using a vegetable peeler or one of those zesters that removes the zest in long strips. Take care to leave the bitter white pith behind. Put the strips of lemon zest into a large bowl with the sugar and pour on 500ml just-boiled water. Stir to dissolve the sugar and then leave to cool completely.

Squeeze the juice from the lemons into a measuring jug; you need about 200ml. Add the juice to the bowl with the zest-infused mixture. Stir well, then strain the mixture into a jug. Stir in 500ml more water (or more, if you'd like it diluted further). Chill in the fridge.

Serve the chilled lemonade in tall glasses with plenty of ice cubes, or crushed ice.

**Variations** There are various ways to scent your lemonade: I like a version made with a handful of young blackcurrant leaves, crushed in my fist, then infused in the boiling water with the lemon zest and sugar. Lemon verbena, lemon-scented geranium and mint leaves work well too – or try a couple of bruised stems of lemongrass.

For a more adult citrus refresher, try a classic mojito: squeeze the juice of a lime or lemon into a tumbler, add 1 teaspoon sugar or sugar syrup and mix well. Add a large sprig of mint, leaves bruised, then half-fill the tumbler with crushed ice. Pour in a double measure of white rum (or vodka). Mix well and drink as is, or top with a splash of soda.

The funs starts when you try flavouring your mojito with alternative aromatics, as in the lemonade above. Lemon verbena works well, with or without a sprig of elderflower. Watermint, if you can find some, makes an intriguing change from garden mint. And a few young blackcurrant leaves, bruised and coarsely chopped, are a revelation, as are fennel, basil and lovage – I've tried and enjoyed them all.

We all know that some raisins flecked through a cake or biscuit will make it a different and in all likelihood more enticing proposition, but let's not stop there. Dried fruits, grenades of sweetness, can have the most dramatic effect on a whole stack of recipes, particularly at the savoury end of the spectrum, and it's my pleasure to pass on some of my favourites. So, for starters, how about folding a fistful of dried cherries through a zesty autumn salad of crunchy red cabbage and apple (page 380), or shaking a few raisins into a piquant pasta dish of cauliflower, capers and chilli (page 368), or livening up a simple soda bread with dried apricots, walnuts and ale (page 384)?

Matching dried fruit with meat is not a new idea – North African tagines have been spiked with sun-dried apricots or dates for donkey's years, as in my goat tagine with apricots and almonds on page 375. But once you begin experimenting, the dried fruit/flesh axis is soon revealed as a rich seam. It works for classic roasts, as in peachy pork with maple syrup (page 376); it works for homey hotpots, as in spiced chicken with dates (page 371); and it works for easy, filling family suppers, as in sausages and lentils with prunes (page 378).

Once you've unleashed their potential, it's tempting to be gung-ho with dried fruits, but less is definitely more. Having lost so much of their water content, dried fruits are far sweeter than their fresh progenitors. So jammy are they with concentrated sugars that a modest quantity will still make their mark.

In fact, due to their high sugar content, dried fruits should form only a small proportion of your total fruit intake. But consumed sensibly they are unquestionably good for us, full of the concentrated goodness of the original fresh fruit, which is largely retained in the drying process. Dried apricots, for instance, are a useful source of iron and potassium, while prunes are a great way to get your antioxidants, and all dried fruits are a good source of fibre.

However, dried fruit by definition is more processed than fresh, and when shopping for it you may find it's pretty hard to avoid additives entirely. 'Vegetable oil' is routinely used to coat the fruit and stop it sticking together, particularly for currants, raisins and sultanas. All too often, this is palm oil – a substance with a large ecological question mark hovering over it. This is a good reason for choosing organic dried fruit, where sunflower oil is more likely to be the coating agent – but do check the label.

Then there is the issue of added sugar, which you'd think unnecessary. Yet some dried fruits – cherries and cranberries in particular – are very hard to find in an unsweetened form. This is perhaps understandable when they are marketed as a snack food, as these fruits are on the tart side. But it can be frustrating for the cook, as it's just this tartness that can offer such character to your recipes. Shop around, and you should be able to find alternatives (organic brands of dried cranberries, for example, are often sweetened with apple juice, and have a nice balance of sweet and sour).

I try and avoid preservatives such as potassium sorbate and sulphur dioxide – the latter is used to preserve a bright colour in dried fruits such as apricots and mangos. The argument as to whether these additives pose a health risk continues, but frankly I think they are unnecessary. And they affect flavour, because they arrest natural oxidation. It's a matter of taste, but I prefer the richer, toffeeish taste of dark brown unsulphured dried apricots to the slightly sherbety fizz of the bright orange, sulphured versions.

These days, modern processing methods mean that most dried fruit comes to us plump and tender – 'ready to eat' is the buzz phrase. Currants like desiccated flies and dried figs you could use for soling your shoes are largely things of the past. But some fruits still need a bath before use; and even nicely soft ones can be enhanced with a soak in something flavoursome. Water will do, but fruit juice that boosts acidity, or tea, which gently aromatises, is more interesting. And booze is always fun. In all cases, the dried fruit in question will need a good few hours in a cold liquid to make a difference – but the process can be sped up if you warm the liquid first.

Thus bathed, dried fruits will readily drink up the flavours of any liquid medium, just as they absorb the character of spices, herbs, aromatics and other fruits – whatever you choose to cook them with. It's this generous give-and-take that makes them such a rewarding group of ingredients to cook with. It's key to the charms of dishes – both savoury and sweet – like my breast of lamb with dates and preserved lemons (page 372), or, at the sweet end, my dried cherry mincemeat (page 392).

It's also something to bear in mind when improvising your own recipes with dried fruits – and I hope you will. The question 'how would this be if I flung in a small handful of dried cherries, raisins or dates' is one all cooks could be asking more often. The answer is, almost invariably, 'delightful'.

DRIED FRUIT

# Apricot and almond granola

**Makes 8–10 servings**

350g porridge oats (or jumbo oat flakes)

150g almonds (skin on), very coarsely chopped

150g pumpkin seeds or sunflower seeds, or a mix

A pinch of salt (optional)

100g soft brown sugar

50ml rapeseed oil

100ml cloudy apple juice

150g unsulphured ready-to-eat dried apricots, roughly chopped

This is a great granola recipe as it is, but of course you can customise it to your liking. Choose whichever blend of nuts and seeds you like and, once cool, add your favourite dried fruits. Personally, I like to allow one fruit and one nut to dominate, rather than have a total free-for-all. You might think along such lines as dried cherry and walnut, or prune and hazelnut, or possibly dried fig and pistachio. See also my naughty chocolatey variation below.

Preheat the oven to 150°C/Gas 2 and line two lipped baking sheets with baking parchment.

Put the oats, nuts, seeds, salt and brown sugar in a large bowl and mix thoroughly. Add the oil and mix well to distribute it evenly, then pour on the apple juice and mix it in thoroughly – I find the easiest way to do this is with my hands.

Spread the mixture out on the baking sheets. Bake for 50–60 minutes, giving it a stir halfway through, then leave to cool and crisp up.

Once completely cool and crisp, stir in the dried apricots. Store the granola in an airtight container; it will keep for at least 2 weeks.

Serve with a little milk or, as I prefer, a couple of good spoonfuls of thick, plain yoghurt.

*Cherry, coconut and chocolate granola*  This is luxury in a bowl, ideal for a very special breakfast (in bed perhaps?), or a weekend brunch. Replace the rapeseed oil with 50g coconut oil (you'll need to melt it first) and add 50g toasted coconut slivers to the mix. When the cooked granola has cooled, stir in 150g dried cherries instead of the apricots, and 100g finely chopped dark chocolate.

# Pasta with cauliflower, capers, chilli and raisins

This is the kind of dish you can throw together in under half an hour when you're tired and hungry and there's not much in the fridge. It's gloriously comforting and warming, yet vibrant and aromatic at the same time. I like to use a reasonably fiery chilli, to create a hot-sweet-sour chemistry with the raisins and vinegar, but choose the level of heat you prefer.

Trim the cauliflower and cut into small florets. Bring a large pan of water to the boil, salt it well and add the pasta. Cook according to the time suggested on the packet until al dente, adding the cauliflower florets to the pan for the last 4 minutes.

While the pasta is cooking, put the extra virgin olive oil, vinegar, garlic, chilli, capers and raisins in a small pan. Bring to a simmer and cook gently over a low heat for about 3 minutes, taking care that neither the garlic nor the raisins burn.

Drain the pasta and cauliflower thoroughly, then combine with the hot oil and all the flavourings. Taste and add salt and pepper if needed (the capers are already pretty salty). Heap into warm dishes and serve.

## Serves 2

1 small or ½ large cauliflower (about 700g)

175g pasta shapes, such as orecchiette or conchiglie

3 tablespoons extra virgin olive oil

1 tablespoon sherry vinegar or balsamic vinegar

2 garlic cloves, slivered

½–1 medium-hot red chilli, deseeded and diced (or a few pinches of dried chilli flakes)

2 tablespoons baby capers, rinsed

100g raisins

Sea salt and freshly ground black pepper

# Spiced chicken with
# dates

**Serves 4–6**

2 tablespoons olive, rapeseed or sunflower oil

1 free-range chicken (about 1.5kg), jointed

2 onions, chopped

2 bay leaves

4 garlic cloves, chopped

2 teaspoons ground cumin

1 teaspoon ground coriander

½ teaspoon ground cinnamon

150g long-grain (not easy-cook) or basmati rice

75g green or brown lentils, rinsed

700ml hot chicken stock

12 Medjool dates, pitted

A small bunch of coriander, stalks removed, leaves torn

20g flaked almonds, lightly toasted

Sea salt and freshly ground black pepper

**This warming, gently spiced, one-pot supper is easy to make. It also works well with pheasant or rabbit instead of chicken.**

Heat the oil in a large flameproof casserole over a medium-high heat. Season the chicken with salt and pepper. Working in batches, brown the chicken pieces well all over, transferring them to a plate; set aside.

Lower the heat and add the onions and bay leaves to the casserole. Cook, stirring from time to time, for about 15 minutes, until the onions are soft and translucent. Add the garlic, cumin, ground coriander and cinnamon, and stir for a couple of minutes. Add the rice and lentils and stir for a minute to mix well with the aromatics.

Return the chicken to the casserole, pour in the hot stock and add some salt and pepper. Cover and simmer gently for 15 minutes, then add the dates, put the lid back on and simmer for another 15 minutes, until the chicken is cooked through and the rice and lentils are tender.

Remove from the heat, taste and add more salt and pepper as needed. Stir in most of the coriander. Serve with the remaining coriander and flaked almonds scattered over the top.

# Breast of lamb with **dates** and preserved lemons

This recipe is the creation of River Cottage head chef, Gill Meller. With its sultry, Moorish fruity flavours, it's a great way to enjoy this inexpensive and underrated cut of lamb.

Preheat the oven to 220°C/Gas 7.

Quarter the preserved lemon, scrape away and discard the flesh, then finely slice the rind.

Trim the lamb breasts if necessary to create tidy, rectangular pieces of meat. Open them out, flesh side up. Sprinkle with a good pinch of chilli flakes and season generously with salt and pepper. Spread the dates and lemon rind evenly over the lamb. Finely chop the leaves from the thyme and marjoram, if using, and sprinkle these over too. Roll up the lamb breasts to enclose the stuffing and tie securely with kitchen string.

Place the lamb breasts in a large roasting tin and cook in the oven for 15 minutes. Take the roasting tin from the oven and cover the meat with foil. Return to the oven and lower the oven setting to 140°C/Gas 1. Cook for 2½–3 hours or until the lamb is completely tender.

Leave the lamb to rest in a warm place for 20 minutes or so, then carve into thick slices and serve. This begs to be served with something that will soak up its juices and cut the richness of the meat – perhaps couscous or rice and a green salad dressed simply with plenty of lemon juice and olive oil. A cucumber salad is another good option.

### Serves 6

1 large preserved lemon (see page 334)

2 boned-out lamb breasts

A large pinch of dried chilli flakes

8–10 Medjool dates (about 200g), pitted and chopped

A few good sprigs of thyme

A few good sprigs of marjoram (optional)

Sea salt and freshly ground black pepper

# Goat tagine with apricots and almonds

**Serves 6**

1 teaspoon cumin seeds

1 teaspoon coriander seeds

2 cloves

12 black peppercorns

2–3 tablespoons olive, rapeseed or sunflower oil

1kg trimmed shoulder of kid goat, cut into 4–5cm chunks

2 onions, chopped

½ cinnamon stick

2 garlic cloves, grated

A thumb-sized piece of ginger, grated

1 teaspoon hot smoked paprika

400g tin plum tomatoes

A pinch of saffron strands (optional)

½ large preserved lemon (see page 334)

250g unsulphured dried apricots

100g blanched almonds

A large handful of coriander leaves

Sea salt and freshly ground black pepper

Although it's not so easy to source, kid goat is well worth buying. Young male goats are an unwanted by-product of the goat dairy industry and often killed at birth: a terrible waste. However, those kids can be raised in high-welfare systems to produce tender, delicious meat – a far saner option, if you ask me. If you can't get hold of kid, mature goat shoulder or shoulder of lamb works well in this North African-inspired dish – you'll just need to let it simmer for a bit longer until the meat is tender.

Heat a large, dry frying pan over a medium heat. Add the cumin and coriander seeds, cloves and peppercorns and toast lightly for a few minutes, stirring often so the spices don't burn. Tip into a mortar, let cool slightly, then pound with the pestle to a coarse powder.

Heat 1 tablespoon oil in the frying pan, add half the meat and brown the pieces well on all sides. Transfer to a plate and repeat with the remaining meat, adding a little more oil to the pan if necessary.

Heat 1 tablespoon oil in a flameproof casserole or large saucepan over a medium-low heat. Add the onions and fry gently for 10 minutes or so, until tender. Add the pounded spices with the cinnamon, garlic, ginger, paprika and some salt, and cook for a couple of minutes more.

Add the browned meat to the casserole, along with any juices from it. Deglaze the frying pan with a glass of water, letting it bubble as you scrape up the caramelised bits from the bottom, then tip into the casserole. Crush the plum tomatoes in your hands and add them too, discarding any stalky bits. Add the saffron, if using, then pour in enough water to almost cover the meat. Bring to a simmer, half-cover with the lid and cook at a very low simmer for 45 minutes.

Meanwhile, discard the flesh from the preserved lemon and finely slice the rind. Add to the tagine with the apricots and almonds and cook for a further 45 minutes, or until the kid is tender. Check the seasoning, then leave to stand for 15 minutes or so. Serve scattered with coriander, with couscous, rice or flatbreads and lemon or lime wedges on the side.

# Peachy pork
## with maple syrup

This elegant dish is based on a recipe from Alexandra Heaton, who used to work with me at River Cottage. From Ontario, Alex naturally insists on using the best Canadian maple syrup...

In a bowl, mix 3 tablespoons of the maple syrup with 150ml boiling water. Add the dried peaches and leave to soak for at least a few hours, ideally overnight. Drain, saving the liquid, and cut into chunky pieces.

Lay the pork on a board and use a very sharp knife to 'butterfly' it: slice it lengthways, but not right through, so you can open it out like a book, to give a reasonably flat piece of meat. Sprinkle with salt and pepper and lay the soaked dried peaches and thyme down the middle. Fold the meat back together to enclose them in a long parcel.

Place a large piece of cling film on a work surface. Lay the bacon slices widthways on it, overlapping them very slightly to form a sheet. Put the stuffed pork loin at one side of the bacon and roll it up in the bacon as snugly as you can. It shouldn't be necessary to tie it, but you can do so. Wrap the roll tightly in the cling film and refrigerate for 30 minutes. Preheat the oven to 180°C/Gas 4 and put in a roasting tray to heat up.

Heat the oil in a large frying pan over a medium-high heat. Remove the cling film then add the bacon-wrapped pork to the pan and brown well on all sides. Transfer to the hot roasting tray. Pour the reserved soaking liquid and wine into the hot frying pan, scraping with a spatula to deglaze it and simmer for a minute. Put the fresh peaches around the pork, pour the hot liquid from the pan over them and place in the oven. Cook for 20–30 minutes, until the pork is cooked through.

Transfer the pork to a warm plate and cover with foil. Tip the roasted peaches and cooking juices into a sieve over a clean pan and press through. Add the remaining 2 tablespoons maple syrup to this sauce. Simmer for a few minutes to reduce and thicken slightly. Add any juices from the resting pork, then taste and add salt and pepper as needed. Slice the pork thickly and serve with the sauce spooned over. Roasted new potatoes and wilted spinach are ideal accompaniments.

**Serves 4**

5 tablespoons good-quality maple syrup (ideally Canadian Amber Grade 3)

About 75g dried peach halves (or use dried pear or apricot halves)

1 outdoor-reared pork tenderloin, or trimmed piece of loin fillet (about 400g)

A sprig of thyme, leaves only, chopped

8–10 thin rindless rashers of unsmoked streaky bacon

1 tablespoon olive, rapeseed or sunflower oil

100ml white wine

3 ripe peaches, halved, stoned and cut into wedges

Sea salt and freshly ground black pepper

# Sausage and lentil hotpot with
# prunes

This easy, hearty winter dish is full of savoury flavours, gently lifted by the rich sweetness of a few prunes. It's already a great favourite with family and friends.

Preheat the oven to 140°C/Gas 1.

Heat 2 tablespoons oil in a large casserole over a medium-low heat. Add the onions and sweat for 10–15 minutes, stirring regularly. Add the carrots and celery, and the bay and/or thyme, if using. Cover and sweat for another 10 minutes or so, stirring from time to time.

Heat a trickle more oil in a frying pan and brown the sausages well all over, then add them to the casserole. Use a little of the stock to deglaze the frying pan, scraping up the sediment, then pour these pan juices over the sausages and veg in the casserole.

Stir in the lentils, prunes, remaining stock and some salt and pepper. The liquid should just barely cover everything. Add a splash of water if necessary. Bring up to a simmer, cover and transfer to the oven. Cook for 1–1½ hours, taking it out to give it a stir halfway through to ensure the lentils all cook evenly.

Taste and add more salt or pepper if needed, then serve. This hotpot is delicious with a baked potato, or a hunk of good bread, and some lightly cooked spinach or greens.

Serves 4–6

About 3 tablespoons olive, rapeseed or sunflower oil

2 large onions, sliced

2 medium carrots, sliced on the diagonal

2 celery stalks, sliced on the diagonal

2 bay leaves (optional)

A sprig of thyme (optional)

8 sausages

500ml chicken stock

150g Puy, green or brown lentils, well rinsed

200g pitted prunes

Sea salt and freshly ground black pepper

# Red cabbage and apple salad with dried cherries

This is the raw, crunchy version of the classic wintry braised red cabbage with apples and raisins. Alongside a slab of nutty Cheddar and some good bread, a bowlful of this makes for a fantastic pared-down winter's lunch as is. But, like the cooked version, it's also great served with roast pork or even venison – cutting those rich and full-flavoured meats crisply with its sweet and sour elements.

Warm the dried cherries with the orange juice in a small pan over a low heat until hot but not boiling. Remove from the heat and set aside to soak for 1–2 hours to plump up.

Separate the cabbage leaves and cut away the thicker white stems. Now pile a few leaves at a time on top of one another and slice as thinly as you can, working across the leaf so you produce relatively short pieces of cabbage. Put all the sliced red cabbage into a bowl.

Drain the soaked dried cherries, reserving any juice. Stir the cherries into the cabbage.

For the dressing, put the ingredients into a jam jar, adding 1 tablespoon of the cherry soaking juice. Season well with salt and pepper. Screw on the lid and shake to emulsify.

Pour the dressing over the cabbage in the bowl and mix well. Quarter and core the apples, then slice them thinly directly into the bowl of cabbage. Toss them in gently, then stir in the walnuts. Cover and leave for at least an hour for the flavours to combine and the cabbage to 'relax' a little.

Before serving, gently turn the salad one more time, and taste and add more salt and pepper if needed.

## Serves 4–6

100g dried cherries (or raisins, or dried cranberries)

75ml orange or apple juice

400g red cabbage (about ½ medium one)

2 smallish, sharp, crisp eating apples (about 250g in total), such as Cox's, Russet or Braeburn

75g walnuts, roughly broken

### For the dressing

2 tablespoons extra virgin olive oil

1 tablespoon walnut oil (or more olive oil if you prefer)

2 teaspoons cider vinegar

1 teaspoon English mustard

Sea salt and freshly ground black pepper

# Dried mango chutney

Mango chutney is such a great standby, not just for serving with curries, but also for adding to sauces and dressings (see page 270), and making a great Cheddar and chutney sandwich. Paradoxically perhaps, using dried rather than fresh mango makes for a fruitier and frankly more mango-y chutney. The spicing here is inspired by a wonderful recipe from Fiona Colonnese, a past winner of the River Cottage Preserves Competition.

If your mango pieces are on the large side, chop them roughly. (If they are very tough and leathery, you might find it easier to do this after they've been soaked.) Put the dried mango slices into a bowl, pour on 1.5 litres water, cover and leave to soak overnight.

Sterilise your preserve jars by washing them thoroughly in hot soapy water, rinsing well, then putting them upside down on a tray in a low oven (at 120°C/Gas ½) to dry out and heat up. (Wide-necked jars make it much easier to pot the chutney.)

Put the garlic, chillies and ginger in a food processor with the orange zest and juice and process to a paste.

Heat the oil in a frying pan over a medium heat, add the mustard and fenugreek seeds and fry for a minute or so until they start to pop. Add the garlicky paste and fry for a couple of minutes, stirring so that it does not burn. Add the ground spices and fry another minute.

Tip the mangoes and their liquid into a large, stainless steel saucepan or preserving pan. Peel, core and chop the apples and add to the pan with the onions, spice paste, sugar, vinegar, salt and pepper. Stir over a low heat until the sugar dissolves, then bring to the boil. Simmer, uncovered, for 1½–2 hours, until rich and thick, stirring frequently – particularly towards the end of cooking to ensure it doesn't stick.

Ladle the chutney into the hot, sterilised jars and seal with vinegar-proof lids. Store in a cool, dry place and leave to mature for at least 8 weeks before using. Use within 2 years.

**Makes five 340ml jars**

500g dried mango slices

1 garlic bulb, cloves separated and peeled

2 medium-hot red chillies, deseeded and roughly chopped

25g piece of ginger, peeled and roughly chopped

Finely grated zest and juice of 1 orange

1 tablespoon sunflower or rapeseed oil

2 tablespoons mustard seeds

2 teaspoons fenugreek seeds

2 teaspoons ground cumin

2 teaspoons ground coriander

2 teaspoons ground turmeric

500g cooking apples

4 onions, chopped

350g light brown sugar

500ml cider vinegar

1 teaspoon salt

1 teaspoon freshly ground black pepper

# Ale, apricot and walnut loaf

This is a simple loaf – a soda bread really – that takes just minutes to knock together, but looks wonderful and tastes great. Serve it with cheese or a big bowl of soup.

Preheat the oven to 180°C/Gas 4. Butter a 1kg loaf tin, about 11 x 22cm, and dust with flour, shaking out any excess.

Sift the two flours into a mixing bowl, add the salt, sugar, dried apricots and walnuts and combine thoroughly. Pour in the ale slowly, mixing as you go, to form a reasonably loose, sticky batter.

Pour the batter into the prepared loaf tin. Bake in the oven for about 1 hour or until a skewer inserted into the middle of the loaf comes out clean and the bottom sounds hollow when tapped. Transfer to a wire rack to cool.

Serve the loaf cut into thick slices, either still just warm, or when completely cooled. It will keep for a couple of days in an airtight container, and also freezes well.

**Variations** As you'd expect, you can play around with the dried fruit and nut combination, pretty much at will. Chopped prunes and flaked almonds work well; so do raisins or sultanas and roughly chopped cashews; or dried cherries and hazelnuts.

## Makes 1 loaf

Butter or oil, for greasing

350g self-raising white flour, plus extra to dust

150g self-raising wholemeal flour

2 teaspoons salt

1 teaspoon caster sugar

100g unsulphured dried apricots, roughly chopped

100g walnuts, roughly chopped

500ml good ale, such as an IPA or mild bitter

# Coconut, carrot and apricot cake

**Makes 10 slices**

200g self-raising wholemeal flour

A pinch of salt

1 teaspoon ground mixed spice (optional)

200g coconut oil

200g soft brown or light muscovado sugar

3 large free-range eggs

200g finely grated raw carrot

Finely grated zest of 1 lemon

150g unsulphured dried apricots, chopped

100g desiccated coconut

**This delicious cake is dairy-free. It uses coconut oil which, being solid at room temperature, can be incorporated into a cake in much the same way as butter.**

Preheat the oven to 170°C/Gas 3. Line a 1kg loaf tin, about 11 x 22cm, with baking parchment.

Sift the flour, salt and mixed spice, if using, together into a bowl.

Beat the coconut oil in a mixer, or using a handheld electric whisk, for a minute or so until soft, then add the sugar and beat for 2–3 minutes until very soft and creamy.

Add one egg and a spoonful of the flour mix and beat until thoroughly incorporated. Repeat with the other eggs, adding a spoonful of flour with each.

Lightly fold in the remaining flour, then the grated carrot, lemon zest, dried apricots and desiccated coconut, folding just until everything is combined, so you don't overwork the mixture.

Spoon the mixture into the prepared loaf tin and gently level the top. Bake in the oven for about 1 hour or until a skewer inserted into the centre comes out clean.

Leave the cake to cool in the tin for 10 minutes, then transfer to a wire rack to cool completely before slicing.

# Fruity
## fridge flapjacks

This unbaked dairy-free flapjack recipe is from Alice Meller, wife of Gill, head chef at River Cottage. It's so easy, so fruity and so good that it just had to go in the book. You can vary the recipe as you choose, substituting different dried fruit and using 100g of any mix of seeds.

Line a shallow baking tray, about 20 x 30cm, with baking parchment.

Put the dates, prunes, bananas, honey, coconut oil and 2 tablespoons water in a food processor and blitz to a thick, fruit-flecked purée.

In a large bowl, combine the oats, raisins, chopped apricots and seeds. Stir in the puréed fruit and honey and mix well (your hands may be the best tool for this job).

Tip the fruity oat mixture into the prepared tin and gently press it out, getting it as even and level as you can. Rolling over the top with a straight-sided glass is one way to get an even top, though you may have to stop and wipe the glass a couple of times as it becomes sticky.

Put the tray in the fridge for 2–3 hours to allow the flapjack to set, then turn out on to a board and slice into bars. Keep in a plastic container in the fridge and eat within a week.

### Makes 18–20

100g pitted dates

100g prunes

2 ripe or slightly over-ripe medium bananas, peeled

150g honey

2 tablespoons coconut oil

325g medium porridge oats, or jumbo oats

100g raisins, currants or dried cranberries

100g unsulphured ready-to-eat dried apricots, finely chopped

25g shelled hemp seeds

25g linseeds

25g sesame seeds

25g sunflower seeds

# Cherry mincemeat

This recipe has everything I want in a mincemeat: lots of citrus zest, a hit of tangy tartness from dried cherries and a generous slosh of booze. But feel free to customise it to your tastes: use chopped dried apricots and/or prunes instead of raisins and/or currants, perhaps; add candied peel if you like it; and feel free to leave out the nuts.

Peel, core and chop the cooking apples (neatly dice eating apples, if using) and place in a large bowl. Add all the other ingredients, except the alcohol, and mix well. Cover and leave to stand overnight.

Preheat the oven to 140°C/Gas 1. Put the mincemeat in a large roasting dish, cover with foil and bake for 2 hours, stirring thoroughly once, halfway through. Leave to cool completely, stirring regularly to help amalgamate the suet as it cools.

Sterilise your jars by washing thoroughly in hot soapy water, rinsing well, then putting them upside down on a tray in a low oven (at 120°C/Gas ½) to dry for 20 minutes. Remove from the oven and leave to cool.

When the mincemeat is cold, stir in the alcohol, then spoon into the sterilised jars. Seal and store in a cool, dry place for up to 2 months.

*Using your mincemeat* There are so many possibilities for this lovely preserve, and you'll have enough to explore all of the following:

- Make mince pies in a bun tin tray, using my sweet shortcrust pastry (see page 177). Bake at 200°C/Gas 6 for 15–20 minutes until golden.
- Use to stuff the cavity of cored eating apples, bake at 180°C/Gas 4 for 30 minutes or until tender and serve with custard or ice cream.
- Spread a generous spoonful over half a freshly cooked pancake, fold in half and then in half again. Serve with yoghurt or crème fraîche.
- Follow the cherry bakewell recipe on page 142, but use mincemeat instead of the cherry jam, and omit the fresh cherries.
- Warm a few spoonfuls of mincemeat in a small pan until bubbling, then take off the heat and stir in an extra slug of brandy or rum. Serve over vanilla or chocolate ice cream – or a scoop of each.

**Makes five 340g jars**

500g cooking apples (or use half cooking apples, half eating apples)

200g dried cherries (or dried cranberries)

350g raisins

200g currants

Finely grated zest and juice of 2 oranges

Finely grated zest and juice of 2 lemons

1 tablespoon ground mixed spice

150g vegetarian suet

300g light muscovado sugar

100g walnuts, roughly chopped

100ml brandy, rum, Calvados or cider brandy

# Date and banana thickie

• • • • • • • • • • • • • • • • • • • • • • • • • • • • • • • • • • • • • • • • • • • • • • • • • • • • • • • • • • • • • • • •

This is a thick, luscious breakfast-in-a-glass: a creamy banana smoothie flecked with lovely little fragments of sweet date and boosted with a handful of oats – it's the oats that make it a thickie. You need the really soft, fudgy type of Medjool date for this; smaller regular dates are bit too tough.

Put all the ingredients into a blender and whiz for a good 30 seconds to 1 minute, until well blended and combined. Pour into glasses and serve immediately.

### Variations

A simple banana thickie can be enlivened by all kinds of other fruits, both dried and fresh:

- Other dried fruits will also fleck the drink attractively with speckledy slivers: try replacing the dates with raisins, cherries, prunes or dried apricots (the soft ready-to-eat kind work best).
- Or, for a fresher, zesty breakfast drink, add a handful of strawberries, gooseberries or raspberries, chilled or frozen (in which case hold the ice cubes).

**Serves 2**

6 Medjool dates, pitted and roughly chopped

2 medium bananas (300–325g in total), peeled

200ml plain wholemilk yoghurt

200ml whole milk

2 tablespoons porridge oats

4–6 ice cubes

The fruit kingdom is too huge and diverse to encapsulate and describe in a single volume. I've chosen to cover in detail a selection of personal and national favourites – those I consider the most accessible and the most worthwhile. But there's another dozen or so I'd like to draw your attention to. Though not readily available 'over the counter', there are some you may meet on your travels, others you can choose to grow at home, and a couple that will fall to the hand of the keen forager. Uncommon they may be, but all are uncommonly good and many can be swapped into recipes in the book with great success.

### Mulberries

These little fruits (pictured right) are very delicate and therefore hard to buy, but exquisitely good to eat. Their flavour lies within the blackberry/blackcurrant/raspberry range, with real depth and intensity. When good and ripe, in late summer and autumn, you can enjoy them straight off the tree or throw them, raw, into a fumble (page 84) or trifle. They also make delicious cooked puds, jams and jellies, as well as ice creams and sorbets. To enjoy mulberries, you'll almost certainly have to grow your own (or make friends with someone who does). The trees are not at all hard to look after – though some varieties take many years to begin fruiting, so do your research first. Once established, however, they grow to the size of an oak and live for hundreds of years: good news for farsighted fruit lovers, and their descendants.

### Worcesterberries

These purple relatives of the gooseberry both look and taste like a gooseberry/blackcurrant cross, though they are technically a type of hairless gooseberry rather than a hybrid. Their flavour is very good, though it can be on the tart side. I like them best when cooked – you can swap them for gooseberries in a cobbler (page 52) or crumble (page 127), or for blackcurrants in a jam or curd (page 58), either alone or mingled with sliced strawberries. Worcesterberries are summer fruits, easy to grow, lovely to look at and generous cropping, though their thorns make picking them a bit of a trial. The jostaberry, a very similar fruit, is thorn-free.

### Loganberries and tayberries

Fat and luscious, these are blackberry/raspberry hybrids (there are others, including boysenberries and tummelberries). Like their parent fruits, they are easy to grow at home and fairly low-maintenance. Both climb well, and can be trained against a wired wall or trellis. The berries tend to be large and long, with a dark, dusky-red colour and velvety drupelets (the individual little juice-filled bubbles that make up the larger fruit). It's easy to pick them too early, when raspberry red, but let them ripen fully until wine-dark purple and their flavour will be rich and floral, and no sharper than ripe raspberries. They can certainly be enjoyed raw, with a sprinkle of sugar and a trickle of cream, but they really come into their own when cooked. You can substitute them for raspberries in any of the recipes in the book, or use them instead of blackberries in my hedgerow fruit chapter (pages 220–51). They make fantastic jam. These berries are in season from late July to early September. You'll find them at some pick-your-own farms and farmers' markets, and the plants themselves are easy to buy.

### Blaeberries/bilberries/whortleberries

These three names – and a few others besides – all describe the same fruit: a wild British relative of the sweet, fat blueberry (which is native to North America). Blaeberries have a sharper, more complex and, arguably, superior flavour, and they

make fabulous pies, tarts and crumbles. I would recommend trying them in place of blueberries in any of my recipes (also instead of blackcurrants in the salad on page 44 or blackberries in the crème brûlées on page 240). You might want to sweeten them a little more than blueberries (or you might not), but you will not be disappointed with their flavour.

Blaeberry bushes love acidic soil and can be found on heaths, moorland and in some woods (most of my blaeberry picking has been done in Scotland). Finding a good thicket of blaeberry bushes, however, does not necessarily equate to finding a good haul of the berries. The fruits tend to be rather sparse and you need to show some commitment if you want to pick a hatful rather than a handful. It's well worth the effort, though. And if you can't muster enough blaeberries for a recipe, just enjoy as you pick them.

### Sea buckthorn

This is the berry *du jour* in many a top-end restaurant, and with good reason since they have an amazing, powerfully sour flavour. The good news is that you needn't pay restaurant prices to sample them: you can forage them for free from spots all around our coast – look out for them from late July onwards. The bright orange berries, growing on small, shrubby trees, are easy to spot. They are not, however, easy to pick, being very fragile and liable to burst, and surrounded by sharp thorns. I take a tip from my foraging partner John Wright (see the Directory, page 403) and 'milk' the bushes, crushing the berry juice from the plant directly into a plastic tub. This, once passed through a fine sieve, can be used judiciously as a seasoning, or in drinks, or, more generously, to make a delicious jelly, combined with cooking apples.

### Japanese wineberries

Do not be put off by the slightly outré name, these are well worth seeking out. Related to both blackberries and raspberries, though a hybrid of neither, they are gorgeous-looking, with bright, translucent red drupelets packed into an almost spherical berry. They are a big favourite of my friend Mark Diacono (see the Directory, page 403) who has it spot-on, I think, when he describes their flavour as sweet and raspberry-esque but 'longer and with a winey depth like that of

well-ripened grapes'. Fruiting in August and September, Japanese wineberries are quite delicious raw, and superb mingled with meringue and cream (page 137), or custard and crumble (page 84). I have never seen them for sale as ready-picked fruits, but you will have no trouble locating a source of the plants. They grow well in most conditions, with little intervention.

### Cranberries

These intensely sharp red berries have become ubiquitous in our supermarkets at Christmas time, usually brought in from Canada or northern American states, where they are grown in the required boggy, acidic conditions. Too tart to be eaten raw, cranberries are generally used in juices and preserves. They make a very good sweet-tart sauce to go with turkey – and other meats, or game – though I tend to use native fruits such as redcurrants, damsons and cooking apples for this job. I do love dried cranberries, though, which have a unique, tart, spicy flavour and a rather lovely, jewel-like appearance; see my mincemeat recipe on page 392.

### Medlars

These curious little brown tree fruits look rather like a cross between an apple and a rosehip. They were popular in Victorian times, but then fell into obscurity – perhaps because they don't offer instant gratification (see below). Happily, however, medlars are on the up again. You'll find them around October at orchards, farm shops and some roadside stalls. Natives of warmer climes, medlars never ripen fully on the tree when grown here. Instead, they need to be picked and 'bletted', or allowed to soften, before you can eat them.

If you have acquired some firm medlars, lay them out on a large tray, stalk end upwards, and simply leave at room temperature, giving them a little squeeze every day or so to gauge their progress. They'll probably take around a couple of weeks to blet. They are best when they give readily between your finger and thumb, without collapsing completely. Once broken open, I like them to have a thin outer layer of still-white flesh, with a soft, fudgy-brown interior. If they're brown throughout and collapsing, or black or showing any signs of mould, then they are past their best.

Once fully bletted, you can simply scrape the soft flesh out of the skins and eat it as it is – it's full of pips though, so it's much nicer if you sieve it first. Mixed with a little sugar, lemon zest and cream, it makes a lovely fool. Still-firm medlars, combined with some softer ones, can be used to make a jelly, which is excellent with game, cold meats and cheeses.

If their charms win you over, you might want to think about planting your own medlar tree. These are low maintenance and very attractive and, once established, will have you cooking up batches of translucent, rose-amber medlar jelly every autumn.

### Bullaces

Related to the damson, these dark stone fruits can be found in the wild, though they are usually escapees from gardens or orchards. You can buy the trees to grow at home too, where they will fruit from August through to October. Rather like damsons, bullaces are generally too tart to eat raw, but come gloriously into their own when cooked with sugar, or steeped in alcohol. Use them in the fruit vodka recipe on page 228, or in any of my other damson recipes. They are also good as an element in hedgerow jelly (page 224).

### Lychees and rambutans

There's something very luscious about a lychee. The pearly-white flesh that nestles underneath its brittle, brownish-pink carapace is sweet, obscenely juicy and full of floral, grapey flavours. Removing the outer shell is akin to peeling a hard-boiled egg and, once you get to the fruit, you'll encounter a large, hard stone inside – but such obstacles seem to make their fragrant flesh all the more delectable.

You can cook lychees but I really don't see the point, and nor do I enjoy the ones you can get in cans or jars, even though the skin and stone are removed. For me, this is a once-in-a-while sensuous treat of a fruit, to be enjoyed after a meal in much the same way I might work my way through a pile of shell-on walnuts, cracking one at a time. They are grown in various parts of the world, including their native China, as well as Israel, South Africa and Thailand, and you'll find them in exotic grocers and swanky supermarkets pretty much all year round.

The outlandish-looking rambutan, which has a bright, orange-red skin sprouting yellow-tipped tendrils, is related to the lychee (it looks like its Rastafarian cousin). The rambutan is larger, but has similar, sweet, fragrant, juicy flesh and is eaten in the same way as the lychee.

### Mangosteens

These Southeast Asian delicacies share something of the floral charm of the lychee and, to my mind, are one of the most delicious fruits on the planet. Inside their thick, purple skins, you'll find segments of pearly-white, sweet flesh with an exquisite flavour. To reveal it, cut carefully through the skin around the equator of the fruit with a small, sharp knife, then lift off one half of the thick carapace. Remove the sweet segments with a fork, and don't think of doing anything other than relishing them just as they come.

### Asian pears

Despite its name, this fruit, which is also called the nashi pear or salad pear, is grown mostly in Chile and New Zealand and is in season during our summer. It's related to the homegrown pears we know and love, the result of interbreeding between different wild varieties. It is rounder, more apple-like in shape, but has a distinctive, dappled golden skin and translucent, slightly grainy, crisp flesh, reminiscent of an under-ripe Conference or Comice pear. It's a lovely fragrant fruit, particularly nice sliced very thinly and used in savoury dishes such as salads. Give it a go in any of the pear recipes in this book.

### Persimmons/sharon fruit

The persimmon, which looks something like a large, orange tomato, is a confusing thing. What you are most likely to find for sale these days, certainly in supermarkets, is a particular variety of persimmon called the sharon fruit. This is, specifically, an Israeli-bred example of the non-astringent, or 'fuyu', variety of persimmon. Squat and chunky, it has the advantage of being tasty and toothsome even if it is only just ripe, and remaining so, becoming sweeter, more tender and more juicy over its considerable shelf-life.

The alternative, astringent type of persimmon, usually the hachiya variety, is mouth-puckeringly tart when under-ripe – or, indeed, even when quite ripe. Not until it's been allowed to soften to the point of near-collapse will it reveal its exquisite, highly prized flavour. It's only likely to achieve this status in the hands of an enthusiast in the know – so you can see why it's failed to find favour with today's fruit growers and suppliers.

Sharon fruit may lack the exotic difficulty of the astringent persimmon, but that doesn't mean there's anything wrong with them. They can be quite delicious, their sweet flesh revealing hints of peach, plum and mango. The skin is edible too. Slice the sharon fruit horizontally to show off its star-shaped core, then give it a squeeze of lemon juice before serving.

Hachiya persimmons are more heart-shaped than sharon fruit. If you would like to join the cognoscenti, your best bets for finding them are specialist greengrocers or market stalls. Take them home and leave in the fruit bowl – perhaps next to a banana, to speed ripening – until very soft and with a translucent look about them. Then slice off the tops, or halve them, and scoop out the middles with a teaspoon.

### Guavas

The guava (pictured right) is a tropical/subtropical fruit native to central America, much celebrated these days for its exceptionally high antioxidant content. There are lots of different varieties of guava and most have a disconcertingly under-ripe look about them, with their bright green skins. If, however, the fruit gives a little when pressed and is at least slightly fragrant, it will reveal ripe flesh when you cut into it, though the texture will still be closer to an unripe pear than a ripe one.

Surprisingly related to cinnamon, cloves and nutmeg, guavas have some of the same flavour compounds, which give a spicy, aromatic quality to their flesh. This may be pink, yellow or white, with a smooth, outer layer giving way to the inner section, which contains lots of small seeds. These are generally quite edible (though in some varieties they are very hard), as is the skin.

If you travel in the tropics, particularly in South America and the Caribbean, you'll find guavas abundant and inexpensive in fruit markets, and they are often served for breakfast in hotels and guesthouses. Don't be shy – this is a lovely fruit. If you do find a ripe guava or two in the UK (most likely in an ethnic market or posh supermarket), just enjoy it *au naturel*, peeled and sliced. Or whiz the flesh into a refreshing drink in a blender – with ice and the juice of an apple or orange to thin it to drinking consistency. In Brazil guavas are used to make a popular sweetmeat called *goiabada*: it's what we would call a fruit 'cheese' – similar to the quince-based membrillo. If you come across it, don't miss out.

### Pomelos and ugli fruit

Should you ever tire of grapefruit, I urge you to consider these two citrus heavyweights, whose outward appearance belies the sweet, delicate flesh within. The pomelo is the forebear of the grapefruit and capable of growing up to 30cm across. Pomelos are usually slightly pear-shaped with a yellow or greenish skin and very thick rind. The flesh can be white or pink and is sweeter than a grapefruit's.

The ugli fruit is a hybrid of the grapefruit and the mandarin. Like pomelos, they have a thick rind which is often pitted and wrinkled. The flesh inside, however, is fragrant and sweet.

In either case, remove the peel and white pith, then slice the segments out from between the membranes (see page 329), which can be very bitter, especially in the case of pomelos. Use the segments in place of grapefruit in dishes such as the papaya citrus salad on page 308, the noodly salad on page 262 or the savoury salad with olives and red onion on page 329.

Both these fruits can sometimes be found in supermarkets but Asian, African or West Indian greengrocers are a better hunting ground.

### Physalis fruit

Also known as the Cape gooseberry, this little smooth-skinned orange fruit is encased within a delicate papery thin husk, resembling a Chinese lantern. It's unfortunate that these fruits have become a culinary cliché – the sweet equivalent of the sprig of parsley – dumped on countless puddings in restaurants because they look good, not because they have anything to do with the dish itself. But physalis fruit are more than pretty – they're tasty too. Actually related to tomatoes (and tomatillos, which have a similar papery husk), they have a nice acid-sweet balance that makes them lovely for munching raw or slicing into salads, sweet or savoury. You can cook them too, of course – they make good jam and are great in a pie or crumble. Physalis fruit that you buy in the shops are most likely to have come from South Africa or South America. But you can grow them here, especially if you have a very sunny, sheltered corner and/or a greenhouse.

# Directory

## Nurseries/plant supplies

**Edulis**
www.edulis.co.uk
01635 578113
Specialists in rare edible plants, including white strawberries!

**Otter Farm Shop**
shop.otterfarm.co.uk
Stocks an extensive range of fruit trees and plants, including more unusual types, such as mulberries, medlars and quinces. Run by River Cottage author Mark Diacono.

**Reads Nursery**
www.readsnursery.co.uk
01986 895555
Has an extensive range of fruit trees and plants, including unusual and exotic types.

**Real English Fruit**
www.realenglishfruit.co.uk
01379 870759
Supplier of fruit trees, including many varieties of apple, plus apricots and medlars.

**Walcot Organic Nursery**
walcotnursery.co.uk
01905 841587
Supplier of organic apple, pear, cherry, quince, plum, damson and gage trees, as well as berries and currants.

## Fruit

**Brogdale**
www.brogdalecollections.co.uk
01795 531888
Home of the national fruit collection in Faversham, Kent, with over 4,000 varieties of apple, pear, plum, cherry, currant and quince. Orchards open to the public; fruit, trees and plants available to buy; fruity events and courses.

**Charlton Orchards**
www.charltonorchards.com
01823 412959
Somerset orchard growing apples, pears, plums, damsons and soft fruits. A variety of fruit and fruit trees for sale and selected fruits are supplied by mail order.

**Crapes Fruit Farm**
crapes.wordpress.com
01206 212375
Essex orchard selling a wide range of apple varieties and other fruits on site and boxes of apples by mail order.

**Cross Lanes Fruit Farm**
www.crosslanesfruitfarm.co.uk
0118 972 3167
Grower of apples, pears and plums, based in Reading, Berkshire. Fruit available in farm shop and at local markets; apples available by mail order.

**England In Particular**
www.england-in-particular.info
Website from Common Ground (see right) that includes a gazetteer of orchards, where you can find orchards and locate fruit growers near you.

**English Cherries**
www.englishcherry.co.uk
01908 587070
Bedfordshire cherry growers. Cherries available in farm shop and by mail, in season.

**E Oldroyd & Sons**
www.yorkshirerhubarb.co.uk
0113 282 2245
Growers of forced Yorkshire rhubarb, available by mail order in season.

**The Orchard Marketplace**
www.orchardmarketplace.org.uk
Online marketplace facilitating the exchange of fruit and other orchard-related produce. Users post requests for, or offers of, fruit – for sale or for free.

**Orchard Network**
www.orchardnetwork.org.uk
A partnership of organisations working for the conservation of traditional orchards.

## Other resources

### Garden Organic
www.gardenorganic.co.uk
024 7630 3517
Based at Ryton Gardens near
Coventry, national charity for
organic growing. Gardening
advice and information, plus the
Organic Gardening Catalogue,
including fruit trees and plants.

### Royal Horticultural Society
www.rhs.org.uk/gardening
0845 062 1111
Useful information on selecting
and growing a range of fruit.
See also RHS Online Plant Shop,
www.rhsplants.co.uk, for a
range of fruit trees and plants.

### Common Ground
www.commonground.org.uk
Charity whose work includes a
far-reaching orchard campaign,
and the organisation of Apple
Day (October 21st).

### Fairtrade Foundation
www.fairtrade.org.uk
An independent non-profit
organisation that licenses the
use of the Fairtrade mark. As
well as information on Fairtrade
the website includes a list of
Fairtrade fresh and dried fruit
available from UK retailers.

### The Soil Association
www.soilassociation.org
Campaign for organic,
sustainable food and farming.

### Local Farmers' Markets
www.local-farmers-markets.co.uk
Nationwide listing of farmers'
markets, plus calendar of food
events.

### Local Foods
www.localfoods.org.uk
Local food-finder website,
including a nationwide directory
of farmers' markets, farm shops
and pick-your-own farms.

### Pick Your Own Farms
www.pickyourownfarms.org.uk
Lists PYO farms nationwide.

### Westmorland Damson Association
www.lythdamsons.org.uk
015395 68698
Cumbria-based organisers of
Damson Day, plus information
and advice on growing and
cooking with damsons. Fruit
available to buy locally.

## Books

### Jane Grigson's Fruit Book
A classic of over 30 years'
standing, and deservedly so,
this excellent book provides an
A-Z overview of fruits, plus a
plethora of recipes. As always
with Grigson, it's a joy to read.

### The Royal Horticultural Society: Growing Fruit, Harry Baker
In-depth information on fruit
and nut growing.

### Fruit: A Connoisseur's Guide and Cookbook, Alan Davidson and Charlotte Knox
Beautifully illustrated, this
compendium explores the
historical and cultural context
of fruit. Also provides detail on
individual varieties and recipes.

### The River Cottage Fruit Handbook, Mark Diacono
Excellent advice on all aspects
of fruit growing.

### The River Cottage Hedgerow Handbook, John Wright
An invaluable guide for foragers
of wild fruit.

### The River Cottage Preserves Handbook, Pam Corbin
Sound advice and a host of
wonderful recipes that will
enable you to preserve fruit
in sweet and savoury ways.

# Index

# Acknowledgements

This book has been an awful lot of fun to write. Not only have I been able to revisit my favourite fruit recipes, tinker with them and fall in love with them all over again, I've also given myself ample licence to try a whole range of brand new ideas – ideas which have been exciting, unconventional, even, at times, eyebrow-raising. It's what I love doing, and I've had a blast. But it wouldn't have been half so enjoyable, or indeed possible, without the commitment and dedication of the talented people who've worked on this project with me.

In devising, developing and testing the recipes, I've had the crucial support of two colleagues. Nikki Duffy has been experimenter, compiler and enforcer par excellence. She has a great nose for a good recipe, and a deft knack for translating blue sky brainstorming into seriously lovely plates of food. Working with her is a constantly fruitful and delicious pleasure.

And Gill Meller, head chef at River Cottage, has once again shared his boundless creativity, enthusiasm and energy and helped to make this book the ripe and vibrant thing I wanted it to be. He is the finest, calmest and smartest culinary collaborator I could wish for. Gill also prepared the recipes for photography with his usual skill and flair (ably assisted by his lovely wife, Alice, who contributed the cracking flapjack recipe too).

Gill's partnership with our co-conspirator Simon Wheeler has ensured that this book is not just useful but beautiful. I'm in awe of the way Simon's images shine a fresh light on familiar things – whether it's making you look at a pear in a different way, or bringing out the quintessential blackberry-ness of blackberries. His work always explores the essence of the dishes we create and I consider myself extremely lucky to have worked with him for the best part of two decades now.

I'm indebted, too, to illustrator Andy Smith, whose wonderful, witty, juicy drawings capture so perfectly the fun and fizz of fruit. I found myself wanting every one of them printed on a tee-shirt... and I may yet get round to that.

At Bloomsbury, my editor Natalie Hunt has, with her trademark charm and elegant efficiency, ensured that this book has not only reached fruition but reached it in style, bringing it together with minimum stress. I'd also like to thank Xa Shaw Stewart and Alison Glossop for their help and enthusiasm. Richard Atkinson, meanwhile, has allowed me the benefit of his vast skill and experience and generously contributed ideas and constructive criticism that, as ever, made a huge and positive difference to the finished book.

I'd have been lost without Janet Illsley, who has managed the whole project with a gimlet eye and superb attention to detail, wielding her editorial secateurs to just the right degree to prune the book to maximum flavour and productivity.

A designer's job is often under-appreciated because you notice it most when it's not done well. I'd like to emphasise that without the talents of Lawrence Morton, this book wouldn't have fulfilled its potential. He has made the words, pictures and illustrations work together beautifully, bringing out the fun, colour and joy of fruit with his clever strategies. He is always a pleasure to work with.

And, for ensuring that the book looks as fresh and tempting as a just-picked strawberry, my thanks to production manager Marina Asenjo.

At River Cottage, Jess Upton and Alexandra Heaton have done wonderful work in managing my schedule and keeping me, and therefore the book, on track, while my partner and friend Rob Love has supported the project throughout.

In imagining and realising *River Cottage Bears Fruit*, the TV manifestation of this book, my thanks to the hardworking, talented team at Keo Films: Andrew Palmer, Zam Baring, Debbie Manners, Stephen Leigh, Nick Shearman, Steve Cole, Mark Davenport, Anna Horsburgh and Annie Coplestone.

For his tireless work on my behalf, and for his invaluable input from the outset, when this book was just the seed/pip/sapling of an idea (he would choose the right word) my thanks as always to my brilliant agent, Antony Topping.

And none of this would have happened, of course, without the love and support of my family. Thanks first of all to my sister Sophy, a wonderful cook, who tested some of these recipes and gave such useful feedback. Thanks to my parents too, who instilled in me a love of good food in general, and fruit in particular, and who have both bequeathed many delicious ideas that have found their way, in various forms, on to these pages.

Finally, to Marie, Chloe, Oscar, Freddie and Louisa, the apples, plums, cherries and berries of my eye, thank you, always, for everything.

For chloe

Hugh Fearnley-Whittingstall is a writer, broadcaster and campaigner. His series for Channel Four have earned him a huge popular following, while his River Cottage books have collected multiple awards including the Glenfiddich Trophy (twice), the André Simon Food Book of the Year (three times), the Michael Smith Award (twice) and, in the US, the James Beard Cookbook of the Year. In 2012, *River Cottage Veg Every Day!* was voted the Best Cookbook in the Observer Food Monthly Awards. Hugh lives in Devon with his family.

First published in Great Britain 2013
Text copyright © 2013 by Hugh Fearnley-Whittingstall
Photography © 2013 by Simon Wheeler
Photographs on pages 6, 81, 145, 164, 321, 343, 347 and 386–7
    © 2013 by Marie Derôme
Illustrations © 2013 by Andy Smith

The moral right of the author has been asserted.

Bloomsbury Publishing Plc
50 Bedford Square
London WC1B 3DP

Bloomsbury Publishing, London, New Delhi, New York and Sydney

A CIP catalogue record for this book is available from the British Library

ISBN 978 1 4088 2859 5

Project editor: Janet Illsley
Designer: Lawrence Morton
Photographer and stylist: Simon Wheeler (www.simonwheeler.eu)
Illustrator: Andy Smith (www.asmithillustration.com)
Indexer: Hilary Bird

10 9 8 7 6 5 4 3 2 1

Printed and bound in Italy by Graphicom

www.bloomsbury.com
www.rivercottage.net